VIVEK M

On the Brink

Travels in the wilds of India

PENGUIN BOOKS

Penguin Books India (P) Ltd., 11 Community Centre, Panchsheel Park, New Delhi 110 017, India
Penguin Books Ltd., 27 Wrights Lane, London W8 5TZ, UK
Penguin Putnam Inc., 375 Hudson Street, New York, NY 10014, USA
Penguin Books Australia Ltd., Ringwood, Victoria, Australia
Penguin Books Canada Ltd., 10 Alcorn Avenue, Suite 300, Toronto, Ontario M4V 3B2, Canada
Penguin Books (NZ) Ltd., 182-190 Wairau Road, Auckland 10, New Zealand

First published by Penguin Books India 1999

10 9 8 7 6 5 4 3 2 1

Typeset in Palatino by DTP Solutions, New Delhi

Printed at Rekha Printers Pvt. Ltd., New Delhi

The photograph of the tiger on the front cover is by Mohit Aggarwal, of the rhino by Vivek Menon, of the turtles by Bivash Pandov, and of the cranes by P. Kumar.
Back cover photograph of the Nilgiri tahr by Vivek Menon.

for
my parents
the shortest line in this book
with love

Contents

Acknowledgements

I am principally thankful to my friend, confidant and editor, Ravi Singh, who never told me that I could write but nevertheless proceeded to commission me to do so.

For being such wonderful characters and helping me spice my book, I thank my friends, in no particular order: Mohit Aggarwal, Bharati Chaturvedi, Rajesh Thadani, Ashok Kumar, Shaila Maira, James Zaccharias, Arun Venkataraman, A.J.T. Johnsingh, Raman Sukumar, Bhupen Talukdar, Pankaj Sarmah, Dharanidhar Boro, Goutam Narayan, P.C. Bhattacharjee, Achinto Barua, Maan Barua, Kamini Barua, Surendra Varma, Biswajit Mohanty, Bhibhu, Mangesh, Fahmida Firdaus, Tara Gandhi, Prakash Rao, Sanjiv Chadda, Anil Mulchandani, Kumi Jr., Kumi Lee Togawa, Masayuki Sakamoto, Narendra Jhala, Hemanto, Esmond Bradley Martin, Iain and Sabah Douglas-Hamilton, Iqbal Malik, D.K. Lahiri-Choudhury, Madhav Gogate, Thomas Mathew, Ulhas Karanth, Alok Malhotra, Atul Singh Nischal, V.K. Karthika, Michael Day, Valmik Thapar, Fateh Singh Rathore, Ulhas Karanth, Gurmeet Singh, Asim Chatterjee, Arun Srivastava and Neeraj Jain.

To my hugely entertaining sister Shailaja Menon and my long suffering parents, C.P. Damodaran and P.S. Rugmini, my gratitude for their understanding and love.

A special thank you to Joanna Van Gruisen, P. Kumar,

James Zaccharias, Mohit Aggarwal, R. Sukumar and Bivash Pandov, for lending their fabulous photographs for this book, and to Virender Kumar for the map.

I cannot thank enough the dozen species in this book in particular and a thousand others in general that have played such an important part in my life. This book, in ways more than one, is for them.

Prologue

The stars in the summer sky hung listlessly from the night. They had absorbed the heat of the day and were now swollen large and white. For a moment, they looked larger than the earth and people who walked under them felt small and ant-like. All life forms were equally dwarfed: the man on the plains, the crane that flapped over his form, the dog that lay hunched at his feet, the paramecium that swam lithely through his blood. There was a strange parity; an unnatural collapse of the pyramid of life that man had drawn up a few centuries earlier. And then the moment passed and people regained control over themselves and the world around them.

~

I did not feel warm but my eyes were reddening as they do when a bout of fever is around the corner. In my bones a dull ache had started up, much like the one that creeps up on you the morning after you bowl fast for a local cricket match after a two-year lapse. Friends were quick to point out the reasons.

'It's jet lag,' said Tara, 'sleep it off.'

'Virus. It is all around Delhi,' said Suchita. 'See a doctor.'

'Absolutely a chill. I've always told you about a change in weather,' said my mother long-distance.

'No, mother, I did not lean out of a window in the plane,' I comforted her.

'Just you wait and see; you have always had this as a child,' she ended the conversation.

'Whisky, my boy, whisky. Why have you stopped drinking? Have I told you about the time I fell ill after I stopped drinking rather foolishly?' asked Ashok paternally. 'Did it for a week. Had to drink water then. What do you think happened?' His face took on a grave expression: 'Jaundice, my boy, almost hospitalized. Never stop drinking, I say.'

At two in the night I woke up, still clammy and burning. The stars were still visible in the sky but they had almost got lost in an enlarging world. As I sat up in bed, the import of the whole thing hit me. There was this insane story that I had wanted to tell a few people for quite some time now. Of the Indian jungles and the life forms that inhabit them. Of a few very endangered species that are fighting to remain under a starlit sky. Of one common species that is opposed to their doing so. In a way, I was glad that the thing had come on in the form of a fever. Such stories should never be told in complete, cold sanity. Rather insanely, I remembered Georges Simenon, a French author whom I do not admire, shutting himself up in a room for days on end, suffering long bouts of labour pain, until, suddenly, a prodigious novel came out. Head first. In this case, though, there was little need for fiction. The story of these wild lives has all the ingredients of successful fiction, excepting that at the

end of the story, the cast of characters cannot shut the
book and laugh it all off.

~

India, the country I was born into, is home to an amazing
variety of life forms. In the high Himalayas, a
near-mythical leopard, its spots melting into the snow,
hunts blue sheep. Slightly lower down, a deer with a
vampirical face skips across alpine meadows, hiding in
its belly a perfume that is the greatest sexual turn-on for
the cognoscenti. In the great plains of the Indian
peninsula, tigers merge into a fast disappearing forest,
playing a game of first-to-vanish with their habitat.
Elephants sail through the subcontinent, being
worshipped when they are not flattening houses. A pack
of hunting dogs whistle to each other as they rip open the
flanks of a still-running spotted deer. In the north-eastern
arm of India, casually flung over an unwilling
Bangladesh, golden langurs cavort over a
five-hundred-million-year-old battle tank, a horn
balanced precariously on its nose. A talking mynah
cackles disapprovingly as it raises its brood on artificial
nests built on stilts. On the coasts, another ancient
creature hauls itself from the sea once every three years
to lay its eggs in the damp sand, surrounded by
thousands of friends in labour. Soaring overhead, a
communal predator looks for an opportunity to pick off
the emerging young, even as reverent Hindus pay
homage to it, believing it to be the carrier of their gods. In
between, tiny emeralds swoop down, sipping nectar
from flowers; a motherly snake, all of twelve feet long,

coils protectively over its nest; and a zillion other forms of life pulsate to an unheard beat.

The wildernesses of the country range from cold deserts, where the wind plays peek-a-boo with errant humans, to hot deserts, where the game includes ten thousand grains of sand as well. From tropical evergreen forests where life begins on towering treetops, to the low thorn scrub that spreads across peninsular India like a two-day-old stubble on the country's face. From the shallow wetlands that squelch and swirl to the footbeats of a thousand waterfowl, to the deep seas that envelop the subcontinent's chin in a motherly fashion. An extraordinary land with extraordinary life.

As a trained biologist, I have wandered amidst this chaos of Indian life for over a decade. Life, here, includes nine hundred million human beings, a figure that haunts my nights and fills my days with dread. This vast number has spread throughout the land obliterating the great wilds that you may still see in Africa or the Americas. Today, wildlife in India live in small safe-deposit lockers, constantly interfacing with humans. In these few unattended corners, getting rarer by the day, thousands of wild species crowd together.

I have been embarrassingly fortunate to have formed a part of their lives for even a short while. On assignments from the World Wide Fund for Nature, the World Conservation Union (through its specialist groups), the Bombay Natural History Society and a host of other government and non-government agencies, I have tramped the forests in which they live, devised strategies to protect them and hunted, predator-like, the people who cause them harm. In this, I have had the co-operation and companionship of three classes of people. The first belong to my own tribe, a rather small but rapidly increasing clan. They include conservationists, ecologists, writers, photographers, film-makers, NGO personnel and general do-gooders. A second lot of people are the officials of the numerous government agencies that have something to do with wildlife. From the ubiquitous forest officers, whom, if I did not know better, I would have introduced as the zamindars of the Indian forests, to police and paramilitary personnel—all sorts of administrators and henchmen to a system that is all of two hundred years of age. These two groups would comprise less than a few thousand individuals. The third group consists of the overwhelming majority who have conserved animal and plant species without even knowing it. Despite the tremendous population pressures and the fast-changing lifestyles, some wildlife has survived. In some ways this miracle is due to the inherent conservation ethic of this country. In most ways, it is because the country itself is a miracle.

~

This story is at least ten years long. From the autumn of 1987 when I first, rather naïvely, undertook a south Indian expedition to be with mountain goats, to the present when much of my time is spent tracking down wildlife criminals. The twelve species that are the prima donnas of this story are all endangered, living on the edge of the chasm of extinction. On the very brink, as it were.

There are seven mammals, three birds, one tree and one reptile that star in the book. Some of them I have worked with and for. Others are species that have come into my wanderings and professional life and provided me with incidents that I can still savour on cold winter days in front of a pine-cone-lit fireplace. The dozen species do not stand on their own. They live in ecosystems that in many ways are more endangered than the species themselves. They are also surrounded by large numbers of other equally endangered species that slip in and out of the story.

It is but inevitable that these meanderings of mine have also yielded a rich crop of human acquaintances, friends and not-so-much-friends, who figure in the whole scheme of things. A melodramatic tiger conservationist broods over his clutch of whisky-toting comrades. A bespectacled Tamil biologist spends his time equally between vegetarian messes and elephant jungles. A heroic range officer plays a flute at 10,000 feet while his flock of endangered mountain goats cavort below him. A young sixty-five-year-old undercover conservationist grows a moustache and shaves off his hair to convince a Tibetan woman that his immediate requirement in life is a rhino horn. And these are people I consider my friends!

Why, the reader may well ask, do I want to tell this story? What makes me love animals and the wilderness so much? I wish I could say that as a child I was reared in the wilds of India. Even if not a modern-day Mowgli, I could then rank with the enviable Saba and Dudu, children of the African sun as much as of their elephant-watching parents, Iain and Oria Douglas-Hamilton. As fate would have it, however, I grew up in urban affluence. The only person in the family who has ever had an inclination to love animals is my maternal grandmother who once stroked the head of a python, muttering, 'How sweet, poor thing,' to the utter amazement of the fake mendicant who made a living out of fooling people in Mussoorie that the snake was a dreaded avatar of Lord Shiva's serpent necklace. Apart from that and nursing a few sparrows that were routinely cut to pieces by a particularly vicious fan in my mother's childhood home, her wildlife ramblings were few if any. My grandmother on my father's side, that beautifully innocent being who shared a bedroom with me for many years of my childhood, usually climbed a dining table on seeing a pet dog. My love for wildlife could not have come from her, although she was invariably supportive in my quests and was the perfect listener to my exploits.

My grandfathers on both sides were equally ecologically unconscious. At least my paternal one was a doctor posted in forested areas, though his chief wildlife hobby was converting the many bones, tusks and antlers that were given to him in lieu of payment by the locals into ornate walking sticks. He must have got terribly carried away, for he managed to convert even the urethra of a sting ray into a stick. My maternal grandfather was an astronomer, mathematician and the first Indian housemaster of Doon School. In those days a wastrel bird-watcher called Salim Ali used to frequent the terai and till his dying days my grandfather used to enquire fondly of easily the most accomplished ornithologist that this part of the world has ever produced. 'Has he come good, young Salim?' he would ask from his frequently prone position—and that statement did not indicate the presence of any wildlife genes either.

Closer to me, my parents and an only sibling, my

younger sister, have never ever entered a jungle. My father used to often join his mother on the dining table at the sight of a family pet. I am convinced that he put up with my large number of in-house animals largely due to his blissful ignorance of their presence. There was an instance when he vehemently protested to having his water cooler used as a winter refuge for two flapshell turtles, but in most other cases my wild charges were well concealed in my room which he did not frequent often. My mother was fond of animals in the way that she is fond of any life, including garrulous relatives and some friends who grew up in part in my house without either they or my family quite realizing it. The only creature my sister was fond of was a cat that ran away and returned dramatically, four years later, sending the entire house into a tizzy searching for its food bowl, which by then was probably being used as a lid in which to dry pickles in the sun. In her adult avatar my sister has taken to children with snot running down their noses and other such human forms that psychologists who specialize in children are wont to love—reasonably far away from tigers, who, amazingly, never have snot running down their nostrils even as cubs.

From none of them, then, could I have got my wild genes. It must have been the stork that brought me, and I often wonder whether it was a black-necked one or an adjutant.

A Shepherd and His Blue Goats

It was one of those mornings when the mist curls up at the doorstep demanding to be let in because of the cold. The Vaghavarai Estate owned by Tata Tea bears the brunt of the mists from the adjoining Eravikulam National Park in the southern state of Kerala. The office-cum-residence of the Assistant Wildlife Preservation Officer was no exception. Swirls of mist had gathered outside the window pane on a colourless September morning. Beside me, Mohit curled tighter into his sleeping bag.

'Kerala is a hot place,' he mimicked. 'Fat lot of good it is to travel with a Malayalee.'

In a neighbouring cocoon Rajesh grunted his approval. I cringed inwardly. There was no escape from either. In the corner, beneath a massive display of assorted smoking pipes, axes and hats, James sat passively reading the memoirs of Neruda. The room, which was still a residence as it was not yet nine o' clock, resembled a monastic cell carved out of a Himalayan rock. Except for the racks that held up an extraordinary array of books and music, it was clear of obstacles. I noticed that this made it extremely easy for Michael, the Man Friday, to sweep up after us. He was up already, and a kettle of tea was gurgling merrily on a wood fire.

Around his neck snaked a multicolour muffler and his body was wrapped up in a shawl. The average resident of the High Ranges dresses to tackle the climate before it gets at him.

'At Eravikulam you normally drink in the weather with the morning tea,' explained James Zacharias, tall, weather-beaten and laconic. 'Both are served up black and unsweetened.'

Neither the black tea nor the huge breakfast laden with wild honey and country eggs, three at a time, were the focus of this trip of ours. We were on a wildlife tour of a newly formed Delhi-based non-governmental organization called Srishti and we wanted, very badly, to see blue goats.

'Blue goats!' my sister Shailaja had shrieked, dancing all around me, when I first announced my intention to go at a family dinner.

'Blue goats!? Eat more! Eat more, fatty. You'll get blue goats in the night after a heavy meal.'

To excite my sister requires very little effort. If she loves the world she will dance with it, laughing and hugging and kissing with unabashed *joie de vivre*. If she does not like it she will dance on it, her hair flying wildly and her feet stomping a traditional dance performed by Malayalee warriors when they see Tamilians. Currently, she loved the world.

'You are going to see blue goats!' she screamed hysterically. 'What about pink fairies and wobbly beasts?'

Srishti was an organization that grew out of a voluntary zoo-help programme. I was its first elected co-ordinator and the two sullen cocoons on either side were part of a five-person executive committee. In 1987, the role cut out for Srishti was quite clear. We would tackle the wildlife problems of Delhi, spread nature awareness in schools and publicly thrash citizenry who went around poking cigarettes into the eyes of silver pheasants at the zoo. It was useful, once we had decided upon this, to know a little bit more about silver pheasants and indeed any other form of Indian wildlife. We could then, rather legitimately, tighten our cummerbunds and go to war to save it. And thus, Eravikulam National Park became our first stop on a south Indian wildlife tour.

Mohit Aggarwal was a Punjabi businessman, inheritor of an iron and steel empire that his father had quietly and unobtrusively built up for him in the backyards of Batala in the Punjab hinterland. Early on in life, he had realized that he preferred the cool feel of a Nikon pressed against his cheekbone than the heat of steel smelting in the furnace. Beginning with the Eravikulam trip he was to slowly inch his way out of the family business and grow wilder and wilder, acquiring a respectable beer belly in the process. His two prime endowments that have remained constant are a smile that warms the cockles of all around him and an engaging quality of forgetting all that is not central to his life—and one or two of those as well.

Rajesh Thadani was a Sindhi botanist in the making, quiet, studious and gifted with the most endearingly miserable expression that God gave man. He had and still has that unique ability of looking utterly miserable with a blue sky overhead and scarlet sunbirds flitting in and out of the blossoms of a red flame of the forest tree. His occasional flashes of pleasure come as suddenly as the Eravikulam sky clears, and he flashes a smile of genuine ecstasy while hopping a curious two-footed wobble known only to him and the rare Bavarian red-crowned goose. Over the years he has developed a life interest in the towering oaks of the Himalayas, a subject he studies assiduously from the confines of a laboratory in New Haven, USA.

Both Mohit and Rajesh have, since the time of the blue goats, become two of my closest friends, surviving my friendship through many a wild year. At the time, though, I was still struggling to graduate from being a student biologist to a struggling biologist.

The creatures that had brought the three of us to the gloom of an Eravikulam autumn were 1000 odd Nilgiri tahr, mountain goats that live on the boundary of the two southern states of Kerala and Tamil Nadu. The Nilgiris, literally translated, are the Blue Mountains and it is only right that the goats living on them and on the adjoining hills should be blue as well. The mountains, like the goats, are not always that colour though. In the goat's case only the adult male achieves the colour and in the mountains it is only when a remarkable shrub, *Strobilanthus*, flowers in single-minded profusion, that the landscape turns a pale blue. *Strobilanthus*, like many bamboo species, flowers only once in seven years. Some bushes flower even later. In a propitious year, when the grasslands flower all together, the skies bend demurely, abashed at being outdone by the earth in shades of blue. On the state boundary, only in the Eravikulam area of Kerala and the adjoining grass hills of Tamil Nadu do the tahr have a protected area to live in. In Mukurthi Wildlife Sanctuary of Tamil Nadu live another hundred odd tahr. All the remaining populations are small and scattered. There are definitely less than 2000 animals, maybe as few as 1500, making them the rarest wild goats in the world and one of India's most endangered large mammals.

~

'What is the difference between a goat and a sheep for a biologist?' my maternal grandfather once asked from a prone position. Having been, among other things, an astronomer, a mathematics teacher and a swimming coach, precision had always been important for him. And so I mulled over his question. Sheep flock, goats herd. Sheep give us lamb to go with the mint sauce, goats give us mutton. Sheep have wool in a woolly manner, goats have hair in a furry manner. Put another way, the hair of sheep tend to curl more than that of goats. So is a sheep a goat in curlers? Not in the least. Both creatures communicate and mark territories using pungent smell markings, like many of my childhood friends at school. All sheepy scent markings are done from glands on the face and feet; the goat has his on his bottom. The sheep has a curly woolly tail, the goat a flat tail that is quite naked on the underside. And for me, most interestingly, the two groups are distinct in the way the males fight for the females. Sheep tend to run in, heads lowered, eyes focused on the spinning ground beneath their hoofs, and meet with an almighty crash. The fact that they still have brains left is thanks only to their unique helmets. The goats on the other hand have a more graceful head-butting routine programmed into their brains. Rival males eye each other goatily, then run in from a shorter distance and, rearing on their hind legs, strike forwards and downwards in a hammer-motion.

Is the Nilgiri tahr a goat at all ? Perhaps not in the true sense, but it is more goat than sheep, more goat than antelope and more goat than wild cow and thus, for all practical purposes, it is a wild goat. The species has all the goat-like characters that biologists have invented for it and reliable sources have informed me that they also have a goaty odour. I have, sadly, refrained from testing this distinguishing factor in the field. Just to confuse biologists, though, the Nilgiri tahr does not have the ubiquitous goatee beard that adult male goats sport and its headgear is rather short, compared to the magnificent horns of its Himalayan goat relatives. Just a variation to the theme perhaps. And variation there is even within the small family of tahr that inhabit the world. There is similarity as well, and it is riveting to think of the Himalayan tahr of the cold Himalayan slopes, the Nilgiri tahr, 2000 km to the south in the peninsular Nilgiris, and the Arabian tahr of the desert mountains of Arabia all doing exactly the same head-butting to win females.

~

Rajesh is allergic to eggs. This is the only thing he cannot eat, other than onions, garlic, capsicum, four varieties of cereals and a dozen preparations that he genuinely does not like. Eggs produce a mysterious rash all over his body that makes him look like a stuffed porcupine boiled tender. This had been drilled into all of us. I was fully sympathetic. I have a Disprin allergy myself that makes me take on a porcine appearance within minutes of the drug entering my blood stream. I have never ascertained the effect of more than one pill at a time but in several nightmares I have turned a light shade of pink, coiled my tail slightly cockily over my rump and rehearsed the oink language just before being saved by my fairy godmother. The last mentioned had a curious resemblance to my girlfriend at the time, allowing my sister to make several psychological analyses.

As Michael slid three of the finest country eggs onto his plate, Rajesh looked sideways at me. James had his head buried in a book. The eggs mysteriously materialized on my plate. The reason Rajesh could not refuse outright was the bearded, curly-haired host, lost in his book, who was yet to talk directly to either of my companions. James Zacharias was the range officer (exaltedly called the Assistant Wildlife Preservation Officer) for Eravikulam and Chinnar and the forests around us were the area where he was king. James had joined the forest department because of his love for the wild and had slowly converted himself into as wild a man as possible. He could walk kilometre upon kilometre of jungle, scramble up precipitous slopes and make all of it look easy. His knowledge of the wilds that surrounded him was phenomenal and it was apparent at a glance that he cared deeply for them. In his short stint at Eravikulam he had already done more than his share of duty, busting illegal marijuana cultivators, censusing his montane charges and introducing new management practices into the park. First and foremost, he walked his forest—sign enough of an officer who wants to do his job. Despite all this, he had a very genuine problem.

James was tough . . . very tough. He was also a Malayalee. Like all members of his clan, he felt slightly superior to the softie, somebody who could not do what he could, not breathe the mountain air as easily as he did or indeed with as much enjoyment. All three of us smelt like softies from a mile off. I had a saving grace: I was also a Malayalee, and the parochial spirit in James was aroused. Somewhere, sometime, since we first met outside the tea-town bus stop of Munnar, he had decided that he would talk only to me. And only in Malayalam. The language was as alien to the other two as English is to most Englishmen.

Rajesh was most affected.

'Can't he ever talk in English?'

'Maybe he's better used to Malayalam,' I ventured.

'And reads Neruda in English . . . Bah!'

Both my companions complained bitterly to me, but in private. I could sense a mixture of fear and respect preventing them from telling James about egg allergies and the like.

'What are these axes for?' Mohit was determined to be friendly. 'Do they protect you from wild animals?'

James looked up with a spreading sneer on his face. 'Axes? On animals! Try it on a tiger when you see one.' He was out and walking and we followed, keeping a respectful distance.

When you wind up to Eravikulam from Munnar, the headquarters of Tata Tea in southern India, the first impression of the National Park is that of a massive football field folded up into hills and vales. For half an hour, the climb up from Vaghavarai is all tea, clumped and clotted green bushes that dramatically give way to the wilds. The grass is short and velvety and the dunes that stretch till the horizon are all grass. All the trees of the area seem to have retreated into small pockets of dense, evergreen sholas. If the football game is substituted for an indoor one, the place could be a billiards baize with clusters of green balls kept ready for the cue in strategic places. The grassland itself conforms to its true nature and hides most of its life beneath the soil. The surface above is too exposed to encourage its survival. Grasses have only their leaves above the surface and the body of the plant is cleverly hidden away under the soil. Even more interestingly, the grasslands are maintained by the most devastating natural force there is on earth—fire.

Fire is used by the wildlife authorities to manage dry, broad-leafed teak and sal forests in India by burning small plots every year or once in two years in spring. During the hot summer months when natural fires or man-made fires sweep the forest, these burnt patches act as firebreaks and halt large-scale damage. Grasslands are traditionally burnt in the cold months, sometimes annually, sometimes once in three years. This controlled burning is designed to bring forth fresh grass, the herbivore's chocolate-cream cake. In a grassland, natural fires occur too, and this burning is supposed to halt the spread of woodlands. Trees ecologically have this bad habit of creeping up on the grass and shouting 'Gotcha' before anyone realizes it. What was grassland yesterday turns into a dense forest tomorrow, a natural enough progression, but one that God and wildlife managers don't like very much. And thus, fire plays fairy godmother to the grasslands.

'The tahr like fresh, young grass,' James explained.

He was using his machete to snip a persistent leech off

his trousers, a more novel use for the weapon than cutting a pathway through the rare shrubby interludes of Eravikulam.

'Wildlife management pundits advocate burning grasslands in a controlled fashion if natural fires are not enough,' he continued. 'In nature, lightning is one of the major causes of fire and when the blaze subsides, regeneration allows fresh grass to come up. The tahr love it. They subsist on the young and tender shoots. If there is one thing they cannot stand, it is coarse grass.' The bearded face wrinkled in distaste as if it were he and not his flock that was being made to eat coarse grass.

'They're not elephants, you see,' he said, half of it in pure Malayalam.

'What the hell does he mean talking away in a language we don't understand?' Rajesh was climbing a small tussock with me.

'He could still be more comfortable in it.' I had started to pant.

'Look at the grass hills. Forget him now.'

Rajamalai was the tourism area of the park and the only place where tourists were allowed without special permission. In 1987 the place was still largely without tourism, although a few herd of tahr, rather accustomed to human presence due to a study done by Clifford Rice, a Western biologist, used to hang around the place. If herbivores love tonnes of grass and green foliage, salt is a must in small quantities. A patch of salt on damp forest earth, and a cloud of thirsty butterflies will descend on it, drinking the saline voraciously through their tubular tongues. The moment the patch is bigger, such as at salt-licks which are clumps of rock salt in a hillside or on the ground, large herbivores come in butterfly-like droves. Clifford Rice had made a salt-lick artificially and the goats responded gratefully.

'Good combination, Rice and salt, eh?' asked Mohit, excited to be on his first field outing.

'Shhhh!' hushed our host, pointing into the mist.

A cold wind buffeted us as soon as we got off the vehicle. Sheets of mist blown in by the wind hung at every corner. We could see each other clearly enough only upto a distance of two feet. The wind was bringing rain as well and the first leeches had started snaking up my trouser legs.

It was a Macbethean scene, with the witch's cauldron overflowing with a vile, thick mist that leapt out of it every time the wind lashed at us rudely. The persistent drizzle only added despair to the scene. In the enveloping mist small bluish-grey lumps were appearing and disappearing. There was no fixed focus, no clarity of sight. The dream vendors were overdoing their bit. Like ghostly apparitions, our first Nilgiri tahr swept through the grassland and Mohit feverishly photographed the swirling gossamer clouds, hoping that in the final result he could wipe the mist away magically and produce tahr from it.

~

The next morning was our first big trek and I was told succinctly in Malayalam that we were to follow the leader without lagging behind. Our goal was the log hut that Cliff Rice had stayed in—a two-hour hike.

'Best way to see the park,' claimed James. It sounded

heavenly. To stay in the middle of the park was a godsend.

'I am bleeding rather badly,' observed the photographer emerging out of his sleeping bag, looking decidedly worried. When he went into the bag, the inner lining was light blue. Now it was scarlet. As scarlet as the body of a yellow-backed sunbird, without question the worst described bird in the annals of Indian ornithology.

'Leeches secrete an anti-coagulant,' explained James, uncharacteristically. 'Put saline on it and it will stop.'

'Where do I get saline from?' Mohit wanted to know the nearest chemists.

'Spit on it.' James was clearly irked. 'Where do you get saline from, indeed. Spit, man, spit!'

Rajesh grimaced. He was brought up in a manner that forbade spitting on thighs and arms.

In half an hour we were ready to set out. My companions, I decided, had a definitely weird dress sense. For Mohit, cameras were his most important possessions. Just after them came his soul. To take out his beloved lenses in the persistently pissing rain made no sense to him. He was the official photographer of the group, however, and knew that he could not afford to leave the camera behind. Those were the days when I was too poor to have my own camera. There was little to do but rely on Mohit. He struck what he considered a decent compromise. He wrapped the lenses in individual plastics, held in place by multicoloured rubber bands, and packed them tightly into his camera bag, loading the intervening spaces with silica gel. The whole contraption was then lowered into another plastic bag, also fastened with a rubber band, and the strap taken out through a slit in it. The overdressed camera was now hung around the neck. All that remained was to get into the raincoat and button it up on top of the plastic-covered, camera bag-covered, plastic bag-covered lenses, and Mohit was ready to look nine months gone with his maternity coat flapping around in the wind. Meanwhile, leeches were dropping out of the rain and especially finding Mohit. While they crawled up our trouser legs and through shoelace holes, they dropped from overhanging branches onto Mohit's nose and ears and managed to progress further up his jeans than either Rajesh's or mine. On all exposed flesh, red welts had started to form. On these, pieces of newspaper were stuck with spit. The paper turned a funny light red, the way damp blotting paper does when a drop of Chelpark's red ink falls on it.

Rajesh had a natural mourning look that morning; not baleful in the least but only celebrating the evils in the world that he had to contend with. He accentuated it by wearing a collarless raincoat with an army sergeant hat on his head, held in place by an elastic band around the chin. On top of this hat, for some ridiculous reason, he had perched the raincoat cap, achieving with great success the double-decker tramp effect. In tow was Michael, who had a chequered lungi drawn up around his knees, a floral shirt open at the chest, and an umbrella to ward off the rain. An alpine woollen cap on his head let us know that he too felt cold. Leading this band was the immaculately forest-attired James, traipsing ahead on the grassy meadows, next to the tahr.

James took the steep climb that cut across the main road, linking the loops of tea like a knitting needle passing through clumsily knotted yarns of green wool. It was shorter, faster and pounded all the breath you had in reserve out of your system. Around us, beginnings of the shola ecosystem started to appear. At every step, beautiful blooms that the teamen had planted alongside the winding roads were disappearing. The brilliance of the red Spathodeas that guard tea plantations in southern India like solitary red militia were becoming rarer and rarer. Instead, the wilds were taking over.

The Eravikulam plateau is a magnificent complex of rolling grass hills and dense evergreen shola forests. The sholas cling to the meeting places of the hills like damp pubic hair nestled between the luxuriantly rolling thighs of Eravikulam. The steam of a humid evergreen forest obscured an unseen life that chittered and twirped in its folds. The grass hills, in stark contrast, loomed lifeless at first sight. Roll upon roll of short-cropped, velvety grass. The sort that cows would pay for in gold nose rings if there was an auction at the village place. We strained our eyes to see if any animal life was visible. Three pairs of straining eyes. The fourth pair was on a hilltop, three hills away and walking fast.

All of a sudden, just as we had lost him, we found James. He was standing on a tussock, one hand on his hat to keep it from blowing away in the vicious wind. He had assumed a frozen attitude, hand pointing outwards and towards the edge of a shola.

'What's up?' asked Rajesh.

'Must be more goats,' said Mohit.

Quite instead, the grass at the edge of the forest parted to send out a sleek reddish-brown creature, then a second, then another . . .

'Dholes,' I whispered. 'Wild dog.'

I could feel the tension in the whole group now. This was definitely more than we had hoped to see. The dog had got scarcer in northern India but was still relatively common in patches in the south. What struck me first, as the creatures emerged, fanning out away from the shola, was their colour. Varying from brick to a rust-blood red, their coats shone with a russet that I was unused to. The paler northern versions I had seen were like dissatisfied ghosts in comparison. The short, rich green grass set off their reds to great effect.

'Fourteen, fifteen, sixteen,' counted James and I could hear Rajesh counting them off behind me as well. 'Where's the camera, Mohit?'

Mohit woke up with an unpleasant start. The dogs had started a curious high-legged lope and all the members of the pack were never to be seen at the same time. There were crouchers and skulkers among the lot while a few led the pack, black-tipped tails held parallel to the body in a defiantly arrogant gesture.

'Mohit, quick! Take the camera out!' James was getting impatient.

Mohit meanwhile had reluctantly taken his raincoat off and was peeling off his baby from his belly.

The dogs had started a hunt.

Mohit extricated the camera bag from its voluminous plastic case, taking care to wrap the rubber band around his index finger so he would not lose it.

The sentinel tahr had got a sudden gust of canid smell now as the wind shifted and he stomped uneasily, snorting briefly as he did so.

Mohit unzipped the bag and got out the camera body and his lens, both individually wrapped in plastics.

'Aahr' said the tahr, sending the Rajamalai herd into sudden panic. They had still not seen the dogs, who, heads held low and bodies close to the ground, were only visible as ripples on the surface of the grass. Now and again, our straining eyes would catch a flash of red streaking across.

'Quick, quick!' exhorted James.

The two pieces of equipment were now free from their mother containers and all that remained was to screw them into position, stash away all the plastics and rubber bands, and Mohit Aggarwal was ready to squint into the mist. The tahr meanwhile had all but disappeared and the dogs were giving up the chase. The wild dog is a powerful runner but seldom gives it a long burst. The hunt is all about stealth and skill, as pack members ambush, head off and tire out the prey. As the last tahr disappeared over the crest, the dogs stood up, all sixteen, on the slopes just above us. The greens glittered with the suddenly revealed jewels. Mohit snapped one, then two frames as the rest of us watched transfixed at what was undoubtedly one of the most unforgettable sights of the trip. As suddenly as they had come out of the forests, the dholes vanished. Prey denied, they merged into the mist in graceful defeat.

James was watching Mohit with unabashed disgust. It was clear that he had not got the camera out in time to get any action. I hoped silently that he had at least got the dogs.

'Aaahr,' grunted the tahr from within the mists.

'Grrumph,' grunted James as he set off in a lope back towards the jeep.

Mohit was carefully securing the plastic-wrapped lenses with his rubber bands, an open camera bag and a raincoat beside him on the grass hill, under a silently glowering monsoon sky.

~

The log hut was a recluse in the valley of grass. A wooden shack leaning against the hillside that sheltered it from a wind that threatened to tear us away. Inside, a fascinating correspondence between the United States Department of the Interior and the log hut formed a perfectly framed farce.

'Dear Mr Eravikulam Hut . . .' the department wrote, supposedly to Clifford Rice. Even the most powerful department of the most powerful country in the world had not heard of Eravikulam. Perhaps not even of grasslands. They did not have intelligence reports that the grasslands of the world were shrinking, contracting into tiny bundles of grass, withering from the heat of a changing climate, cringing from the onslaught of the advancing tree line, dying wholesale at the hands of man. Much like foresters of not so long ago who planted grasslands with large, woody trees to afforest them, the department did not realize the value of a grassland left alone. There was no one to tell them or the world that grasslands are not wastelands, orphans of the wonderful mother who has produced rainforests and savannahs as elder siblings; that the sheaves of uncut grass are not lost commerce, nor an unsightly stubble to be shaved off the armpits of forests. There should have been someone to tell them that the grass contains a unique set of animals and birds, insects and fish. Like the tahr, the rarest mountain goat of the world, almost pushed, by the ignorance of man, off the very precipice on which he stands silent sentinel.

Mohit was slowly learning that James would be a tough nut to crack. James was fast learning that Mohit was a nut who could be cracked. The contest was fascinating to watch from the sidelines. Our second day at the log hut dawned surprisingly clear and from his favourite corner James spied unseen ghosts in the forest behind the hut. In a flash he was out, a hop down the courtyard, two unhesitating steps onto the single-pole bamboo bridge and a jump into the forest fringe beyond. A few feet below the bamboo, a small stream chortled merrily.

I had followed James into the courtyard and watched as he shaded his eyes from the dishevelled sun and peered into the lifting mist. A large herd of deer had just emerged from the forest and were nervously tugging away at the fringe vegetation.

'Grrmphhh,' said James, making the situation obvious to the uninitiated instantly. I saw a short frenzied wave and knew immediately that this was unusual. I decided to join him. A hop down the courtyard and I was at the edge of the gully. The bamboo swayed enticingly.

'Sambar,' pronounced James, speaking in English as there was no one else around. I put a tentative foot on the pole and the stream spun a lazy half circle.

Sambar are the largest of Indian deer, huge shaggy brown beasts with a wide forest distribution.

'Could be fifty, maybe sixty . . . whew . . . very rare.'

He was not looking backwards. As my second foot left terra firma, the pole finished its circular motion and I swung, seasick for a moment, contemplating life and possible death.

'Have never seen more than a dozen or two together at any time.' He was being loquacious.

My hand had miraculously gripped the green slime-covered bamboo and I was proceeding cautiously like a three-toed sloth. Two feet and one hand planted successively on the bridge, facing downwards in real alarm, a free hand pointing to the sky in an attempt to balance the whole body.

'Forty-five, forty-six . . . damn . . .' I got to the other side and slowly righted myself. James had still not turned around.

'Should have got the binoculars.' He turned as I looked up. 'Ah! there you are . . . look at this. Quite rare to see this congregation . . . I need those binoculars.'

The binoculars were in the hut. He had three options. He could go back and get them himself, or ask me to do it for him, or, perhaps, ask one of the three people back there to get the pair for him. I was watching the sambar herd intently now, but I could feel the minor conflict in his voice. Perhaps, he knew what he wanted anyway.

'Mohit!' he called out suddenly. 'Mohit, get me those binocs!'

The sambar were mostly hinds and fawns but a few stags stood out amongst them, russet-black in their mature testosterone colours. Most of them were in velvet although some had started rubbing the skin off, revealing the new year's hard, smooth antler. By November almost all of them would have headgear that deer ought to wear. Even illegal shikaris like to see them in hard antler and only a Chinese medicine hunter would smack his chops at the sight of large stags in velvet. For him, it could mean a cure for rheumatism or adenoids, fatigue or sexual failure. Mohit had got out of the hut and was slowly making his way to the bridge holding the binoculars up in one hand, the other pressing his thigh in a pressure grip. A small trickle of blood stained his leg.

'C'mon, hurry up, will you,' James yelled; the first deer were beginning to turn their backs on us.

At the sound of James' voice, a stag jerked his head up in alarm. A small velvet sore had formed on his throat, something that would gradually become a runny mess and a quite distinctive feature. There are many theories about the throat gland but the one most widely accepted is that it plays a role in the deer's mating ritual. Maybe they just like each other with runny necks.

I looked back just in time to catch a look of genuine horror pass over Mohit's face. He had never ventured into the back courtyard before and the sudden sight of the bamboo pole seemed to have given him a morning wake-up call.

'C'mon, give it to me, these sambar are going away.' James was imperious, legs apart, arms akimbo.

The sambar dhonked in alarm. Mohit tentatively touched the pole with his right toe. Now, there are bamboo poles and bamboo poles. Some move rather churlishly, others rotate on a good day and yet others love to do themselves a good turn once in a while. This one was a bloody pinwheel. The softer you trod on the pole the more it turned. The trick was to place your weight confidently on it, once and for all reminding the bamboo of its rightful place in the world. But a toe . . .? The pole spun viciously, evoking a sharp 'Yeeow' from the bleeding hero. He quickly backed away like a scalded cat. James was tapping the ground impatiently with his left foot. The sambar stag was tapping more firmly in alarm with his right foot. Mohit was tapping away at the edge of the pole with both his feet. First left . . . the pole spun, then right . . . the pole rotated.

'What's the matter with you, are you afraid?' James knew these Delhiwalas were softies. I saw a grim look of determination cross Mohit's face. He advanced threateningly now and I could see him mutter silent curses at the water.

'What's the use of giving it to me after the bloody deer have gone, eh?' Mohit placed his first firm foot forward. The pole held. His jaw clenched, he put his next foot forward. James had turned to start counting with his naked eye.

'Won't make it, I'm sure . . . Twenty-two, twenty-three . . .'

Mohit had reached the middle of the bridge. His arms were held apart, scarecrow fashion. His leech bite, freed of its previous stranglehold, had begun to flow. Looking back on the event now, either James or I could have stretched our hands out and taken the precious cargo away from him, allowing the tension to leak away. But I was too caught up in watching the enthralling contest between the two. James, of course, was enjoying the advantage; he wasn't about to spoil it by offering to help.

'Forty-eight, forty-nine, fifty . . . have you got anywhere at all?' James half turned, taking his eyes off the last of the big herd. Only a few scattered ones remained to be counted.

Suddenly, as if on cue, the bamboo decided that

enough was enough and turned upon itself.

'Ooh,' said Mohit, suddenly on all fours, clutching the bamboo with both hands, the binoculars dangling perilously from one thumb. 'Oooh!'

'Watch out!' I cried helpfully. 'Get up very slowly.'

There was no getting up for Mohit though. His eyes were glazed over with horror, his hands turned to stone. 'C'mon, c'mon,' yelled James, enjoying this hugely.

'Oooh!' said Mohit.

'Dhonk!' said the deer.

James had slowly advanced to the edge of the bridge. There were ten, perhaps twelve feet separating the two of them. James bent down, bringing his eyes level with Mohit's, and for a moment I thought he would hold out his hand.

'Crawl!' he cried out. 'Crawl! Now!'

And as if struck by the velocity of his words, Mohit Aggarwal started crawling the last few feet on all fours. James straightened and turned back to count the few remaining.

'Fifty-five, fifty-six.'

Mohit had reached the end and I heard a huge gasp of relief as he stepped onto firm ground.

'Seventy-two . . . and . . . seventy-three. That's it—seventy-three, now is that not a large herd?' James asked me in Malayalam now that Mohit was within earshot. '*Ende ammo!*'

Mohit had slowly got up and was proffering the binoculars.

'Thank you,' said James graciously, then added, 'finished counting the sambar anyway,' and with two lithe steps he crossed the bridge again.

I noted with concern a strange colour suffusing Mohit's face, a curious shade of red-purple that matched the fast-spreading stain on his thigh. It was then, he later told me, that his fever started escalating rapidly.

~

The weather changes rapidly at Eravikulam. Breakfast had just finished for most others. I was struggling with fried egg number three that had been slid onto my plate by Rajesh. James was already donning his khakhis with a matching hat perched jauntily on his head. Rajesh was studiously wiping his boots clean, sitting on the front doorstep, a ritual that he followed religiously throughout the trip. The night before, there had been talk of trying to climb Anamudi, the Elephant Peak, in the morning. At over 9000 feet, the peak is the highest you can get in India south of the Himalayas. It is peninsular India's Mount Everest. To climb it would be a challenge and an achievement. Mohit was slowly crawling back into his sleeping bag.

'Fever,' he muttered, to no one in particular. 'You guys go on. Today . . . not for me, thank you. Fever.'

Nobody answered him. I gulped the last egg down and wiped the honey from the plate with my forefinger.

'*Poova,*' said James from the doorway and stalked away into the morning.

'That means, let's go,' I translated. 'The weather is rather misty now, I'm not sure if we can climb Anamudi.'

I was talking to Rajesh. Mohit was well into the sleeping bag and beginning to snore gently to remind us that he intended to sleep. James was striding rapidly away and there was no time for questioning. I grabbed my rucksack and camera and ran out. I could hear Rajesh following close behind.

Eravikulam is a beautiful park. It is also a remarkably featureless park. Especially if you are trekking in it for the first time. Most definitely so if your friend, guide and counsellor is walking a dozen kilometres in front, glimpsed occasionally in the distance.

'I saw his hat,' I panted.

'Where?' Rajesh was rolling his eyes about in a hopeless gesture.

'There! It just went down into the valley.'

'I can't see a damn thing except for elephant shit. Come to think of it, we are wading in the muck. Did you know there were elephants here?'

I hadn't and I told him so. I thought the tahr were very much alone except for the deer and dholes. But we were ankle deep in fibrous dung cakes broken open by the rain and gently steaming from the insides.

'Does the steam mean it's fresh?'

'Perhaps,' I ventured hopefully, 'it's just the mist around it.'

'I don't think so. They are all around us. It is just that we can't see them. Just like James. Now where the hell *is* he?'

'Just follow your nose, he's bound to be waiting for us at the next hilltop.'

'What nose? I can't feel it for the cold. Did you say that Kerala was hot?'

'Okay! Okay! I've heard that one before. Come on now, walk faster.'

'I can't, and I won't. Just because our guide is a

mountain goat ... Actually, I am just about getting fed up with all you Malayalees.'

At this he broke into a nursery rhyme at the top of his voice:

'Cock-a-doodle-doo, the king has lost his shoe.'

'I don't think it is a king, anyway.'

There was no answer. Rajesh was panting away, head down, camera lolling, and still singing.

'Cock-a-doodle-doo,

We-e-e've lost Jame-e-es.

Whenever we find him,

I'll know what to doo . . .'

In the distance the hat bobbed up again and for once held still. As we climbed the crest of a hill the rest of his body became clear as well. He was sitting on the far side of the mountain top, legs dangling over a sheer precipice of a few thousand feet. He was bunched up over himself as if he was working furiously away on a laptop. Except that all he had in his hands was his axe.

'What are you doing, James?'

The silence echoed. All around, hills rolled away to infinity. Once they reached there they turned and rolled all the way back again. Erumapatti, the cliff that James sat on, dropped like a stone, for ever, till the mists swallowed the valley up. I went up to James to see what he was doing on the very edge of the precipice. He was holding one hand above his lap, palm facing sideways, and with the other he was swinging the axe casually around, chopping his nails! When I say swinging, he was not going full pace, but was definitely briskly carving away, stopping ever so briefly to re-position the hand and then clipping away again.

'Wild! Absolutely wild!' whispered Rajesh who had come up behind me.

I did not know whether he meant the occurrence or the person. Probably both.

Typically, James stood up abruptly and walked to a small crag.

'Gaur,' he announced and pointed imperiously to a hilltop a few hundred metres away. Sure enough, four Indian bison or gaur were slowly rolling up the slope. Columbus missed India by a few thousand miles, but Buffalo Bill, it would seem, had found it long ago. The Indian bison, however, is in actuality not a bison at all. It may look like a bison to most people who are not biologists, but then during biology lessons I had learnt that God was superseded by taxonomists in matters such as this. We trained the binoculars on the animals. Even in the distance, they were massive, heads bent down to the grass and backs humped in gargantuan churlishness. Before we could ask him the next question, James had turned the other way and was peering at the opposite hilltop. 'Saddlebacks,' he said. The one-worders were becoming a habit.

'*Gaur se dekho, tahr dhole baja rahe hain,*' chanted Rajesh in Hindi, which roughly translates into 'Look carefully, the wires are playing the drums.' It was an attempt at a triple pun. He was slowly cracking up.

On a crag, three saddlebacks were silhouetted against the sky. Male mountain goats. It was a bachelor party unusual for August as the rutting season had started and males would normally join in with the female herds for the period. It can be safely presumed that mankind has never ridden a wild Nilgiri tahr, but looked at from a distance, the white saddle looked inviting. The young males are grey like their mothers, achieving a more brownish-yellow hue as they grow older. The browns soon predominate and the older the goat gets, the darker it becomes, until finally it is the colour of ash and grime; a dark slate. From a distance the saddlebacks looked ashy-blue. The phantasmagorical blue goats of the Nilgiris.

With a flourish that was by now characteristically James, a flute was produced from the inner jacket pocket. With one foot perched higher than the other, James the Shepherd put it to his mouth and played an indecipherable tune. Below and beyond, the saddlebacks started moving as if galvanized into action by the lilting melody. We watched spellbound as for five minutes and more the bearded shepherd played to his goats. James was in all probability playing to the winds, but to us the tahr seemed responsive. All of a sudden, the world seemed to be a better place to live in. A wave of a misty hand enshrouded the tahr as James replaced the flute in his jacket pocket.

'James the Shepherd,' muttered Rajesh and then, more respectfully, 'Saint James the Shepherd.'

'Are there elephants around?' I asked, when we had all settled back on the mossy slopes for an unspecified rest period. Rajesh was slowly taking off his left shoe and I wondered whether he intended to clobber his nemesis at an opportune moment. There was no need to worry though, he was more interested in cleaning it of strands of elephant dung.

'Plenty. Hah!' James laughed like he spoke, in monosyllables. Perhaps if he learnt to laugh in

Malayalam he could go into peals of it.

'Anaimudi. Elephant Peak. How do you think the name was given? Plenty. We have not seen one today, however.'

That seemed reasonably obvious.

'Are we trying to climb Anaimudi today?'

In reply James got up and, hand on hat to keep it in place in the torrential, truant wind, walked away down the hill.

'Let's go,' I said wearily. 'Put the shoe back on before he has a two-hill lead'

'Cock-a-doodle-doo.'

'Oh! Shut up, will you!'

'Okay then. Twinkle, twinkle, little star.'

As the hat bobbed away over the horizon, I began to worry about my two companions. One was obviously a leech-bitten, James-ridden creature shivering in high fever in a blood-stained sleeping bag. The other, who had by now abandoned his trousers altogether in trying to keep track of the leeches that kept crawling upwards in a stubborn climb to salvation, was repeating his four words of Malayalam in tandem with his nursery rhymes.

'*Onne, rande, moone, atta,*' he chanted— 'One, two, three, leech.'

'Now where the hell is that hat?'

'Cock-a-doodle-doo. Poor James has lost his shoe.'

As the last strains of his nursery rhyme with the newest twist wafted over the hillside, we were presented, literally out of the blue, with the broadside of the Eravikulam stream. As the land sloped all around, the waters gathered speed. A regular habit, I have since noticed, of all mountain streams. Like all high altitude waters, the Eravikulam stream also has a tendency of bearing very cold, icy waters.

'Where the hell is James?' shrilled Rajesh.

'Can't say. I saw the hat sort of come in this direction.'

'What do you mean sort of, eh, sort of? He could be on any hilltop by now and we are stuck with this bloody river. I think we are totally lost.'

Having moaned his lot, he went off immediately into the newest rendering of cock-a-doodle-doo.

I was practising my rudimentary wildlife tracking skills. James had footprints sufficiently distinct from Nilgiri tahr and elephants and tracking them was easy. They came all the way down the hill we had just come down and then stopped abruptly as the waters began.

'He's gone across,' I said.

'What do you mean, gone across? Where's the boat?'

'He has walked across. Waded.'

'What!' Rajesh on his best days looks shell-shocked. At times such as this he looks as if he has been caught in his middle by a particularly strong pair of buffalo horns.

'You mean go across . . . that!'

'No choice, friend.'

'And what if he is not there? What if he went some other way?'

I pointed at the footprints.

'Oh! Well, all right. If you think so.'

I had begun to take off my shoes and roll up my jeans. Rajesh tucked in his raincoat as the trousers were already off. Both of us tied our cameras around our necks, winding the strap around like a Himalayan mendicant does with his cobras before taking an icy river bath. For a moment we looked at each other pityingly.

'Let's go then,' he ventured, holding out his hand for me to grasp.

'Thank you for that. You know that I can't swim, don't you?'

As the first streams of icy water clasped at our ankles we sucked in our breath. As the tide grew, we let it out in cautious pants of anticipation. And then we started falling.

'One,' I counted.

'One for you, too,' he retorted.

We were stumbling in midstream now, falling every now and then but being pulled up by the other from a certain wash-away. The bottom was covered with green algae. They look beautiful when lazing next to the river and watching from the bank. They turn treacherous when you try to put your feet on them.

'Eight,' I said.

'Seven for you. Don't worry, you'll catch up.'

'What if I let go of your hand when you fall down next?' He was getting hopeful.

Fifteen full minutes later we were on the other bank, drenched head to toe in the montane waters, absolutely lost, clueless about our current positions and cursing our guide. And then, as if God had ordained, the hat came bobbing towards us again from the opposite direction.

'See, what did I tell you? He has missed us and is coming back to look for us.'

'Thank God for small mercies. There he is now, hat and axe and . . .' Rajesh broke off and then piped more shrilly, '. . . but where are his clothes?'

And indeed James was coming back with hat and axe but sans all clothes except his underwear.

'What the . . .' I began.

With measured strides James approached us, passed us, laid his hat and axe on the bank and wading in knee-deep into the waters, started having his daily bath. Unknown to us, we had reached the back of the hut, taking a huge circular sweep of Eravikulam in our day-long march. Hidden by the crest of the hill were our log hut and a fevered Mohit. James had reached ahead of us, stripped to his bare essentials and had come down to the river to bathe, completely oblivious to our plight.

'I am killing him . . . now,' whispered Rajesh ferociously, marching resolutely towards the waiting axe.

'No!' I cried. 'No!'

'Why not?' asked James. 'It's a good place to bathe, come in both of you. *Va do, va.*'

~

Ten years passed eventfully after that first encounter with the misty goats of Rajamalai. I was back at Eravikulam with Surendra Varma, an elephant researcher working with the Asian Elephant Conservation Centre, to which I was a Senior Consultant. Varma is what Wodehouse described as the Euclidean definition of a straight line. All length and no breadth. A scraggly beard fills out his sucked-in cheeks. His eyes wander dreamily in forest lands, exploring the air, the land, the water. If you do not know him well, they are the eyes of a person twenty-two hours into a combination of ecstasy and marijuana. I knew him better. It was completely the effect of ten days in the city, writing out an interim report on elephant censusing techniques. They were the eyes of a hunted man who had suddenly spied the magic invisible bush to hide in.

'Give him a pair of good boots,' a friend confided, 'and he will walk the country in twenty-one days.'

Varma, left to himself, would walk for twenty-one years. It was good that he had only an old pair of hunters at his disposal.

A tahr sentinel snorted his alarm as we approached. He was not looking at us but into the mists at an unseen foe. Around him, two dozen goats were spread evenly on the velvety baize. Most of them lay with their legs bunched up below them, like schoolgirls at the tiffin hour, munching contentedly at their chewy cud and looking up only to giggle gurglingly at one another. The saddleback lay a little distance away, the phantom blue of his uniform merging well with the darkening skies behind his shoulder. A few youngsters butted around us in a casual expenditure of their energies.

The number of people around the tahr had changed, though not dramatically. A few hundred more tourists in a week; a building pressure, but still far away from the insanities of an African savannah safari. A forest checkpost had sprung up at the corner to monitor these changes. The essence of Eravikulam was still in evidence. The goats and the grass, the mist and the rain, the leeches and the sholas, the Spathodeas and the *Strobilanthus*. Elements of a giant jigsaw puzzle that fused intangibly into an alpine grassland. Varma was musing in the distance. I was clicking away furiously, trying to use the cameras, which I had procured by then, to better effect than Mohit.

'How did they come out, Mohit?' Rajesh and I had

chimed in unison as soon as we reached Delhi from the earlier southern expedition. 'How are the pictures?'

The leeches and a sick grandmother and perhaps, just maybe, the effect of James the Good Shepherd had driven a defeated Mohit back to Delhi two weeks before us. As James swung around the curling paths on a motorcycle and we hung on, triple-pillion, riding back to Munnar, Mohit had made his decision not to come with us onwards to Silent Valley. His grandmother had mysteriously taken ill in those twenty minutes. He was to keep the official photographs of the trip ready for us by the time we got back after our rainforest sojourn.

'Oh, those!' He was dismissive, waving a hand in the air as if to clear the mist. '*Woh to chur chur ho gaye* (They have disintegrated into nothing)!'

Even blue goats on a blue hill had not been able to do just that.

Whistling Dogs

It was the beginning of summer and dusk was falling on Rajasthan, wiping away waves of dust and daytime heat. A hysterical night was about to unfold at the Sariska Sanctuary in the northern part of the state, just three hours from Delhi.

Those were the days when the managers of Sariska had little clue of the potential that Kalighati had to add excitement to the lives of tourists, and still permitted them to use the forest hides at night. Kalighati or the Black Valley is a slight depression in the park with waterholes dug for thirsty wildlife. The aridity of Sariska makes it imperative that such waterholes are dug and maintained by man for animals. The Kalighati waterhole is a particular favourite with deer, antelope, langurs, monkeys, peafowl and the occasional big cat, especially in the blistering hot summer months so characteristic of Rajasthan. For me, the adjacent ground hides were a favourite watchpoint.

On this particular occasion, Mohit, Rajesh and I were joined by two girls from our university. Shailaja Raman was a quiet bespectacled Tamilian, one year senior at college. She was part of the original team that had set up Srishti and contributed in all its activities very seriously. Her dedication shone through her lenses in a fiercely concentrated manner, and people tended not to fool around too much with her. Bharati Chaturvedi, who studied in a neighbouring college, was almost instantly renamed Doracs by me. This was a short form for Doracouli, a South American monkey with dark circles around its eyes. In her case the dark rings set off large, lustrous eyes that dominated her palely beautiful face. When you know Doracs well, you realize that she possesses oodles of imagination, and the powers of absolute and instant entertainment.

The five of us were crammed into a four by six by four mud hide with two oblique windows and a fragile tin door, left for the night by the guard in a safe, dark tiger jungle. Mohit instantly occupied both windows and stuck out all the lenses that he had through them. Rajesh retreated to a corner near the door to sulk about this selflessness displayed. Shailaja quietly merged into another one. I sat beside Mohit and Bharati plonked herself on my lap.

'Can you give me some space?' I asked as she was neither on nor off.

'I know I am going to feel cold in the middle of the night'—a usual Doracs prophecy—'I might as well start using your muffler now.'

She unsnarled a bit of my bright blue-banded muffler, a loving present from my mother, and curled it around her neck. I was now joined inextricably to her, neck upwards, in a replay of the original Siamese twins.

'Can the two of you stop moving around! I can't get my focus.'

Mohit was trying to size up peafowl that had by now started crowding the waterhole. A pair of langurs sat on the bank undecidedly. A herd of spotted deer had broken cover and were slowly making their way to the hole. A tree pie rattled overhead. Rajesh continued to look mournful. Shailaja concentrated on her toes.

The spotted deer or chital had reached the waterhole and one by one they spread their forelegs and bent their necks down to the water. A lone male kept watch, sniffing the untrustworthy dusk air. Now and then he would catch the click of Mohit's camera and raise his right foreleg slightly, pausing undecidedly before giving his alarm stomp. He was reassured by the sudden appearance of two male nilgais, blue bulls. These, the largest of India's antelopes, stand horse-high and adult males are the colour of their southern cousins, the Nilgiri tahr. To set off their lanky blue legs they wear black and white ankle-socks which muddy ever so often to turn brown. A slight beard reiterates their manliness. As the nilgais approached, two of the peafowl took off in laborious alarm. 'Piaaaow,' they cried, 'piaaoow'.

'Now, be quiet all of you,' said Mohit addressing himself mainly to Bharati and the peacocks. 'Any moment and a tiger is going to appear. I am taking no chances.'

As he bent over his lenses he panted and wheezed. Mohit vocalized most of his spurts of concentration. As his mind focused, the extra steam that accumulated in his lungs was let out in rasping streams through his nostrils and half-pursed mouth.

Bharati was chattering away nonchalantly about tigers and college mates. Rajesh had started to look up at the ceiling.

'Look,' said Mohit pointing to the edge of the waterhole. 'Tiger!'

The chital had finally decided to stomp as hard as he could, and now wheeled around with a startled 'Ackk!' 'Piaaaaoow' replied the peacocks running a few hundred metres to begin their laboured ascent. The peahens beat them to the air by a few minutes, unencumbered as they were by a few feet of trailing, iridescent blue. The nilgais turned silently and broke into a trot. A male langur bounced up and down on its pads, tail curled elegantly over its head.

From the edge of the jungle, two pale shadows broke cover.

'Not tigers.' I was removing the muffler that had begun to wrap itself obstinately around my eyes, while trying to inch forward towards the peephole.

'Wild dogs,' whispered Mohit. 'Dholes.'

'Don't pull me along, you Puchchkii, you,' screamed Doracs as silently as she could scream. She was being involuntarily dragged nearer the peephole, trailing on the muffler.

'Shhh! Quiet!' commanded Mohit, clicking away rapidly.

The wild dogs were an absolute bonus. We had heard that two dogs had been sighted in Sariska, although they had not been known there for very many years. People knew of the amazing fluctuations in numbers that wild dogs go through, but even accounting for that, Sariska was not thought to be wild dog country. And now here they were, light, ghostly versions of the Eravikulam animals. They pattered confidently up to the waterhole and drank singly, the other watching cautiously. They did not seem as cocky and self assured as the dogs in Eravikulam, nor did the dry, salt-crust-coloured Sariska earth do much to enhance their colours. Behind them were the peacocks, and there were langurs hanging like dissatisfied souls on the pipal near by. A few dozen deer peered out of the surrounding vegetation.

The wild dog is spread over much of Asia, having somehow missed Japan, Sri Lanka and Borneo. Not too much of an island dog, perhaps. In India, at least three and perhaps four sub-species of the dhole exist, ranging from the heavily furred Himalayan one to the pale northern dog and the red southern cousin. Much like the tahr being an almost-goat, the dhole is a member of the dog family but special in a way. Taxonomically, the domestic Pomeranian is more closely related to the wolf than to the wild dog. In fact the wolf, the jackal, the fox and our domestic dog all start their names with *Canis*, an indication that they are closely related. The dhole, which has one molar tooth less than the other dogs and two teats more, is called *Cuon*. It also has more rounded ears and a shorter muzzle that lets it bite more ferociously.

('Teats and teeth,' sang Bharati at Sariska in that high pitched, mad melody that sets her apart from nightingales. 'Teeth and teats.')

Other than these two anatomical peculiarities, the dhole is very much a dog. Very keen powers of smell and hearing allow it to detect food; powerful legs that are built only for running let it get close to the prey. Once it is there, rows of forty teeth make sure that the dinner does not run away. In all this, the hungry dhole relies also on the strength of his fellow dogs. Dholes almost never hunt alone. Even during those mysterious times when their numbers drop alarmingly, there are at least two of them that hunt together. When they are in full strength, they set the forest on fire.

Suddenly, as if to dramatize the scene, a wet wind blew across the waterhole, the sky darkened to the colour of a ripe jamun and the first fat drops of a desert rain pittered on the asbestos roof.

'It's raining,' observed Shailaja, the first words she had spoken in the hide.

The dholes heard her and looked up nervously. The clouds were a juicy purple now. The bitch took the lead and walked away. Mohit clicked in desperation. No tigers, but this was a predator, at least. Like most wildlife people, Mohit was fascinated by teeth, fangs, claws and the hunt. It could be a tiger, a dhole, a goshawk or an owl, just so long as it was a hunter and not the hunted. Occasionally on birdwatches in Delhi, half an hour without a predator would be punctuated by the excited shout of 'Shikra! Shikra!' A confused blue rock dove would fly noisily away. The shikra, a small sparrow hawk, is easily the most common wild predator in the capital and a favourite with Mohit.

The male dog followed the bitch into the forest, and the rain set in.

'Piaaow' shouted the peacocks in great excitement.

On the opposite shore, peahens were pecking away at the earth as the dampening surface started to yield interesting food possibilities. The males, as males are wont to be, were only interested in sex. With a ruffle of his tail feathers, like an experienced card sharp shuffling his pack, a male produced the best hand displayed in the Indian avian world. A thousand blue-green eyes shimmered in iridescent lust at the sombre females. With quickening steps the cock started a slow rock and roll.

Arching his neck skyward, he called cat-like, punctuating every routine with a collapse of the tail. A few minutes later his tail feathers fanned out again in glorious celebration of the thundering rain and the lovers around.

Rajesh had retreated to the far corner. Bharati was puffing frenetically away at her inhaler. The rest of us were watching spellbound this meeting of heaven and earth. A slow leak had started from the corner directly over Rajesh's head. The drops would collect on the eaves and drip down, finding a soft landing ground on his thinning hair. With a curse, he got up and shifted near me and for some strange and inexplicable reason hugged my legs tightly. Bharati was trying to re-choke me by winding the muffler desperately around my neck. I felt like an apprentice deer caught in the coils of a two-headed snake.

'Now, the tiger will come,' decided Mohit hopefully.

'Before that I want to go to the bathroom,' declared Bharati gaily.

'Where are you going to find that, pray?' I was trying to kick softly upwards into Rajesh's ribs to persuade him to go back into a corner. My legs were going to sleep.

'Just outside. You'll come with me, won't you?' Shailaja looked shocked.

'No. I'll come to the door and you can run out and do what you like.' I gave up friendship and kicked Rajesh a little harder. With a soft moan he got up and selected a different corner.

'Will you let me out of this muffler wrap if you want me to come?'

Doracs started spinning slowly away from me and bumped into Mohit who was just about to get a covey of sandgrouse that had come down into the waterhole. It was the last shot he could have got before it grew too dark.

'Will you get out if you want to go to the loo,' he snarled, 'and leave people who want to do serious wildlifing alone?'

The last coil of the muffler had unwound and I gulped in the stale air of the hide gratefully.

I was starting to realize that I possessed legs after all. The deer was winning.

Doracs groped her way to the door, there being no lights to frighten away the potential tiger. A large spotlight had been kept ready for that wonderful moment when the tiger would come to the peephole and declare its presence.

I accompanied her to the door.

'Shit!' cried Rajesh in alarm. A line of raindrops had followed him to his corner and started to drip directly onto him. The corner that he had earlier evacuated was now bone dry. 'Nobody loves me,' he chanted. He had a habit of going into rhymes when his misery exceeded certain fixed quotas. 'Nobody loves me.'

Bharati had disappeared into the darkness and I could hear her fumbling out there. Just beyond her I heard the sound of other feet.

'Tiger!' she cried from the gloom. 'Help! Tiger!'

'Only wild boar, I'm sure,' said Mohit starting to pack his gear up pertly. 'I am sure I heard some.'

I could hear Doracs pounding towards the door.

'I think it could be a tiger. I saw something move,' I said.

Mohit seemed to think a little highly of my wildlife abilities, for he sat bolt upright, his face suddenly losing some of its incipient colour.

'Tiger? Did you say tiger? Shut the door. Shut the door. Quickly!' He was up and running towards the door. In the darkness I could hear Doracs a few hundred yards short of the door.

'Just a minute, Mohit,' I got between him and the door. 'Bharati is outside.'

'First . . .' panted Mohit, 'first shut the door. Then we will see where she is.' He had thudded into me and was scrambling around to reach the latch. At that very moment Bharati screamed in from the night. 'I saw it! Promise! Promise! Tiger! Tiger!' I shut the door and latched it and Mohit immediately leant on it heavily to stop the charging tiger. There was no sound from outside, though, except a few hesitant shuffles. There was definitely a sounder of wild boar about as well, I noted.

'Nobody loves me,' declared Rajesh. 'Nobody at all.'

As it turned out, the dholes were the only predators seen that night from the hide. An year earlier, the brilliant reds of the Eravikulam creatures had been a preview. The dogs of Sariska, dusty and bleached, had completely changed my image of the dogs. This was also the beginning of the end for the dhole in Sariska, for the animals disappeared soon after and have never re-appeared. Dholes, like lemmings, fluctuate greatly in numbers in successive years. The sudden decline in numbers keeps their population in check, allowing them to use the resources around them optimally and more sustainably. (Like the lemming hero of Thurber's short story, I have often wondered why the human race does not evolutionarily adopt the suicide strategy.) Unlike lemmings, however, nobody has seen dholes go and jump off a cliff. It is theorized that the dogs either emigrate out of the pack and its home range or else die out naturally. Packs of fifteen and twenty dwindle to four and five over a year. Just as suddenly as they go down, they build up again, as nature fluctuates around an unseen optimal line.

In Sariska, the dholes had come only for Mohit Aggarwal, as compensation. The tiger never kept its tryst with Mohit's multiple lenses that waited like a jilted lover all night long. But when we opened the door to the early morning air, there was a strange offering deposited just outside it. A trail of a large adult male tiger came up to the door and then turned and led away from it. Was Doracs right or was the tiger a later visitor? Had he visited us at our back door? A tiger sees you a hundred times for every time you see the tiger, goes an old jungle saying. Make it a thousand times and it may still hold true.

'Did I not tell you to shut the door firmly?' asked Mohit.

'Nobody loves me,' moaned Rajesh, 'not even the tiger.'

~

There are only two biologists who have done any work on the wild dog in India. They are separated by twenty years and twenty inches. A.J.T. Johnsingh is tall, lithe and gleams like polished ebony on a moonlit night. Arun Venkataraman is on the shorter side, with large glasses and a halo of dark, curly hair framing a cherubic face. Johnsingh is a pioneer species, a sal tree, who colonized the Indian wildlife scene with a classical study of the wild dog in peninsular India. Many years later, Arun, who had doctored in the social behaviour of wasps, decided that dogs were bigger and easier to see. It was also in their favour that they do not sting but whistle in a manner that no self-respecting wasp would. Infinitely better manners, he thought. So he switched to studying packs of them in Mudumalai Sanctuary, the Tamilian part of the tripartite protected area that spreads across the Nilgiris.

This was during those pleasant times when the sanctuary was called by its original name. Later, as the reins of the state passed on to the omnipresent, omniscient mother of Tamil Nadu, a huge granite nameboard sprung up in the middle of the dappled deciduous forest. On gleaming black granite, in brassy letters eight inches tall, the new name of the sanctuary shone forth at alarmed chital deer. PURAITCHI THALAIVI DR. J.J. JAYALALITHA SANCTUARY AND NATIONAL PARK, it boasted. The new Chief Minister needed immortality and a large number of sycophants were there to provide it. They were not very bothered about the fact that a national park is not something you just add to a Sanctuary. One extra adjective according to her worshippers did not matter much . . . Arun Venkataraman and A.J.T. Johnsingh were lucky not to have to work under the glare of the burnished gold.

The subject of their studies, on the other hand, is a little low on luck. It is an animal as misunderstood as the many mythical creatures of the forest night, the yeti of the high Himalayas, the mokele mbembe of the African rainforest and the Loch Ness monster, a creation of the Scotch drinker. The conservation world has never been kind to the dhole, and even today, the big problem that the wild dog faces in India is its image. It badly needs a public relations exercise, and a candidate who automatically disqualifies for the job is Fateh Singh Rathore, the flashy Rajput with a big hat and even bigger heart. For Fateh, the world is a tiger world, and as with all cat lovers, dogs come a distant two thousandth. '*Kutte hain, saale, kutte,*' he gestured dramatically, sitting before a blazing fire at his mini-fortress in the wilds of Rajasthan one night. 'Dogs! Bloody dogs.'

Fateh was referring to the reputed killing technique of the dogs. Not having that tennis-player forearm of the tiger and the leopard with which to strike down its potential dinner, the dog relies on its powerful jaws to do the job. In case of prey that it feels it can tackle, a bold dog may go and hold on tenaciously to the animal's nose or ear while other dogs disembowel it. Catching a deer by the nose is a favourite technique as this rather restricts the animal's chances of using its antlers to any effect. At other times, packs run in from all sides in an apparent mêlée and snip flesh off the running prey, killing it by loss of blood, disembowelment or sheer shock.

'*Chhee*! Horrible!' spat Fateh, squeezing drops of Scotch from his spreading moustache with the back of his palm. I am unsure of what he would say in that characteristically colourful language of his when he is told that the dogs sometimes bite the testicles of a male prey as well, castrating it before killing!

Fateh should be spared the critic's sword in his rapid assessment of the dhole. Many before him have done the same thing with equal vehemence and venom. British foresters were quick to dub the dhole 'bloody' and a 'perfect swine'. Hundreds of them were shot in peninsular India during the middle part of the century. There was money to be got from the government for destroying the killer of deer, the depletor of game, the pest of the jungle. In central India, where dholes are reputed to take livestock, their dens were dug out with iron crowbars and their pups battered to death. It has been left to scientists such as Johnsingh, Arun and the tiger man of Karnataka, Ulhas Karanth, to redeem the reputation of dholes. Man and dog; centuries of trust, friendship and loyalty. Man and dhole; centuries of uncertainty and mistrust, violence and bloodletting.

In defence of the dogs, their attack is almost always a well-planned and militarily executed one. There is very little time for the prey to realize what is happening before it goes down, in no doubt a gory fashion. Unlike tigers and leopards, which slowly consume the prey, sometimes keeping it for a few days, dholes tend to finish it off fast. With ten or more dogs chomping away with those extra long jawbones—which is what gives the dog its fantastic grip—the average-sized prey is pared to its bones in quite a short time. As a predator the dhole is unmatched in India for achieving what it sets out to do with the least amount of energy wasted. Not the most elegant predator, perhaps, but Alan Border is still worshipped by the cricketing fraternity, Juergan Klinsmann by the footballers and Al Pacino by the rest of the world.

The first story that I heard about the powers of the wild dog was from the pioneer himself. Johnsingh has a peculiar way of attracting wild dogs. It is a well-known fact that to attract an animal a fake call of its mate is often very useful. Birdwatchers carry bulky tape-recorders that sing like the bird that they want to see, moose hunters in America rend the morning air with calls from their blowpipes, and tiger guards at Ranthambhor make a tiger look up for the tourist by making an exaggerated call: Aaahrroomph! Johnsingh produces the same effect by blowing into an empty, medium-bore rifle bullet case. It may be strange to find a tall, dark man walking the tall, dark jungles of India blowing into a bullet to attract wild dogs, but that is exactly how he took to studying them in the southern forests of Bandipur in the late seventies. The bullet works the best according to Johnsingh, although in its absence the biologist also has the option of plucking a large enough leaf, plastering it to the face and blowing through the green surgeon's mask. The resultant shrill shriek is that of a dying deer fawn, a dhole dinner gong.

'I was walking the forests,' said Johnsingh, launching into his story as energetically as he actually walks the forests. 'All of a sudden, I heard a noise in the bush. Dhole! Had to be! As is my usual practice, I stepped slightly away from the road, and taking my bullet, whistled into it.'

At this point he took an empty cartridge shell from his pocket and blew into it as if his life depended on it. The fact that he was talking to a hundred-odd spectators in a large auditorium in the capital did not inhibit him. Half the audience looked fearfully around, expecting wild dogs to appear out of all the curtains in the hall. A particularly excited old lady in the front row screamed in tune with Johnsingh's performance. The showman was back to telling his story .

'You know that wild dogs don't attack people. Wolves and hyaenas may occasionally attack human beings but dholes never do. So I was standing quite close to the bush, expecting two or three dogs to come out of it attracted by the call, and then finding no other dog, go away peacefully.'

He paused for a moment, a slight hesitation before jumping at the audience.

'Imagine my surprise when a large male tiger jumped out of the bush.'

At this Johnsingh jumped and gave a realistic roar that had half the audience screaming again.

'Luckily,' panted the dhole man, 'luckily, there was this rosewood tree right next to me.'

Johnsingh has a funny relationship with rosewood trees. A cousin of the northern Indian shisham, the rosewood spreads over most of southern deciduous India but is increasingly becoming rare, and is now found only in certain patches. Man normally finds the rosewood irresistible for its poetically coloured wood, a king among timber. (The encyclopaedia of Indian Natural History describes the wood as 'gold-brown to rose-purple or deep purple heartwood streaked with black'. Sheer poetry.) Johnsingh finds rosewood trees conveniently large wooden natural towers that spring out of the woodwork just when he has to climb to escape from leopards or to look out for tigers or just to look at dholes.

There was nothing to worry about, however, as the tiger was more interested in its own safety. Hearing the shrill whistle of the bullet it had thought that a pack of dogs were out hunting and decided to make good its escape. Not even noticing a terrified Johnsingh, the tiger looked first to its left, then to its right, and then ran away into the forest with the ghosts of imaginary dholes in close pursuit. The uses of an empty bullet case! I was particularly piqued when I heard that overzealous airport officials had confiscated Johnsingh's favourite dhole-call as he readied to board a plane with a pocket full of empty cartridges. Whatever did they think bullets were for, anyway? To hijack planes?

If Johnsingh did not need to worry about the tiger, the striped pussy cat need not have worried about the dog either. In nature, wild dogs don't often attack tigers and leopards. The three large predators of the Indian jungle lead by and large a conflict-free life. If food is aplenty, they just choose according to size. The tiger will have more of the sambars, the leopard more of the chitals, the dhole more of the fawns. It is known that dholes kill either young or old prey, easier targets during a full-blooded chase. Tigers and leopards kill the biggest they can get, easier to expend energy on when you hunt by stealth. Another theory thought out by Johnsingh, possibly when up a rosewood tree during the good old days, is that dogs take more male deer while the big cats prefer the females. When food becomes scarcer, the leopards and the dogs sometimes compete, but very rarely. Usually the leopard takes the night shift and the dhole takes the day. Wildlifers talk of times when hungry dogs get together to tree a leopard. While some dogs guard the base of the tree to make sure that the leopard does not come down, others eat their fill of the contested prey.

~

Other than the Sariska episode, I have seldom seen dholes in northern India. In the south, on the other hand, they have been constant companions and Arun an accomplice on several occasions. In Mudumalai we watched his study pack attempt a hunt. Around us, herds of chital munched the sprouting grass in silent mouthfuls.

'Tribals,' said Arun, 'are responsible for a large number of kills being stolen from the dog.'

Kethan, his tribal tracker, smiled and listened, ear cocked for the rustling of grass. Out of nowhere, the lead dog shot, tracer-like, across the road and disappeared into the grass. Two more followed, snapping at his heels. The chital on the left had broken up into two herds, both flowing liquidly away into the slope above the tourist reception centre. The dogs were already red ripples in the green; rustles of burnt grass, the crackling of fallen bamboo leaves. One herd of deer was forgotten, the main body left alone. The smaller herd had a foal whose mother was trying her best to push it back into the herd. The dholes were manoeuvring all around, silently pushing away at the grass, playing a delicate chess game where the final push could turn the pawn into a queen.

The bonnet macaques, who hang around the reception centre in the hope of free handouts, started a chattering alarm. Their hair neatly whorled into a bonnet, they dominate the south much as the rhesus monkeys do the north. In Mudumalai they are by far the most ubiquitous monkeys, seen in groups of ten to twenty. The dholes had caused a commotion in the otherwise orderly lives of the bonnets. The long tails that normally swirl placidly behind were half-cocked in alarm. The chital sought comfort in the company of the monkeys. The dholes subsided into the grass, only an occasional ear cocked in anticipation could be seen over the settling grass. Another chase, another hunt. Still failure. Contrary to popular belief, the dogs never run relays, tiring the prey in long-drawn-out chases. Theirs is a swift try and, if successful, equally swift retribution.

Arun was whistling to get Kethan back. He had disappeared into the grasslands to look for the dogs or the signs of a kill.

'The tribals may take it later if they find one,' confessed Arun. Kill steals by humans is a common problem that dogs face all over the south. In Gujarat, maldhari herdsmen try to steal a lion's kill, tugging at the victim even while the king of the jungle is feeding on it from the opposite end. A dhole is easier prey for the southern tribal.

Kethan appeared, disappointment writ large on his face. He had collected a handful of mushrooms as compensation. The dogs had vanished quickly. As in Eravikulam, they did not wait to share the gloom of a failed dinner. Arun and I had to wait another year for a better sighting of the wild dogs together. It was 1997 and we were in Thenkanikottai, on the Karnataka-Tamil Nadu border, together once again.

Thenkanikottai literally translates into Honey Fruit Fort. It is in actuality a dusty Tamil township that borders the Hosur forest range, a few hours away from Bangalore. The Asian Elephant Research and Conservation Centre, which is headquartered in Bangalore, had surveyed most of southern India for elephants. The work done by the centre was a thorough, professional one, the first if its kind for India. But, as is normally the case, they had not looked in their own backyard. There was a need to check out the elephant status in Hosur and Arun wanted to confirm the dhole status as well. The chaotic traffic of the Bangalore-Hosur road had spilled us onto Honey Fruit Fort. Geographically, we were on the Pennagram plateau, a place as renowned for its natural beauty as for its 'comely lasses'.

'Look out for them,' Arun instructed, driving the Mahindra jeep rather too fast for me to catch sight of anything half-way beautiful. 'The Pennagram plateau,' he recited from memory, eyes closed in appreciation, 'a land poor in soils and rich in girls.' Women on either side of the vehicle seemed to be as dark, dumpy and frowzy as the average Tamilian villager keeping alive a husband and five children. It was difficult under the circumstances to attain comeliness and I could quite understand.

'Keep a sharp eye out,' Arun persisted, 'Kenneth Anderson has said so.' I did not want to contradict his guru and therefore kept my eyes glued to the road.

The Range Officer at Thenkanikotta was disarmingly welcoming and made it clear that we could see the forests as long as it did not involve him having to accompany us from the comforts of Honey Fruit Fort or send his hard-pressed guards with us.

'There is a watcher at the gate. He will show you the rest house. Nobody has gone there for a l-o-o-o-o-ng, l-o-o-o-ng time.'

The length of his 'longs' was ominous, but we decided not to pay attention.

The forest as we drove through it turned out to be a dry evergreen one, a less glamorous relative of the rainforest. I was familiar with it from my Point Calimere days but had not seen it for many years. The rest house was just as the range officer had promised.

'Nobody has stayed here after a British *saar, saar,*' said the gate watcher, a charming name that you give the nearest human being to the gate. In northern India he is given the rather more lowly name of chowkidar, who is watchman, gatekeeper, attendant and sometimes cook all rolled into one decrepit creature between a hundred and a hundred and fifty years old. He is paid the princely sum of three hundred rupees for his job. Quite naturally, he cultivates green swathes of crop cut into the poor forest soil and, bone weary, snores inside his self-constructed hovel while poachers, infiltrators and local couples inclined to discreet amour pass through the gate unchallenged. But our friend did not seem the type, although his belly was pressing rather alarmingly to his backbone, a sure sign of poverty.

'How can you stay here, *saar*?' He was quite incredulous.

So was I. The rest house consisted of four whitewashed mud walls with a half roof. There were no doors or windows to be seen and this left rather large holes in the walls through which most of the resident wildlife could visit us for the night. The wood had probably ended up as local fuel after all the furniture had been used up. A coat of white Pennagram dust had cloaked the floor and it was clear that no one had set foot inside in a long time. We found the main door in the backyard and managed to fit it in the gaping hole rather precariously. I had to be absolutely brave about it.

'Of course we can stay here,' I said to the gate watcher. 'Just clean the floor and put a jug of water for drinking in the corner.'

'A bucket of water for the morning would be more

handy,' interjected Arun.

'But where will you sleep, *saar*?' queried our watcher. 'No cots, *saar*, no beds to put on top also.'

Tamilians always put their beds on top of cots, the former being called mattresses in other parts of the world.

'Don't you have two mats to put on the floor?'

'Yes, *saar*, in my house, *saar*. But what about dinner, *saar*?'

'Whatever your wife cooks. And now we will go to the forest for a drive and then come back.'

'But *saar* . . . only rice, *saar* . . . only rice?'

I thought of Mohit and knew he would have suffered if his rotis were not made in time, but the two of us . . .

'That's fine. Rice is okay.'

Arun had already got into the jeep with the bottle of rum and the coke bottles that had been taken out by mistake during the unpacking. At least he had his priorities right.

'But *saar*, only rice, *saar* . . .'

'I said that is fine, didn't I?' The watcher still hung on and his pathetic face had taken on a new dimension of pity for these crazy officers. He had clearly not worn that expression in a long time. There must have been very few more pitiable than him in his immediate vicinity. The pity came out unused and fresh on his creased face. Arun was the first one to catch on. The watcher meant only rice, *saar*—*only* rice. Nothing to go with plain, parboiled rice. This was a bit too rich.

'No curry?'

'No, *saar*, no vegetables.'

'No pickle?' A firm shake of the head.

'Any nearby town to buy provisions?'

Honey Fruit Fort.

Arun and I exchanged despairing looks. Was this going to be the final straw that broke our camelian humps? From near the small shack that sprung out of the forest fringe like an upstart mushroom and that the gatekeeper called home, a familiar noise arose and filled the dusk air. A chicken clucked its way into view. Not the cocky gait of the male grey junglefowl that is protected and cannot be eaten, but the unmistakable gait of the next-door rooster that most definitely can. The macabre signboard I'd seen outside a Punjabi dhaba swam in front of my eyes. The board had a plump cocky rooster painted on it, puffing an exaggerated breast and proclaiming in large maroon letters: 'Meet me anywhere, but eat me here.'

'Whose is that?' Arun and I spoke almost in unison. 'Why not cook that and give us dinner?'

The man's face had gone ashen grey. For a long minute, I thought the rooster was his childhood companion or a venerated local deity.

'That, *saar*, will cost you thirty rupees, *saar*,' he wheezed, unshakeable in his belief that no sane person would offer that sort of money for a night's dinner.

'Great,' I said, dipping eagerly into my wallet and handing him three crumpled tenners. 'Here you are. Now tell your wife to make the rice and the best goddammned chicken curry there is in the world.' I swung into the Mahindra just as Arun started the engine ecstatically.

'Thirty rupees,' he muttered, a broad grin spreading across his face, 'too much, actually, but what the hell.' He revved the vehicle onto the reddish path that cut the forest diametrically. 'Now for dogs and elephants.'

The old watcher watched us now with a look of horror mixed with gay abandon at the sight of the money.

The first sign of life came just as we were passing God's own tank, or Swamiera. The water was to our left, slightly below us. Suddenly I heard a huge splash and Arun braked abruptly.

'What was that?'

In response two more splashes were heard, each a successively bigger one.

'There is something inside,' I said.

'It's big.'

'Huge. Let's have a look.'

As we scrambled down it was apparent that whatever was in the lake was having a whale of a time. Splashing around like an errant schoolboy in the local village pond, the creature was producing a mini-tidal situation. As the last bamboo fronds parted, the grey outline of the creature was clearly visible.

'Elephant,' whispered Arun.

'Elephants,' I corrected, as, slowly rising from their watery playground, twenty-six massive pachyderms formed a single file on the verdant shore across. This was beyond our wildest imaginations and quickly the cameras were put into position and a spot chosen in which to crouch down and observe them. Careful not to crackle the drying bamboo underfoot, I sped upwards to replenish the film stock and descended rather rapidly, braking just in time to prevent another splash in the lake. For an hour and a half we sat on our haunches watching the elephants at play. For an hour and a half they obliged, bathing, rolling, splashing and gurgling in huge delight. Young calves wandered drunkenly on the water's edge, slipping comically and falling in with huge splashes to the accompaniment of reassuring thwacks on their bottoms from their mothers. As dusk approached, squeals, grunts and rumblings rent the air, an occasional trumpet indicating an irate sub-adult demanding its fair share of the pool before closing time. The elephants filed three and four at a time back into the evergreens, and I turned to catch Arun's eye. He was already trying to catch mine. We were not going anywhere for the night. We sped back to the rest house for the promised dinner of chicken curry and rice, and returned to the sporting elephants. They were still at their water games, and we settled down in the shadows. A bottle of Old Monk rum slowly cracked open with a sweet crick.

As Arun brought out the coke bottles, I tried a shrill version of '*Hum yeh multinational zahar nahin piyenge,*' the slogan that Bharati normally greets a bottled soft drink with. Arun's Hindi was probably rudimentary and he did not get it. (For people not familiar with our national language, it means, I will not touch this multinational poison.) And then we discovered that we were without an opener—I was going to be denied the multinational *zahar* after all!

'Shit,' said Arun, a dreamy expression of gloom creeping into his eyes. He has a dozen or so different dreamy looks, the best of which creeps out of him, coyly, after a few drinks.

'Mouth,' I decided and putting the bottle into my mouth, cracked it against the molars. I could feel the tooth giving way. The Honey Fruit variety of the drink came with welded caps. There was only one way. The stepnee! The spare tyre had holes in the hub that resembled a bottle opener, the same way a rock hyrax resembles an elephant. I put the bottles in two at a time and tugged. The tops of the bottles gave way.

'Shit! Shit!' exclaimed Arun. His vocabulary was getting rather repetitive. Draining the life-fluid through a handkerchief had the desired effect, and we toasted the elephants with shredded glass and rum.

'A perforated oesophagus, that's for sure,' Arun commented.

'Better than a perforated penis. Make sure it does not get that far down. Digest it. Pray for dogs.'

The morning dawned clear and red. As we got back into our jeep, pockets bulging with a gift of yellowing guavas that were given to us instead of breakfast, I spotted a leopard track next to the vehicle. Two hundred yards from our open window and creaky door. Fresh.

'It had come to pay its respects,' I joked.

Arun did not seem to like it very much.

'It's eerie, this,' he declared. 'We were up till two in the morning and then this chap decides to do his house call. Or do you think he came while we were swimming our senses into that delicious curry?'

The thought of the night's dinner warmed the cockles of my heart. Never before had plain rice and a coconut chicken curry tasted so heavenly. As the flesh of the bird melted and the grains of the coconut brushed huskily against the palate, a big cat had come a-visiting. Arun swung back towards Swamiera, and even as the thoughts of the curry filled the crannies of the brain, he braked hard on his nose.

'Dogs,' said the dog man. And who would not believe him? 'I can smell them.' Wonderful.

'This pungent, acrid-acid smell of a wild dog,' he diagnosed.

Absolutely brilliant. No wonder they called this child-man a good biologist. He could smell the cussed things without getting out of the vehicle. The wonder of the uninitiated can turn to near worship in some cases. Take the case of Neeraj Jain. A businessman with a reputation of a playboy, he was a friend of Mohit's who had turned up one day in a flashy Toyota, wanting me to take him into Sariska National Park. I had never gone into a wildlife park in a Toyota, definitely not a red one. Very reluctantly I agreed, looking at Mohit's disappointed eyes. Surprisingly, Neeraj turned quiet and attentive and horribly decent when I was around although he was his boisterous and philandering self the moment I went out of view. Some years later, a full-fledged and established friend, he had confessed why.

'Your bloody wildlife eyes, man. Couldn't handle it. I had difficulty seeing the bloody sambar and chital you were pointing out. Mostly shadows in the bloody bushes.' His voice grew more respectful: 'Just as I saw it, you would go and sex it. Male sambar, you would rattle off, or sub-adult female chital. I never figured out how you could see their bloody balls at that distance.'

As the surrounding wildlifers dissolved into hoots of laughter, Neeraj continued his rumination. He had completely missed the antlers. In the males. It was good to be a one-eyed king amongst the blind.

In Hosur, Arun was turning out to be three-nosed. He was smelling dogs all the while. I wondered why I could not, especially after I found out that we were actually driving along a shit trail left by them. Every two hundred yards or so there were two or three blackish-brown cylindrical offerings. Their ends were curled like toffee-wrappers. A few of them had disintegrated, and a most acrid-acidy odour was wafting upwards. Fresh dung is the most recognizable smell in the forest, followed by a decaying kill and Mohit Aggarwal's unwashed feet. Arun was quick on the trail, his face pressed six inches to the ground, a plastic bag-wrapped hand picking up samples with the eagerness of a squirrel gathering its winter nuts.

'Must send them to Front Royal,' he declared, everting the plastic bag outwards and over the sticky mess.

'Lovely stuff. Great samples!' He was not exactly a coprologist, which is a scientific term for shit-gatherer, crap biologist, turd scientist. He did enjoy his samples though, like most ecologists working in tropical forests where there is not as much visual contact with animals as with their morning offerings. Some biologists deduce whole life cycles, nutrition and social behaviour by looking at these samples under a microscope. It is a studied science. If it evolves further, human misery can be solved by looking at a decent human sample. It may contain the answers to broken marriages, work stress and manic depression.

Shit and urine bind Arun and Johnsingh to the dogs. Arun's favourite story is of his tracking dholes in Mudumalai one summer morning.

'You know dogs, they are fast and you have to go quite fast to keep them in view,' he wheezed, picking up lumps of chocolate-brown dog-turds with infinite care. 'They were going up this incline and I was hot on their arses . . . heels, I mean.'

The dogs were gathered at the top of the slope, having temporarily lost sight of their pursuer and, much like dholes, had immediately forgotten all about the human being. Dholes have a wonderful knack of pretending that you do not exist at times, going about their daily lives with complete nonchalance and a hint of disdain. One of the dogs then decided to empty its bowels, a good morning routine.

Arun surfaced on the slope just as his favourite samples came tumbling down and onto him.

'Just missed me,' he chortled, wheezing with the effort of bending down and remembering the past. He looked happy and contended.

Johnsingh's favourite dhole legend I had heard on a cliff in the Garhwal Himalayas, where the only dogs are massive bhotia sheepdogs with iron-studded collars around their necks. We were watching gorals, small, elegant mountain goats, browner, nimbler versions of the tahr.

'Urine!' Johnsingh had declared suddenly, inexplicably, talking to the mountains all around and, through the echo, to me.

'The stories about wild dogs and urine! Hah!' He was now looking at the rapidly dissolving shadows of the far-flung gorals, reliving Bandipur in the Himalayas.

'The tribals say that the dogs urinate in the eyes of a deer to blind it before killing it.'

Good aim the critters must have.

'Or else that they urinate into bushes and then force the prey to run through it. Blind, of course! What absolute bullshit, eh?'

It was difficult for dog piss to be bullshit, but you don't

press these points with Johnsingh. He had already moved back to the gorals and to the mahseer that swam ever so rarely in the deep swirling riverine pools of the Alaknanda below us. Only the flitting genius of Johnsingh could produce work on so many unrelated species—dogs and tigers, goral and elephants, mahseer fish and ungulates.

But to return to Hosur, Arun was bent double over his precious samples, and from behind his proffered backside, a couple of dogs came into view. They let out curious, low whines and Arun straightened up alarmingly fast. The dholes produce a variety of sounds, the most spectacular one being a low whistle, a let's-get-together-and-hunt-boys call. The whistle is never used during a hunt, though, serving more as a contact sound to get the pack together. They also grunt, moan and whimper. All that they do not do is bark. Much like the Ambassador car that comes out brand new from the factory—in a day or two you realize that every part in the vehicle makes noises, except the horn. Not what you expect. Horns should honk, dogs should bark.

Twenty-five feet from the jeep, the two dogs settled on the road completely unconcerned about a gaping biologist and his shit-collecting companion. As I watched them my mind flashed back to the grasshills of Eravikulam. The swiftness of the chase, the precision of the ambush, the grace of defeat. Sand-red blotches packed with power and verve. Today, the dogs were at peace. Innocence their byword, bloodletting a pastime of the past. For twenty minutes they lolled around, courting briefly, a light, low seduction routine that rarely went beyond foreplay. They were not serious, almost as if exhibitionism was their only purpose. Then the bitch, as women are wont to do, took the lead and led the male off into the bushes.

'The dogs of Hosur!' I exclaimed. 'Now, dog man, have we seen them all?

Twenty-six elephants and two dogs, Old Monk rum and a curry from heaven, a leopard's pug mark and a prize rest house. All in a day and a half, in a reserved forest, two hours from Bangalore. This country of mine never stops throwing up the most pleasant of surprises. The gatekeeper was ready with one more.

'No, *saar*, no,' he exclaimed, his eyes rolling skywards, as I offered him payment for his services, the meal, the hastily bundled breakfast.

'You gave me yesterday, *saar*. Thank you, *saar*.'

Thirty rupees was not just for the rooster, it was also for the preparation and the rice, the guavas and his gnarled care. I pressed twenty rupees into his hands as a tip. He smiled briefly, lighting up the forest with unexpected joy. The sum was exactly the same as what he would have got for producing an ear and the tuft of the tail of a dhole to the Nilgiri Game Association in the early part of the century, as proof of his having destroyed the bloody vermin of southern jungles. The wheel had turned almost full circle.

The Nun and the Adjutant

P.C. Bhattacharjee, or PCB as he is endearingly called in the student slang of Assam, popped up to his feet with a startled 'Hoi!'

PCB is short and rotund, not quite flabby but portly in a restrained manner, a physical state academics at a certain level must acquire. He has small, piercing eyes framed by a pair of owl-glasses and a thin Bengali moustache that pencils masculinity onto his upper lip. Most of his remaining hair forms a skullcap at the base of the head and that day a single swathe was plastered onto his forehead with the fevered sweat of excitement. If you knew PCB, you knew that this excitement was his basal state, peace an unusual blip on the life screen. His name had just been announced at the podium and he responded with great alacrity.

'Good morning, ladies and gentlemen. I am Dr P.C. Bhattacharjee from the zoology department of the Guwahati University. I welcome all of you to visit Assam.'

We were at the annual conference of the International Wetlands and Waterfowl Research Bureau. There were more than 200 wetland managers, bird scientists and amateurs in the hall. The hall was in Karachi, Pakistan. I do not know how many took up his opening offer. I definitely did and he may well have rued his generosity a few years down the line when I descended on Assam for my rhino work. On the podium, he bounced up and down, effervescence bubbling over in ecstatic froth.

'When our study started,' PCB explained as an image of the greater adjutant stork flashed on the screen, 'we had first to find out the number of wetlands in Assam . . . You see?'

We saw. The greater adjutant is by far the most endangered stork in India. It gets its rather martial name from its habit of stomping a military dance in the marshes of the north-east in search of food. It is a large black and white scavenger, with an estimated global population of less than 1000 birds. Like most of the species in danger stories, it once had a much wider distribution, ranging over much of south and south-east Asia. Less than 500 birds, half the world population, are now restricted to north-eastern India—PCB and his students from the Guwahati University have counted 126 nests of the bird in the Brahmaputra valley. Another hundred birds definitely exist in Cambodia, and the rest are scattered in fragmented pockets of Nepal and south-east Asia. Not a pretty situation to be in.

On the screen, the bird seemed to be sullenly contemplating its next move. It glared malevolently at us, fleshy head and neck stretching forward and a tiny stubble on its bald pate standing up in excitement. The huge yellowing bill was overshadowed by a pink, cadaverous pouch hanging from the neck like a vocal scrotum. This is what distinguishes the bird from the far more common lesser adjutant, a close cousin on the paternal side. The white feathers on the body parted at the shoulder to reveal more pink flesh, a bladder-shaped baldness starting at the wing-edge.

'You see, in Assam it is very difficult to tell how many wetlands there are.'

PCB spoke with a slight pout and a strong Bengali accent, both contributing a child-like coyness to his speech. 'When there is no rain, there are hundreds of wetlands. When there is too much rain, we have only one wetland. The state of Assam.'

Wetlands, according to experts who should know these things better than politicians, are areas of shallow water, marshes and fens, peatland or swamps; standing or flowing water with submergent and emergent vegetation. The politician, who in real life knows these things far better than a scientist, thinks of wetlands as real-estate submerged by water. Areas that can be drained and transformed into housing colonies and parking lots. Land that can be de-silted and from where water can be diverted, to transform a natural ecosystem into a new-generation playworld for the children of the neighbourhood. The playworld would make lots of money for the politician while being built and afterwards. The parents of the children might also vote for him. Wetlands and waterfowl indeed!

PCB, however, was no politician. He spoke with much gesticulation, his small frame reaching out into space in frantic gestures as he held forth on the stork and its habits, its threats and the conservation solutions possible.

'We have many problems in conserving the stork.' A slide of the Guwahati garbage dump was now being screened. Thirty-five of the most endangered storks in India rifling through Pepsi cans, chicken entrails and a hundred plastic bags. 'One, of course, is just working in

Assam. So many kinds of people, so many languages, so many customs.'

He was bursting the bubble that the state of Assam was a single entity. The many people of Assam—the Bodos, the Karbis, the Misings, the Rabhas, the Bengalis and the Ahoms—were also busy bursting the bubble using explosives and firepower, letting flow the blood in a thousand mutinies. It was 1990 and the state had just started experiencing violence in its Bodo regions.

'When we printed the brochure for the stork,' P.C. Bhattacharjee explained, 'the most important thing was colour. We sent a red-coloured brochure to a Bodo area and they chased us out with sticks. You see . . . they think yellow is a good colour. Red is for war, for bloodletting.'

By now, people were sitting closer to the edges of their seats, looking at this bouncing man, an anachronism in the dignified world of high scientists.

'Terrorism, now that is one problem. But the biggest problem for the storks are the trees,' confided PCB. '*Gos*, you know *gos*.'

In the state of Assam the three 'G's dominate conservation problems: *Gaur, gos* and *goru*—rhinos, trees and cattle. The rhino, a state heritage species, is falling every day to a hail of poachers' bullets. The tree count in Assam is at an all-time low, with the timber and tea industries having ravaged the land. There are also, of course, the low-milk-yielding holy cattle eating up the forest—India's single largest problem in all protected areas.

'The big trees are all cut for timber. Only smaller ones remain. Then you see . . . the funny thing.' Conservation is a glum business at most times. Luckily for PCB he has plenty of funny things up his sleeve. 'The stork is a big bird and the nest is a big nest, but the tree is a small tree. The bird . . . it lays two eggs and in about a month's time there are two big chicks to feed; babies that get bigger by the day.' Big was explained in mime, by reaching out to embrace the universe, and the audience, who pre-empted his joke, tittered appreciatively.

'Then, one day, comes the mother bird to feed the two big chicks and lands on the nest. That day, by coincidence, comes the father bird too! He also wants to see his chicks and lands on the nest. One big mother, one big father and two big chicks. See . . . the funny thing. The tree falls down . . . Big problem.'

Earlier conservation problems described at the conference were loss of genetic variability, felling of riverine forest patches and the hunting of cranes by organized crane-hunting camps in Afghanistan. PCB had brought the conference to the ground with trees. See the funny thing!

~

Four wild birds captivated me that winter month in Karachi. All four loom four and a half feet off the ground, the Gullivers of the bird world. All four are threatened species. Two of them are definitely endangered, and attract world attention. The other two are near-threatened, waiting in the wings, hoping that the world will discover them before they go extinct. In a conservation world dominated by charismatic mega-mammals, birds come a distant second.

The four birds belong to two families, unrelated but

similar-looking to urban man whose familiarity with birds extends to the sparrows beneath a park bench. There are seventeen species of storks; long-legged, voiceless birds that inhabit both the temperates and the tropics. Most of them are predominantly black and white, like characters from a silent movie. None of them have in their throats the soundbox that allows other birds to coo and trill, warble and cheep. It must be hard being a bird and not being able to wake up the neighbourhood with the mellifluity of being. Angered by the rather unfair evolutionary disadvantage, the storks rattle their beaks instead, which are huge sabre-sized appendages that dominate the face of the bird. Their necks stick out from their bodies at sixty degrees to the vertical. All of them build large stick-nests perched awkwardly on any available platform with no attempt to conceal their homes from predators. Many of them are colonial, though a few are highly territorial and suffer a solitary existence. When they fly, they stretch their massive wings outwards, trail their legs behind a rather short tail and alternately sail and flap into the twilight. Some are conventionally ugly birds, others pass muster till they take off in an ungainly fashion or open their mouths to let loose their castanet-ramblings. They are nobody's favourites except of mother storks and pregnant human mothers who associate them, rather strangely, with their babies.

The cranes on the other hand are grace personified. The family is a 600-million-year-old one, a hundred million years older than the rhino family. The ancient cranes resembled the modern day crowned cranes of Africa. Fifteen species of cranes have today colonized the world; all except South America and the Antarctic. They are as tall as the storks, sometimes taller. Their legs too are as long as those of the storks', and sometimes longer. Most cranes are white and grey birds with a touch of red; just a wee bit of blood, to excite the onlooker. They are mostly feathered delicately on their backsides like samba dancers or Hawaiian welcome-girls. Some extend the feathered charm to the side of the head and neck. All of them dance exquisitely and while they do so, render the latest avian musical hits in a stentorian operatic tenor that beats the beak-rattle of the storks rather handsomely. The cranes are among the most loud-voiced of the birds and their song-and-dance repertoires have fascinated millions of people of different cultures and races across the world. The elaborate courtship dance of the cranes may be a means used by individual birds for establishing species and gender, according to some scientists. That makes the birds seem rather silly, as if they need to dance to know who is who. Others maintain that dancing is usual foreplay before a rather ungainly and short sex act. Bernard Shaw, as usual, puts it far more succinctly than an avian biologist. 'Dancing is the vertical expression of a horizontal desire,' notes the veteran Irish ornithologist who wrote plays in his spare time.

The two waders, for that is what the long-legged storks and cranes essentially are, make for fascinating comparison. The stork is the gawky, long-legged adolescent girl, croaking her first notes at her debutante ball. The crane is the poised demoiselle, long and loose in the limb, with a spring in her gait and a song in her throat. They have both fascinated me in equal measure. At Karachi the prima donnas were the Siberian and sarus cranes; the debutantes, the adjutant and black-necked storks.

While PCB and his group were espousing the cause of the adjutant, two other groups were saving the cranes. The International Crane Foundation set up by George Archibald in the United States was the Siberian crane's saviour. Its Indian-born representative, Minnie Nagendran, long-legged and lanky like the crane, was there with some of her Russian counterparts. For the sarus, the one-man army of Prakash Gole fought handsomely. The quiet, unobtrusive Pune-ite can pass off as a small-town academic. He is actually a big-time dreamer. For many decades his work on the sarus crane in particular and other wintering species of crane in India have made him a popular figure in Indian conservation. There was no champion for the black-necked stork as such, although in my presentation I had highlighted the stork and the Indian skimmer as birds vanishing over large parts of their range where they used to be common.

The black-necked stork is found throughout its range in solitary splendour, although rather sparsely and in decreasing numbers. In some parks such as Keoladeo Ghana, it still survives in large enough numbers along with the Siberians and the sarus.

Keoladeo Ghana is the big bird park of India. More popularly known as Bharatpur, the name of the small Rajasthani town near which it is situated, the park is one of four internationally acclaimed wetland sites in India. They are called Ramsar sites after the Iranian seaside town where the decision to honour such areas was taken in 1971. High time too that the decision was taken, considering that a large percentage of India is under water, and wetlands are the most neglected of all wildlife habitats.

Wetlands, ecologists try to tell the politicians, contribute to human beings just as much as they help the birds. They control floods and erosion, recharge the groundwater that man has tried very hard to drain away, are a source of water in arid areas, have plants that are an economic asset to man, regulate water quality by detoxifying the water that passes through them and influence the global cycle of nutrients like carbon, nitrogen and sulphur. They also provide a habitat for wildlife, like at Bharatpur. Come winter and a huge congregation of migrating waterfowl skid in to land in the park, joining hundreds of bird gazers. Gathered to watch the tourists are the shovellers and snipes, pintails and pochards, gadwalls and garganeys, grebes and geese in the water. On the sand *bunds* that run through the park, there are the Germans and the Gujjus, the British and the Bengalis, the Japanese and the Just-for-fun-ese. Taking advantage of the commotion, a few lily white birds try to sneak in every year with a red cowl pulled low over their yellow eyes. They fool nobody. The whole world and their Indian nannies wait assiduously year after year for the arrival of the Sibes. Allen Hume, who when he was not the father of Indian ornithology also formed organizations such as the Indian National Congress, described the Sibes as the snow wreath, the lily of birds. The Germans call them *nonnenkranich*—nun cranes. The white feathers of the bird bunch up into a cowl at the neck, framing its rather red face. This, I am told, reminds German birdwatchers of nuns. A nun with a red face! Decidedly German!

One of the more memorable trips that I have made to Bharatpur was with my sister and three other friends. Taking my sister Shailaja to a national park is like boarding a high security jet with a time bomb strapped to your waist. There is always the chance of detection because of the noise. Even if past the first layer of security guards, there still remains the very real possibility of a premature explosion.

'I like birds, I like birds,' she shrieked, dancing around the hotel room, sending everyone else scurrying to the four available corners. My old buddies Rajesh and Mohit occupied the two farthest from me and the nearer one had Ruchika, Shailaja's classmate and an equally new entrant to the world of nature and birds. Ruchika is a big, dark girl with a husky sensuality that she tries to hide rather ineffectually, and an extraordinarily deep voice that is created for singing sad songs. Mohit was doing what he does on the eve of a trek into a wildlife area, cleaning and caressing his lenses. Rajesh was swatting mosquitoes with his glum look and a roll of newspaper, while Ruchika stared at him with great fascination.

'You must show me those black-necks and blue-bills and red-whatnots, okay, okay?' Shailaja was still dancing her high fevered trot.

Fine, I agreed, if she could get up at five in the morning.

Five! Nobody got up at five. Only demented souls and total idiots. Ruchika looked at Rajesh rather pointedly.

Rajesh had not managed to get a single mosquito. He had, therefore, done the next best thing. He had wrapped a large, coarse, black and maroon blanket over his head and shoulders. He had his hands carefully hidden in its folds. For mobility, his feet needed to be kept outside the blanket, so he put them into twin blue plastic bags held in place by rubber bands at the ankles. Ruchika's wide nostrils flared slightly wider. She whispered something into Shailaja's passing ear.

'Gussssiiieee,' shrieked the sister, 'Gussiiee Fink Nottle.'

'Do you collect newts?'

'No, I don't.' Rajesh was trying to be cold. Botany had nothing to do with newts and he was sure that Shailaja was insane.

'When he wears shorts, are his legs bow-shaped?' she was shrieking into my ear now, a sordid secret that only I was supposed to know.

'No.' I was the absolute authority on Rajesh's legs.

'But, look at him, he's sooo much like Gussie.' Even Wodehouse had not seen his character as clearly. Ruchika decided to do a rendition of a sad romantic Hindi melody. Her baritones drove the sadness from Rajesh, wiped clear Mohit's lenses, soothed the banshee in Shailaja and lulled me into a premature sleep full of cranes and ducks, storks and geese.

The morning dawned on the hinges of the music of a million waterfowl. Bharatpur demands an early morning wake-up, a drowsy walk to the chai-shop, a stumble to the park gates and then a full awakening by a chorus of assorted birds.

'*Oi, vekho, ji, vekho,*' one of Mohit's Punjabi friends had enthused on first catching sight of Bharatpur's avian spread, '*eh vekho. Storka te gheessan de jhund pe jhund.*' (Look, look, clusters of geese and storks!)' And indeed, spreading in ripples of clustered bodies were a mass of waterfowl: ducks and geese, storks and cranes, egrets and herons, cormorants and darters, waterhens and lily-trotters. A world of water, a water of wings. December was bang in the middle of the migration and a large number of the migrants had reached the refuge of Bharatpur to mingle with the resident species. The birds arrive by October and leave by March, a pre- and a post-migratory congregation exhibiting the largest variety at a time. During those special weeks, certain birds like the delicate garganey teal, a small pink-brown duck with a white ear tuft and a green wing, are suddenly seen at Bharatpur.

I was especially interested in checking out if the Siberians had come in as yet. I had been monitoring the park for the Sibes the last two years in a personal capacity and as co-ordinator of the Asian Waterfowl Bureau's mid-winter waterfowl census for northern India.

The Siberians and Keoladeo Ghana are linked together for posterity. True to its name, the Siberian breeds in Siberia. Ornithologists have a great capacity to come up with descriptive names. Nine times out of ten, if a bird has pink feet and a yellow bill and lives in Mongolia it will be the Mongolian, pink-footed, yellow-billed bird and not the weeping wydah. And so the Siberians breed in Siberia during the Russian summers when the ice thaws sufficiently for the birds to find food for their chicks. Come winter and the big migration starts. Migration comes at noon, with a southerly wind blowing across their tail feathers. As the wind gains favour, a flock rises into the air, spiralling upwards and leaving their already cold homes in a V formation. For many years, I have struggled with the V. It is strange to think that in all these years I have not seen birds coming in to land in any other formation. No other letter of the alphabet gets used except occasionally the I when a straight line is formed. The V according to many biologists is a means of reducing wind resistance, a ploy so clever that aeronautical engineers had to learn from the birds.

One lot of the Sibes goes off, in this holy V, to the southern coast of China to spend the winter. At last count there were two thousand or more there. Another lot decides to fly longer and more to the west and comes in through Afghanistan and Pakistan to India. Even this flock splits over the Afghan ravines and a smaller number move to an Iranian wetland. The ones that come into India use the Himalayan flyway or migratory pathway that is the main road in the skies for more than 300 species of bird forms that migrate into the country. The country has over 2000 bird forms of which a sixth are foreign visitors. Incidentally, form is not a scientific word, just a convenient usage that clubs together species and sub-species and races and all other such technical terms that people would love to forget altogether. The Sibes are the stars of this migratory show. For many years, Bharatpur has remained the last stand of the Indian wintering population of the species—Custer's Last Stand, Nelson's Trafalgar, Rana Pratap's Chittor.

'Are these egrets, egrets, egrets?' chanted Shailaja as plumes of white rose daintily from wattles, dipping their toes into the water.

Bharatpur is a chequered land, sloshing with shallow water that a special water-regulating system maintains. Along the borders of the checks run earthen *bunds* or raised ridges on which we were walking. In olden days, kings and visiting English gentry shot birds from these *bunds* and the legacy of the bloodletting was carved on a stone plaque in the middle of the park. On average days a few hundred birds fell victim, on a special day as when the Viceroy of British India himself came down for a shoot, it would be in the high thousands. Today, tourists use the very same *bunds* to admire the birds.

'Yes, these ones are intermediate egrets.' I pointed out the little egrets on the edges of the water and a solitary large egret further off. These are the toughest to differentiate. The cattle egrets are easy because of the yellow suffusing their heads. The herons are all sufficiently different as well—the purple, the grey and the night; names that come on with a sunset.

In the distance, two nuns stood in white. White and Bugle. Strange names for nuns. Nuns hand-reared by Minnie Nagendran trying to look like a mother crane. This was an exciting concept. To imprint young captive birds on their wild mothers, Minnie wore outsize gloves that looked like the top half of a crane's body. The clothed forearm was what the chicks got used to and so mother-crane was Minnie-crane. This was a wonderful way to make sure that the cranes didn't recognize human beings and run to every Japanese tourist in Bharatpur with loud cries of affection. Instead they were released there to watch and wait for the actual Sibes to come in. They could then recognize them and mingle with them. Probably if everything went right they might even be accepted by the flock to go back to Siberia. The re-introduction would be a success. There was, however, one small problem. The wild Siberians had not come this year around.

In 1964 there were 200 Siberian cranes that landed at Bharatpur. By 1984, twenty years later, there were only forty-one. A decade later, there were none. The year before, five birds had landed, giving some hope to the project. White and Bugle had been transported to the park just before their arrival. The idea was to fix radio-transmitters onto the young ones and follow them back home. The young ones, however, fought shy of the new birds and did not fly back. Too little time, wept conservationists; give them more time. And so in 1993 they were ready and waiting. For non-existent cranes. The reason for the decline of the Siberian is a hotly debated point. The ruddy Afghanis shoot them down, of course, say one group of people; stupid birds to fly over a war zone. Too many pollutants in the waters, say one lot. They are dying just like the sarus are, declare another. They are just going elsewhere, just not coming to Bharatpur, claim a third. But the most interesting hypothesis by far is that it is all because of buffaloes and *paspalam*.

The buffalo and grass story is one of my favourites in demonstrating the arrogance and ignorance of man. Man, who wants to manage wetlands just like every other habitat. Man, who therefore removes the buffaloes who have been grazing in the park for centuries and throws them outside newly built stone walls. Buffaloes that eat grass, including one special one called *paspalam*. *Paspalam* which without the buffaloes grows high and luxuriant and spreads like a thick mat over the wetland. A mat that suppresses sunlight and competes with other vegetation including some which have tubers that the Siberians eat. Tubers that the cranes dearly love and that they probe out of the slime with their delicate red beaks. What a bother! The buffaloes are killing off the cranes. Or is it the manager? The man who knows enough to take decisions to change ecosystems? He should go out and look at the night stars that come out swollen and large, like I did.

On the half-submerged stumps that rose dissatisfied from the water, a line of black birds were drying their wings.

'Look, Ruchika, look! These ones are spreading their wings like Christ on a cross. See! Like this.'

Shailaja had assumed a classic Nataraja position, not at all like Christ's and completely unlike the cormorants that were sitting on logs with spread wings to dry themselves. The long-necked snake bird or darter also joined them on the black clothesline; two of the few birds not blessed with the waterproofing that most other waterbirds have.

'If you make so much noise, the snakes won't come out,' threatened Mohit, his lenses searching frantically for pythons as we approached Python Point. This was a favourite draping point for the Indian python and trees and mud banks often camouflaged this massive reptile coiled in a deceptive slumber, taking in the heat of the sun.

'Snakes! Snakes! I don't want snakes!' Ruchika was definite. 'They are slimy.'

'Of course not, silly,' Shailaja had to say something. 'My brother has told me. Rough. Like ladies' handbags.'

'Do you like them, then?' Rajesh was willing to spoil her outing. 'There are a hundred and two of them in the park.'

'Not entirely,' Shailaja was edging away from the water.

'Don't talk so much. You just scared away the nilgai, see.' Mohit's photography was never successful with a lot of people around.

'What's a nilgiri? What's a nilgiri? I want to see a nilgiri.' Shailaja had caused the first smile of smugness to shine on Rajesh's face. He knew more!

The sun had got hotter overhead, as passing the Keoladeo temple, from which the park gets its name, and Python Point, we headed out away from the water into the drier and arid parts of the park. The girls were lagging behind, the soaring heat sapping enthusiasm and vocal cords. For a sudden moment or two the sun was blocked by twin shadows and the four of us squinted skywards to look at a pair of black-necked storks flying overhead. From down below they were white birds with black necks, heads sticking out in front and black tails fanning out at the back. Across the predominantly white wings, two bands of black made an interesting pattern. In the glare, the deep red legs trailing behind looked black as well. The jaundice in the eye was hidden by the distance.

'Black-necked, black-necked!' danced Shailaja.

The black-necked stork has been dealt a low blow by evolution because of its territoriality. If there is one thing a male stork cannot stand in his territory, it is a second black-necked stork. Unless it is a female and he is in breeding season. Even then, he may chase her away with the religious fervour of a Christian missionary banishing infidels and heathens from his home turf. His iridescent head, largely violet, turns a purplish blue and his yellow eye sears through the mauve. Long orange feet stomp a celestial tandava and the intruder retires quietly to a nearby area. This is very good for the individual stork. It is disastrous for the species. In a world where every inch of habitat is fought over by man and beast, no species can afford to squabble among themselves over what is still with them. Yet, evolutionarily this is not possible. And so they duel and posture, squabble and peck, threaten and maul, all in order to draw their own lines of territoriality over a chosen area and around a favoured mate. Very beastly. So much like man.

~

Years passed and I visited Bharatpur on an annual basis. Once in a while a season would go by when I could not go, but the very next year I would visit the sanctuary a couple of times and atone for my ornithological sins. Cranes and storks remained in my life, but came in stronger than ever over New Year 1998.

'Where have you bin all this time, eeh? Fucckker you are, yaar,' drawled Anil Mulchandani. I was meeting him after nearly ten years, although we had kept up a Gujju-English dialogue for nearly all that time. Letters were received regularly from Anil *bai.* (*Bai* in Gujarati is brother, in neighbouring Maharashtra it is the maid; Indian cultural versatility at its best.) His letters were always written on bright yellow writing paper with numerous animals crawling all over the top in an unabashed display of his love for wildlife. Anil had branched away from a family textile business to start a travel agency that explored the wilds. In this move away from the world of business into the world of creepy-crawlies, he resembled Mohit. There the resemblance ended. It was now 1998 and I was back in Amdaavad (Ahmedabad for the uninitiated). Anil *bai* was there to greet me. He was subdued, very subdued and I felt that either the years had mellowed him or that he was uncomfortable with Kumi Junior sitting beside me.

Kumi was Japanese and I had first met her in Tokyo where she was my translator for my talk on elephants. You need translators in Japan. Especially ones like Kumi. I had liked her the moment I set eyes on her. She was very young, with an open face that had still not been closed over by life. A Japanese hair fringe framed the Oriental guileless look. 'She is pure girl,' Kumi Senior had assured me as if her virginity was under discussion. At the talk I was faced with an audience of inscrutable Japanese whose only connection with elephants was the ivory name seal that lay in a drawer of their study tables. I desperately needed translators like Kumi. As it turned out, she seemed to have been sent to me by Ganesha, the elephant god.

'The elephant is a god in distress,' I began.

Kumi Junior pulled up her chair nearer the table, fiddled with her hair band twice and began to translate earnestly. Her face shone with the excitement of translation but like all good Japanese (a term that she loves to hate) she put on her best 'inscrutable' make-up just before beginning. She translated my opening sentence in five minutes. I drank a glass of water, nodded appreciatively and wiped my brow seven times.

'In India they kill our god in five ways,' I ventured.

Kumi translated it in four minutes. I finished my talk

in one and a half hours. Kumi spoke for an hour out of this. The Japanese were stunned into applause by the translation and I had won a friend. Six months later, on a trip to India to help the Missionaries of Charity in Calcutta, she decided to visit me in Delhi.

'Can I be of some help?' she asked, very Kumi-like, full of solicitous concern.

'Of course, of course, you can,' I replied, and took her on a one-week, two-thousand-kilometre car journey, bumping across the driest part of the country in search of elephant ivory. But that is another story. At the fag end of it we sat together in a hotel room in Amdavaad with the benignly large presence of Anil *bai* beaming in front of us.

'What wildlife can we show her in a day and a half, Anil?' I asked, guiltily aware that her spare week in India had been spent driving through dusty towns and out-of-the-way villages negotiating for ivory, instead of relaxing in the middle of tiger-jungles listening to the reassuring creak of a herd of elephants ambling through bamboo thickets.

'The Rann is veeery faaar, Veevek *bai*.' Anil knew the Rann of Kutch very well but was too busy to come with us. Vistas of open salt desert with galloping wild ass and flocks of flamingoes swam before our eyes.

'Maybe Velavadhar.'

Velavadhar is a patch of golden grass in southern Gujarat where corkscrewed black buck spring around in gay abandon. The male buck is a handsome critter, gleaming chocolate-black above and white below, rather overshadowing the fawn doe by a bit and more. On his head he sports a pair of perfectly honed corkscrew horns.

Antelopes have horns, deer have antlers, and that is one easy way of distinguishing the two. Horns are not branched, are not hollow inside and are not shed once they have grown; antlers are all the opposite.

In Velavadhar, the black bucks were pronging in the air in graceful parabolas over liquid-eyed does; an exhilarating sight amidst golden sheaves of grass.

'Are there cranes in Velavadhar?'

Kumi wants people to believe she is not Japanese in the true sense. The whole world and their grandmothers come to India to see the tiger, and Kumi-*san* wants a crane!

'There are thousands in Keechan, eeh,' drawls Anil *bai*, 'maybe only hundreds in Velvadhar, eeh.'

For the first time in the trip Kumi's eyes brighten.

Till I met the Japanese Wildlife Conservation Philosophy Society, I thought that cranes were the only wildlife that lit up Japanese eyes. With a thousand-watt Sanyo luminescence. Despite the fact that they are not manufactured by Mitsubishi. Cranes are long-legged, delicate, white-skinned and paired for life, highly desirable attributes that the Japanese search for in cranes and geishas alike. The Japanese, I thought foolishly, can only munch whale-burgers with much baleen-crunching delight, turn elephants into drawerfuls of name seals and kimono drawstring beads and pass bowls full of tiger penis soup around in a devout awestruck manner. Nothing moves them beyond an occasional '*Tso-tso*'. But give them a crane or two and the Japanese go misty eyed. Through the mist they see the peaks of Fuji-*san*, the clear flowing waters of mountain rivulets, the green of paddy fields around their country home. The courtship call of the crane is the Japanese conservation conscience awakening after a brief ecological hibernation cushioned by the warmth of the rising yen. Or so I thought, for quite a long time. These views of mine have altered greatly after meeting the three musketeers of Japanese conservation. All three as different as they come. Professor Hideo Obara, snow-capped like Fuji-*san*, bent with respectability, the voice of the Japanese soul. Masayuki Sakamoto, dark-eyed with impatience, hair flopping over his face with the onslaught of ideas, rushing through life with a mission of rebellion. Kumi Lee Togawa, the gender-balancer in a modern musketeers' world, a minstrel with a smile that spans continents and a heart full of cherry blossoms. Their fight for tigers and elephants is a great story but luckily for them they have not yet had to fight for cranes.

Kumi Junior and I decided to look for cranes on a drive starting from the golden heart of Velavadhar and ending in the dusty heart of Delhi. I owed her one and if it was cranes that she wanted, cranes she would have. The belt is definitely crane country. In our wake at least four crane species could occur. The increasingly uncommon common crane, the tiny ballerina demoiselle crane, the resident sarus and the avian star, the Siberian. I did not tell Kumi, but the black-necked stork could also be seen rather plentifully along the way, once upon a sunny time. This was not science, it was more fun. Utilizing time that would otherwise be spent munching salted peanuts and ridged potato crisps. In Indian lingo, time-pass. We had two days and 2000 kilometres.

The count started auspiciously enough in Velavadhar. It was getting to be dark and the last light of the day was spreading like a tea-stain on muslin. Whatever it touched turned to a shade of yellow-brown. The grass was yellow-yellow, where it was burnt it was brown-brown. The female blackbucks clustering in the centre of the grass were milky coffee-brown, the soaring spirals of their males a rich black-brown. The dust track ploughed by passing jeeps was rust-brown and the edges of Narendra Jhala's field camp where we sat drinking cups of the quintessential tea-brown chai, were suffused with ochre. Narendra Jhala is India's wolf man and is currently with the Wildlife Institute of India. He had radio-collared wolves in the park and was not averse to the idea of going out and having a 'hear-see'(radio-tracking parlance).We could look for cranes as a bonus. Jhala drove his jeep with a skilled single hand and gestured with the other to show us the sights around. Indians are wont to use their hands generously.

'A cobra-tail, a cobra-tail, a classic mating posture.'

Jhala was pointing to a male nilgai, horse-high and pitch blue. The females are fawn brown. An aroused male was advancing gingerly on his white-socked toes up to a young female, his short tail curled above his rump like the spread hood of a cobra. Jhala is a mammal man and is widely respected in conservation circles for a fine mix of grimy fieldwork and sound theoretical biology. His students swear by his teachings as well. A formidable combination. I had known Jhala little and this was my first time with him in the field. His eyes were glued to the antelope couple.

'Look at the birds.'

Kumi tried to distract his mammalian attention. In a flock of wheeling beauty, a dozen common cranes took to the skies, legs trailing behind limpidly. Their bodies gulped in the dusk air in huge considered wing-beats.

These ash-grey cranes with a black neck bib and a red skullcap are fairly common in India during winter. Breeding in the inhospitable swamps of northern Asia and Europe, the cranes wing across the Himalayas and enter the northern half of the country before winter sets in fully. In protected areas like Velavadhar and in completely unprotected maize and corn fields, flocks of the three-foot cranes then set the cold air ablaze with their largely welcome presence. Almost throughout India, the cranes are welcome birds, farmers tolerating their crop raiding because of old fertility beliefs and perhaps charmed by the grace and elegance of the ballerinas.

'I'll show you more,' Jhala promised and we cut across the main tar road that divides the park into two distinct cleaves. Around a bend, a small patch of water mirrored a smaller flock of cranes. These were common cranes as well—fifteen of them. On a sand mound beside the water, six painted storks perched, their pink-flushed feathers rippling gently in the breeze.

'Can we get out? Can we get out?' whispered Kumi.

In India, moving out of the vehicle in a forest full of tigers and elephants is not advisable for tourists. On the open plains of Velavadhar with storks and cranes and blackbucks trotting around, the dangers were slighter.

'Okay, keep the silhouettes down and creep towards them from around here,' I instructed. As we got down, the birds took off in an alarmed squawk, legs trailing behind, a loose V formation appearing even in their hasty flight.

The trip began at five the next morning. From the Rann

to Rajasthan. More than a thousand kilometres. No cranes. I had done drives like this a number of times in the past looking for the sarus and the peacock, two large, magnificent birds that symbolize northern India like no other avifauna. Species associated with wheat and maize fields, with the torrid yellow of the mustard crop, with sugarcane. At dawn and dusk, they would be in the fields picking away at their chosen diets or displaying with the lazy elegance of a showperson, the spectacular bodies that both are endowed with. Year after year, the counts became lesser and lesser, the numbers lower and lower. There could be a host of reasons for this, among them poaching, habitat loss and pesticide poisoning. The sarus is the tallest flying bird in the world. That itself should have got it enough conservation importance to ensure its protection. It is also the only crane that breeds in Asia south of the Himalayas. Unfortunately for it, the bird is also considered one of the most adaptable and common of the crane species of the world. It is only recently that the cries of conservationists, notably Prakash Gole, have been heard and the species put in the list of endangered birds of the world.

The trip was a craneless and storkless one till we reached Bharatpur once again. Kumi seemed tired by the exertions of the drive. The birds woke her up rather well.

'Let us finish Bharatpur in an hour or two so that I can take you past the Taj on the way back.' I was still trying to compensate for her lack of a holiday.

Kumi lengthened her pout. Her ponytail flew about in consternation

'Is it possible that we go and see the Taj tomorrow instead?'

This was unusual. Most visitors started with Agra as a Mohammedan starts his day with the Ka'aba.

I said that it was.

'It is just that I did not want to spoil the effect of the birds with the Taj! Not on the same day anyway.'

Kumi was definitely not a typical Japanese. The birds heard her say that as well. It was an unusually glorious day at the Ghana. Waterfowl sparkled everywhere like diadems on a tiara. All of a sudden, from amongst the cacophony rose the clear clarion unison call of the sarus.

'Look!' I whispered, 'the sarus dance.'

In front of us not more than ten feet away from the *bund* a pair of sarus were just starting up their performance. They twirled around, twiddling their pointed ballerina toes delicately in the water. The dance of the sarus is as spectacular a performance as you will see by any bird. The pair stood close to each other with their feet apart and probed the ground with their bills looking apparently for food. Food was not on their minds, however, I reminded the by now enraptured Kumi-*san*. They were establishing proximity, the first important step in their courtship ritual. Now, who would have thought that you needed to get close to each other to have sex!

All of a sudden one bird looked up and away and started ruffling its feathers and shaking its body in excitement. Unfortunately its mate continued to feed. The time was not ripe as yet and the two waited for another moment. Once again the initiator tried to excite its partner and this time there was a response. Now, the posturing could start. Neck held low and tail extended, each bird proffered itself to the other. Wings outstretched, they seemed to embrace their wetland world in symbolic love.

And then slowly, pirouetting and side-stepping, the pair broke out into a dance that is the pinnacle of the bird world. As the big birds wheeled and twirled, flapped and danced duet, the five feet of ungainliness was forgotten in a spectacular display of balance and tone. Suddenly, the male gave a series of low, long calls—the unison call. The female responded with shorter, higher notes. The pair had bonded. For life. Kumi-*san* had justified her trip to India.

~

Back in January 1990, the conference in Karachi was winding to a close. I had not attended the penultimate day because of ticket and visa complications. Now, the office of the Governor of Sind had promised to bail me out and in fact put me on a boat to cruise the Indus valley while the papers were being put in order. When the visa ran out and the airlines refused to take me out, I had cursed Pakistan's cussedness. When I had to present myself at a police station every day like a common criminal, I knew why we had fought two wars with them . . . But then, suddenly I found myself with the man in the street who offered me discounts on the food I ate because I was Indian, gave me letters to post back home to his various relatives in India and addressed me as brother. Why did we fight the wars, I wondered. Now that the Indus trip was confirmed, I could attend the last session without the thought of Pakistani jails. The mangrove along the coast provided a far more interesting option.

At the conference, preparations were afoot to receive abstracts and full written papers from the delegates which would then be made into the proceedings. Hussain saab, the genial organizer of the conference, accosted PCB in the corridor leading to the main hall.

'Dr Bhattacharjee,' he wheezed, smiling all the while, 'you will give us your paper on a floppy won't you?'

'No, no, *bhai*, no floppy and all that,' PCB seemed quite perturbed and his pout had lengthened. 'I'll give in typewritten sheets.'

Hussain saab was the meticulous organizer looking at the most minute detail.

'But, you know, we have to key it in again if you give us typewritten sheets. Can't you give it in a floppy?'

PCB had drawn himself up to his full height. He replaced his few strands of hair on his forehead with great dignity.

'You see, Dr Hussain, that is very difficult for me because I am not used to these PCs. You see . . . the funny thing. The only PC that we have in the north-east is P.C. Bhattacharjee.'

The conference closed amidst much mirth.

The Horn of Sorrow

Muhammed Aslam moved cautiously through the burnt grass of Pobitara Wildlife Sanctuary. It was the wee hours of a February morning, chilly but frost free, the short ankle-length grass skirting the fringes of bald open spaces. Dawn was still a few hours away but there was sufficient moonlight to allow a sepia visibility. In the haze, the Mayong hills blurred into infinite shapes and the highway to Guwahati seemed waterlogged. It was a perfect day for Aslam; good visibility, good weather, and in the far horizon, the reassuring hump of a rhino's back. Just the right combination for a rhino hunt.

Pobitara Wildlife Sanctuary lies fifty kilometres off the Guwahati-Kaziranga road, a main highway that cuts through the arm of north-eastern India arterially. Pobitara is Assamese for the Sanskrit *pavitra*—pure or virginal. It is named after an ancient Mayong princess of the same name, only now the park is known more as one of only ten places in the world where the great one-horned rhinoceros can be found. The park is just sixteen square kilometres in area, not enough to hold sixty-five rhinos within the sanctum sanctorum. They often graze on the boundaries, sometimes getting bold enough to stray into nearby agricultural fields. Just as the farmer around the world chases errant cows, the Pobitara farmer picks up a crooked stick and runs after the rhino yelling nonsensical war cries. India is absolutely special in such marriage of man and beast. In the Gir forests of Gujarat, maldhari cattle herders pull a joint of meat from the jaws of an adult Asiatic lion. In northern Bengal, crowds paint the night with flame torches pushing back a herd of marauding elephants into the forest. At Pobitara, the buzzword is *gaur*, Assamese for rhino. With the highest density of rhinos in the world, the park is a haven for both the rhino viewer and the rhino poacher.

Aslam had started his night's work three hours earlier, checking the peripheries of the park for a stray rhino in the paddy fields. He knew that it was easier to kill the animal on private land. The shot of his muzzle-loader might be heard by villagers waking up early but would not create enough panic to start an investigation. The carcass would probably be discovered in the morning, by which time he could be several hours en route to Kohima in neighbouring Nagaland. He would use the autonomous hill district of Karbi Anglong for his getaway.

But today there was no rhino in the fields and Aslam had perforce to switch to his second plan of action. Slinging a cloth bag over his shoulder and armed with a long bamboo pole, he made his way through the *dandis* that criss-crossed the park. *Dandis* are rhino lanes, torn through the low bush by the bulk and power of the behemoths in search of fodder. One-way lanes that the rhinos habitually frequented for food, and if Aslam could help it, for death. Ten minutes down the *dandi*, he looked skyward and found what he was looking for. In a few moments, he was on his hands and knees assembling a death trap that he had devised a few seasons ago when conventional methods had failed to get him his prey. He had with him a long bamboo pole with a metal hook attached at its head. Passing above him were two high voltage 11,000 kilowatt cables that run through Pobitara. Taking a length of wire from his satchel, he attached it to the tip of his bamboo pole. Slowly, very slowly, he inched it up towards the crackling wires. Aslam knew that without the protection of the insulating bamboo, his life would only be worth a few seconds. He could feel his heart pounding. As the metal tip hooked onto the power lines, he could hear the current lapping at it hungrily. He let go of the pole, leaving the wire dangling waist high in the air. At times, helpful farmers would poach electricity to run their irrigation motors and Aslam would get a mesh of finer, smaller wires at more accessible heights to lay his trap on. This *dandi*, however, was on the high-tension route and from his observations over the past two days, he knew that the Big One would come this way in half an hour. Work over, he sauntered into the nearby bush, a couple of hundred yards away, and sat on his haunches beneath a silk-cotton tree. The *semul* blessed him with a new shower of silken white wisps. Time to wait for the Big One. The Habitual One. The Lucky One!

Dawn had still not broken when Aslam heard the first wheezes of his quarry. Within moments, he could perceive the bulk of a rhino grunting its way through the grass. A mammoth beast, a male one-horned can fairly tear through the bush. Aslam caught his breath as he looked at the horn on the rhino. It was a large one. Almost certainly more than 800 grams. Perhaps as much as a kilo. The price he would get could sustain his immigrant family for more than a year. Even as his eyes followed the slight curve of the horn, the rhino came upon the wire. With a surprised snort, it tried to back away. As the massive bolt of electricity charged through its body, it wheezed twice and with an amazing hastiness crumpled in front of Aslam. With a whoop of joy Aslam rushed to his quarry. The huge beast lay on its side, dead in less than a second. This was what Aslam had waited for the whole season, and with practiced hands he hacked the horn off. He was careful to cut from the base, eager not to lose any of the valuable shaving that might add to its weight. With a sharp knife he sliced off one of rhino's ears and wrapped the horn in it. He knew from experience that the Marwari at Kohima would ask him to prove that his horn was genuine. Aslam laughed a hollow laugh. You could fake a rhino horn with a buffalo horn, but who could fake a rhino ear? Large, soft and fleshy with blotches of fresh blood on it, the ear told a story that the horn could not. Aslam hurried away from the scene with his bag, slung over his shoulder, and the bamboo. Half way home, he threw the bamboo into the undergrowth. He did not need to hunt for at least a month now and for the next time he could easily cut a fresh pole. What he needed to carry from now on was only the one kilo or so of the horn.

Aslam was not to keep this horn for long. His misfortune was a revolutionary range officer called Bhupen Talukdar. I met Bhupenda in Pobitara, fresh from a confrontation with Aslam. He sat on a metal standard-issue cot in Pobitara flanked by two World War II vintage guns. A ·315 rifle lay on his left, a double-barrelled shotgun on his right. He had just finished retrieving the Pobitara horn from Aslam's village in a daring counter-attack planned over many months. No officer had done a raid in this manner before him, but then few range officers are like Talukdar. Outside, the park was quieter than ever before, but through the silence filtering in, Bhupenda could hear the rumblings of discontented villagers and a troublemaker politician.

'I have six bullets, three in each gun,' he pointed to his weapons, 'standard forest department issue. I have to explain to the department after I use up three, so that I get three more.'

On his gaunt, bearded face, a betel-stained mouth pouted. His laugh was red with betel vehemence.

'I think they will come tonight. I can get six of them. What do you think?'

He is polite enough to ask you what you think. He is rebel enough not to care about your answer.

Talukdar's men had developed the intelligence that led to Aslam in a village on the north bank of the Brahmaputra. A deal was struck by a covert officer. The horn was to be delivered mid-river in a boat and an unmarked briefcase containing three lakh rupees, in unmarked notes, exchanged for it. Talukdar packed a suitcase with newspaper cuttings. He laid his men out on their stomachs in a melon field on the river bank. They waited through the night and tensed as they saw the outline of the boat in the early haze of dawn. There was only one hitch. The melon-field owner was coming to have a morning look at his crop. If he raised an alarm, all would be lost. Talukdar never wasted time. He barked a short order. An extended leg tripped the farmer who found himself lying cushioned against a melon with a rifle down his throat. The boatmen never suspected. In ten minutes they were within firing range and the guns of the department opened up. Three dead, four injured and the horn safe in the custody of the government. A brilliant retrieval planned and co-ordinated by men who are tree growers and park managers. Whose last weapons training was three decades ago. Who have three bullets in each rusty rifle and for whom 'undercover' had thus far only meant running for cover from poachers' bullets.

'In other parks,' Talukdar smiled, 'they say that only God can protect the rhinoceros. Here we do the work ourselves.'

~

There are five species of the rhinoceros in the world, of which two are in Africa and three in Asia. The black rhino is the African rhino whose plummeting numbers sent the conservation world into a great tizzy. Slightly better off is the white rhino which, when you see it, is no less black than its cousin. The 'white' is a Dutch Afrikaner word which means wide, a reference to the animal's square Muhammed Ali lips that are suited for grazing, in complete contrast to the pointed Narasimha Rao lips of the browsing black rhino. Both these rhinos have two horns. In Asia, the Sumatran rhinos also have two horns. Less than 300 of these exist on the Indonesian island and the species stands on the brink of extinction. Better off than the Javan rhinos, though, of whom there are less than a hundred left.

The greater one-horned rhinoceros, found today only in India and Nepal, is so named because the Javan rhino is smaller and known as the lesser one-horned rhinoceros.

At one time, the greater was also called the Indian rhino, but the Nepalese took offence to this, as the rhino was a creature of the mountain kingdom as well. A brilliant bureaucrat came up with the double barrelled name of 'Indian/Nepali rhinoceros', a name as cumbersome as the system he represented. Unlike the Indonesian rhinos, the greater one-horned was once extremely widely distributed, spread throughout the Indo-Gangetic plains and the Brahmaputra riverine tracts. The destiny of the pachyderm flowed with the waters of these two mighty rivers of India, or so it seemed. It was befitting, considering that like the Ganga and the Brahmaputra, the rhino is also part of our heritage. Five hundred million years old, this large land mammal has both the majesty and the wisdom of the ages on its side. There is only man on the other.

With the advent of tea in the drawing rooms of the West, the rhino, peculiarly enough, felt the first strains of civilization. Tea companies cleared natural forests and grasslands and planted the olive bush over vast tracts. Darjeeling tea, which today epitomizes quality in the beverage, is a product of the north Bengal terrain once inhabited by the rhino. So are the Dooars, the Assam and the Brahmaputra teas. For the rhino, tea spelt tragedy. Nearly a century of conservation measures later, there are less than two thousand greater one-horned rhinos in India and Nepal, the last refuge of the species. Is the rhino slated to be the most endangered land mammal in India? There are approximately four thousand tigers left in the country and about twenty thousand elephants. That makes the rhino population less than half the tiger and one-tenth the elephant population of India. True, there is the lesser known and the less glamorized pygmy hog or hispid hare that could be biologically more threatened with extinction than the rhino, but it can be safely said that the rhino is the most endangered charismatic Indian mega-fauna.

Unlike the tiger and the elephant which reproduce prolifically given stable conditions to do so, the rhino is at best a very hesitant breeder. Even if the one calf, born after a very long gestation period, can stave off natural threats of mortality and grow into an adult, it faces a serious threat from an unnatural enemy: man. It is clear that the immediate problem confronting the rhino is not habitat loss. Of the two thousand animals, approximately fifteen hundred are in eight separate protected areas in India. In Nepal, too, two parks contain most of the rhinos. These parks are not shrinking by the day, so the habitat available for the animals is more or less the same as was fifty years ago. But while habitat loss has been more or less arrested, the rhino continues to die because of the presence on its nose of what can only be called the horn of sorrow.

The horn on a rhino's nose is a compact mass of hair, much like human nails. Keratin is what the biologists like to call its composition. Medicine is what most Orientals like to call it. The rhino is killed in India for a demand that originates in the Far East. The poacher sells the horn into a well-knit trading conglomerate that operates mafia-like in India and Nepal. Many miles away and across the seas, the horn finds its away into Taiwan and China, South Korea and Japan. In Taiwan, the Asian horn is called the horn of fire, as opposed to the horn of water, which is the African horn. Worth between five and ten times as much as the African horn, the Asian product is used in a variety of traditional Chinese medicine preparations. For many years, Western scientists could not read Chinese properly. With the wisdom of the West they proclaimed all such medicine mumbo-jumbo and the myth that rhino horn was used as an aphrodisiac spread. When in doubt, give it a sexual connotation; less questions are asked as a result. Then, Chinese scientists started to learn English and write papers in it. An age-old belief was shattered. Doctors in Hong Kong proved that rhino horn reduces fever in rats and that it has antipyretic properties much akin to paracetamol. The rhino is being killed, therefore, for an alternative to paracetamol, an essential drug and not a luxury commodity. Chinese Crocin!

The attitude of conservationists has thus to change accordingly. Finger pointing at alleged Chinese mumbo-jumbo will not wok. It is time to tell the Chinese that Paracetamol off a chemist's counter is cheaper, as effective and ecologically a whole lot better than rhino horn is in bringing down fever.

~

In June 1991 I had written an article on the illegal bird trade in an Indian daily. Wildlife trade, I later learnt, was not something that people wrote much about. Biologists avoided it as it was not science. Managers and foresters avoided it as courting it would be too much like Pandora opening her box of little evils. Enforcement officers avoided it as it was not as sexy as narcotics or arms running. Only a few people loved tackling the challenge. A few days after the piece appeared, I received a call from

Ashok Kumar of the World Wide Fund for Nature-India. I met him four days later and that afternoon I had a job. It was a job with a mission; to help start up India's first wildlife trade monitoring unit in WWF. I have always had a weakness for starting things. It is only in completing them that I have had problems. Srishti was Delhi's first wildlife organization and I was happy that I had something to do with its formation. The time seemed ripe to move on and do some other useful job in wildlife conservation. Nobody was talking about poaching and the trade in wildlife products with any seriousness. Create protected areas and let traditional foresters protect wildlife, seemed to be the general consensus. The idea of exploring a new possibility excited me. Besides, Ashok's enthusiasm was infectious. He sat hunched on a chair that seemed to be too small for him, and I sensed in him an unease that implied a knowledge that his was not a job suited to sitting. His close-cropped white hair spread unevenly over an emerging pate. Years of business management experience had taught him the most effective combination of looking completely disinterested and faraway when in conversation and then pouncing on a loose word that anyone let through. His hands were forever clenching and unclenching. I was not to know then, but he was to prove much more than a boss in the years to come.

'You take on the *gainda-shaindas* and the *haathi-waathis*,' he said with characteristic nonchalance and a half chuckle. His laugh is most reminiscent of the chirrings of a spotted owlet at its roost. His was the tiger realm in those days. Much later, weakened by the air of the terai forest and the effects of rum, he confessed his true love for the elephant, but in 1991 he was very much the tiger man of WWF-India. The *gainda-shaindas* were the 1500 or so greater one-horned rhinos left in the grasslands of Assam and north Bengal. I remembered PCB's invitation at the Karachi conference. This was the opportunity. I took the first train to Guwahati and reached it a short forty hours later.

Four hours down the highway from Pobitara, a small climb marks the beginning of Kaziranga National Park. From the elevation, the spread of the park can be seen, stretching 430 square kilometres upto the mighty Brahmaputra. Twelve hundred of the remaining rhinos in India inhabit the park. PCB invited me to Assam, Manju Barua called me to Kaziranga. Idealism strains through Manju's whiskers as he speaks the slow, long drawl of an Assamese aristocrat. His is an old Guwahati family and living by culture and the sword comes equally easy for Manjuda. Aristocracy is evident in the erectness of the being, but there is great humility in his personal life. An early ideologue of socialist movements in the north east, there is a hint of disillusionment in his body language. At times he reminisces of Assam's forests and their systematic rape at the hands of outsiders.

'I am not a conservationist, I am a businessman. What do I know of saving rhinos and all that?' he says slowly and softly.

He is referring to Wild Grass, a luxury hotel that he has set up on the outskirts of Kaziranga. There is an old elegance to the new construction, and with an equally old-world charm he invited me to be his guest in Kaziranga. There is a story that the conservation of the species in the park started with only a dozen animals.

Today it protects sixty per cent of the world's greater one-horned rhinos. The last safe deposit locker for the species protected by brave fighters and modest ideologues. Also, surrounded by a gang of lock-breakers and pilferers, bank-robbers and masked gunmen.

There are five ways to kill a rhino in India. You can shoot it, poison it, trap it in a pit, electrocute it or hang it. Of these, shooting is by far the most popular and most simple. To kill an elephant, poachers use home-made guns with crude bullet-shaped pieces of window grill. To kill a rhino, poachers have even used a semi-automatic weapon fitted with a silencer. Like those used for executing the president of a country. With the influx of arms into Assam, an AK 47 is as easy to procure as a muzzle-loader. The only problem with shooting is in escaping enforcement authorities who may be alerted by the sound of the shot. This is, of course, presuming that enforcement men are in the park. In Kerala, a poacher was once arrested on charges of shooting over a hundred elephants in an area.

'Whom did you pay money to, for getting into the forests?' asked the prosecuting lawyer in court, sure that such a large scale of crime indicated complicity of the authorities.

'I am not the sort of person who goes to people's homes to give money,' retorted the accused sharply. 'Who has ever heard of forest staff inside forests anyway!'

Before arms became easily available, a more traditional method of poaching was used extensively. A trapezium-shaped pit, about five to six feet deep, is dug on the rhino *dandi*, lined with sharp bamboo staves and then covered up with branches and leaves. Once a rhino falls in, its neck is forced upwards, making it easy for the horn to be cut off by the poachers. Pit poaching is used extensively on the north bank of the Brahmpautra where the terrain is more suitable to do so. Poisoning and noose-trapping are far less common and are used only when essential. Poisoning has occurred in the past in the hill tracts of Manas where pesticide was left out on natural salt licks. Salt licks like waterholes are areas of great animal concentration and the method causes indiscriminate killing of other animals as well. A steel noose, hung about three feet above the *dandi,* is sometimes used. All methods are planned to perfection by very clever poachers, and their job is made easier by the terrible stupidity of the creature in following its rigid habits. Five hundred million years is a long time, I suppose, for a creature to form its habits. Whatever the method, the end is clear. One very valuable horn and one very dead rhino.

In 1996, Kaziranga was as safe as it gets, because of three dedicated men. Poaching was the lowest in many years. It was rare to have the three men most responsible for the turnaround in one room. The Kohora Range Office was using up most of the furniture it had, as all of us crowded into the room. Bhupen Talukdar occupied the central chair. His beard sprang on either side of his face in continuous defiance. Alongside me sat a small, bald ball of muscle, porcine eyes leaping out of an intelligent face. Dharanidhar Boro was a Boro tribal. The woodlands of the eastern range, where the elephants roam, was his charge. In a corner, surveying all around him with elegant disdain, was Pankaj Sarma, tall and well built, goatee well trimmed, cap in perfect position, hands in pockets of well-cut khakis. The three musketeers of Kaziranga were as different as they come. To save the rhino, they employed techniques as different as those come. It was a relief that the cause was the same. Around us were scattered two dozen rhino horns. It was an annual stock-taking exercise and I was a guest allowed to measure, photograph and pass the odd comment.

Talukdar had done very well in Pobitara, in fact he had done even better at Orang Sanctuary on the north bank of the Brahmaputra on his earlier posting. In the middle of a poaching wave, he had come up with a zero poaching year and followed it up with a single poaching year. He was rewarded with a transfer to Pobitara. Then there was the wonderful operation at Pobitara. He was shunted out without a posting. It was the Indian government system at its best. The Assamese had merely perfected a two-hundred-year-old bureaucracy. There was a hue and cry in conservation circles. Talukdar was not an easy man to ignore. He wrote poetry in Assamese newspapers. Revolutionary verse. The conservationists loved him. The system did not. For once, the system seemed to bow slightly to pressure and Bhupenda was back at the helm of a range. The most coveted range in Assam: Central Range, Kaziranga National Park at Kohora.

I had visited each of the three musketeers in their ranges to get an idea of their protection methods. On the western side, almost at the border of the national park, is Baguri range. Beside it lies the hilly range of Burrhapahar which is not really a rhino area and is therefore often forgotten in the final tally. An April morning in 1994 and Shaila Maira was with me on an elephant at the break of dawn in Baguri. Shaila was a colleague at WWF, an honest, uncompromising friend who alternately lifted me out of deep depression and pushed me back into it with her frankness. In the dawn-light of Baguri she looked radiant. Clouds poked pink fingers at the earth. The earth responded sullenly, changing colour from pitch black to grass green in a matter of moments. A transient world of magic enveloped us. A small *beel* separated us from a herd of swamp deer. The *beels* are the lifelines of the park, shallow lakes that drain away from the river and secret away a hundred fish, a thousand types of vegetation and a few rare mammals. The otter and the river dolphin in Kaziranga are creatures of the *beel*, the latter coming in from the main river for moments of solitude or breeding secrecy. As the elephant lurched towards the waters, the surface parted abruptly and a rhino grunted out.

'I thought it was a log,' breathed Shaila and indeed for a good ten minutes the horn and the ridge of the back had been visible like a piece of flotsam in the waters. As the sun rose, the creature emerged from the waters. A few dozen egrets took off in hasty flight, legs trailing across a rosy sky. Pankaj Sarma drove up in a jeep. He was back from a sleepless night in the forest. A shot from the forest had drawn him into the night. An encounter with three fleeing men had kept him there. The rhino in front of us was possibly the one who benefited.

'Patrolling incessantly and good intelligence is the secret,' Pankaj confided over small cups of red-green tea, 'but this is only possible if all the higher-ups help.'

Anti-poaching as an ideal had come early on in life to Pankaj. Almost cushioning the city of Naogaon there is a sanctuary called Laokhawa Wildlife Sanctuary. Even today, remnants of the protected area exist but I had heard that the sanctuary was now more of a large, cultivated field. Pankaj accompanied me to the potato field. This was a pilgrimage for him. A return to his first wildlife posting. A cascade of a million memories. A forest that spread to the banks of the great river, a thousand pressures, the violent mob, the axe slashing his scalp, the end of naiveté. It was a pilgrimage for me as well. Along with Narayan Sarovar and Darlaghat, Ranthambhor and Chilika, Laokhawa is a constant reminder of protected areas gone bad. But Laokhawa is a unique sore. Nobody has heard of it. Those who have, do not want to go there.

The *bunds* that raised the jeep a few feet over ravaged earth were potholed and cratered. In a country where main roads without potholes are commemorated with signs of 'pothole liberated stretch', not much should be expected from forest roads. The range office was a decrepit structure, the entrance hidden by a massive pile of logs. Seized contraband. A funeral pyre for the forest.

'This is terrible,' Pankaj moaned, 'nothing has changed. Only become worse.'

The range officer could not receive us. He was in hospital recovering from a head injury. He had told the villagers that they could not cut down the forest. A cardinal sin in Laokhawa. He had also told them that they could not fish inside the sanctuary without permits. They showed him forged and fake permits that had been issued by his own department mates. He was tough. They were tougher. Pankaj felt his own scalp gingerly.

All around were the remains of a park. Trees had been felled rampantly and on the peripheries there was now almost no cover. Towards the interior a few clumps of narrow-sized trees remained. Even the grass had gone.

There were more than 5000 cattle grazing inside Laokhawa at the time. There were fishermen fishing in the *beels*, and farmers sowing potatoes and beans on the periphery. Clusters of huts marked the boundary, pushing inwards, incongruously and insidiously.

'This is gone, brother.' I could see the pain in Pankaj's eyes. 'All of Laokhawa is gone and nobody knows about it.'

That in fact was the bigger tragedy. Seventy odd square kilometres of forest. Fifty-six rhinos. Six weeks of mayhem. The rhinos gone, the forest ravaged. Two years of court fights and political interference. The death of a sanctuary.

'The rhinos of the north bank, you know, Vivek,' a forest officer in charge during those dark days confided in me much later on, 'on the north bank of the Brahmaputra, are a new sub-species.' Laokhawa itself is on the south bank but it connects with the Burrhasapori population on the northern bank. In fact most of the rhino populations in Assam were at one time connected through tenuous links of wilderness. Describing sub-species was a favourite pastime of aspiring forest officials. In a world where the knowledge of the scientific name of the species raised a few eyebrows, sub-species was a social propeller.

'I nearly wrote a paper on it, you know. All those skulls lying around. It was so easy to measure them. In France somebody has also measured skulls, they say. What do you think, eh?' he was leaning forward, conspiratorially.

'If I wrote it up, do you think I will be able to prove it is a different sub-species?'

I knew what I thought, but could not vocalize it well enough. He had watched, perhaps with legitimate helplessness, the 1983 massacre. He had been witness to an entire population of rhinos being wiped out. All that was left for him to do was to measure their skulls and write a scientific paper on the remains.

'I do not think that is possible, though.' I was as diplomatic as I could be. 'There was another paper published in Germany, you know, which said that all these methods were bunkum.'

German was beyond his comprehension. I hoped that he had given up his research and left the rhino remains alone.

The middle range was the area that I had covered the most thoroughly even before Talukdar took over. Other than the range officers, Kaziranga was lucky to have had a succession of good higher-ups as well. Pankaj had for a boss in those days a Divisional Forest Officer who wanted to patrol in the nights. The very presence of an officer of that rank in the forests at night gave strength to the ragged band of guards and foresters. Men who are underpaid to the point of poverty, undermotivated to the point of ridicule and underarmed to the point of death. I spent many a night in the park with the forest officer. He showed me most of the central range of the park. Kohora at night took on a completely different shade and the air smelt fresh and sweet as if perfumed with the expectations of a new day. The nights at Kohora also brought the life of the forest guard into sharp focus. In ramshackle guard posts and camps, the true men of the forests led lives unseen and unheard by the outside world, walking the forests on foot and in the harsh discomfort of the bottom rung of a service. Lives commanded by those other men who had day shifts and offices and vehicles of comfort. I sat on the forest floor beside their wretched thatch-roofed huts, drinking their midnight tea and sadly, involuntarily, thanking the heavens that mine was only a romantic foray into the forest, not the daily grind of an invisible man. The melancholy of the dark disappeared when the night brought out creatures that were difficult to see by the day and even rhinos that were seen day in and day out assumed shapes of significance and terror as they loomed a few feet away in the cloak of indifferent light. The night also brought forth the occasional new species.

'Vivek, I want to tell you something very important,' the forester with me said, his eyes twinkling in anticipation. 'I have discovered a new species.'

After the sub-species of Laokhawa, I was reasonably well prepared.

'A new species! What is it, then?'

'That I cannot tell you, except that it is a mammal. Everything else is top secret.'

The last large mammal discovered in India was the golden langur and forty years had passed since then.

'Very well then, let's get to this camp of ours. I would like to discuss the patrolling beats in this area with you.'

'No . . . this beast, you know, seems to be very rare.' He was raring to get back to the topic.

'When the patrolling beats are planned out, does the range officer consult you?' I was pretending not to be interested.

'Of course . . . of course . . . But you see, this new species . . .'

'Either tell me about this species of yours or let's forget it, okay? Let's get on with our work.'

His face was set in grim lines of determination.

'Well, you see, it is a cat species, a new wild cat species.'

'Fantastic! Those are the best for publicity. What's new about it, then?'

'It's black. Like the black panther, but is as small as a domestic cat.'

The black panther is a melanistic form of the common leopard. There was nothing that small and that black.

'Fully black ? Or splotched or blotched or . . .'

'No! No!' He was getting impatient. The jeep was fairly flying in his hands. The forest revolved by like a racecourse in velvet.

'It is a fully black, new cat species, I tell you. And besides what! I'll show you the species if you want. I know where it will be at this time.'

This was getting more fantastic by the minute. A rare creature who was punctual.

'Beneath the palm tree near the *beel*.' He was certain, and sure enough a dark shadow detached itself from the base of the trunk as the jeep rolled towards it. It had been feeding on a fallen cluster of palm fruit. As it crossed the track parting the short grass, a clear view could be had.

'My new species!' the forester was ecstatic, 'and just where I predicted!'

The palm civet is a creature known to science for many hundreds of years. It is the most common civet in India, a family that is feline in its movements but shares some of the low-slung mongoose body architectural plans. It was not a cat. It was not new. My guide was a good forester but he had been fooled by the light.

'Let's get out and have a bite.' I needed a little time to break the news gently.

We sat in a line-dhaba, the Assamese version of a Punjab roadside eatery.

I plucked up courage and told the truth gently.

'That was a palm civet, my friend. Not a cat at all.'

His face puckered in disbelief, then withered like a mango in the sun. For a moment I thought that he would cry. Just as fast as the storm cloud arose, it blew away.

'Never mind,' he brushed aside my consolations, 'never mind, Vivek.'

He gripped my arm tightly like a drowning man. 'Never mind. I still have a violet sambhar!'

As midday approached, the next day at Wild Grass, I spent a few moments under a creaking bamboo grove beside the river Dirring. It was hot in the first week of May, but beneath the *kakobans* it was cool and pleasant. A light breeze sprung up from the south and the bamboo bent accommodatingly, stirring up a mild protest from its weary joints. Around me the voices of nature asserted their right to life. The cicadas were all around, chirruping in notes that rose to a crescendo and then tapered off like the winding of a rusty clock. Two lineated barbets called for their mates from atop two mango trees. Whether it was their maddening guttural calls or the season, I was unsure, but the trees were shedding small, unripe fruit, littering the short grass with green and golden balls. A royal blue butterfly, the colour of a silken night sky, flitted across my face. Two bulbuls and a magpie robin orchestrated their notes from close by and then from a little further off. Bosagaon on the banks of the river settled into the smooth cycle of a summer afternoon.

The river Dirring separates Golaghat district from the hill regions of Karbi Anglong. Known for centuries as the Mikirs, the Karbi people were gathering together in an uprising, claiming their rights to development and a new identity. There were no *kakobans* in the hills opposite me, no trees above a certain girth either. Raw logging trails snaked their way up the base of the hills, the short vegetation torn up by the dragging of timber through them. Every now and then a truck roared into life, its load of bamboos and logs, ever decreasing in girth, destined for the paper markets. *Vang Ik Nom*. Welcome! a Karbi sign proclaimed across the river. 'We want development. Education for all.' Was scrawled underneath in sprawling graffiti. My eyes wandered across the hillsides and were suddenly drawn back to the river by a streak in the water, a rippling sensation in its sub-cutaneous regions. Slowly, the sensation rose and then, with the graceful artistry of a performing gymnast, a water snake raised its head over the water. Neck downwards, it still remained submerged, but through the water I could see the rough diamond-shaped scales, keeled strongly. The snake coiled through the water, swimming powerfully and intelligently, manoeuvring its form across and around the currents. I stood up to watch it more closely. The footfall on the drying bamboo litter caused it to start and veer away towards the opposite bank. Suddenly, a brown patch on the nearby bamboo clump burst into a brilliant blue form streaking across the river in full-throated alarm. A white-breasted kingfisher in flight is a marvellous sight, often underestimated because of its abundance. The snake, startled still further, coiled tightly against the bank, perfectly camouflaged, discernible only to the already alerted eye by a gentle rustle in the flowing waters.

I settled back into the welcoming shade of the bamboos with a thousand images of Kaziranga flashing through my mind. Where I sat was the farthest corner of the Wild Grass compound created by the love and wisdom of Manju Barua and his team. In front of me lay the barren hills of Karbi Anglong, a land laid waste by his short-sighted fellow Assamese. Five kilometres away was the treasure house of Kaziranga National Park. A small spider, its back streaked with yellow and its nervous legs brushed with rufous, scuttled past me. Then Kamini Barua appeared through the culms with a drawn and agitated face. He was a friend and partner of Manju's and an instantly likeable person. Behind him appeared Hemanto, the most trusted guide at Wild Grass, waving his hands about through the bamboo leaves. The cane hat on his head was momentarily dislodged by a branch and he picked it up with a small grunt. His permanently pasted smile was missing and Kamini seemed serious as well.

'He was nearly killed by the rhino,' Hemanto explained as if it was a natural occurrence that took place at regular, reassuring intervals. Kamini had just got back from a rhino census in the park. Normally censuses are a totally official affair but with younger and better informed park managers taking over and with criticism from a number of quarters, outsiders have started getting involved. Kamini was the Wild Grass representative at the year's rhino count. The count was done on elephant back. He had sat sandwiched between the mahout and the guard.

'We were seated like wildlifers, you know,' explained Kamini.

When tourists ride an elephant they sit on a mattress-base with four corner wooden posts to hold on to and in extravagant cases, a metal bar across the body to act as a life belt. When foresters or wildlifers sit on an elephant, they straddle it, letting the pelvis get stretched like in pre-natal exercises. In rare cases, they straddle it bare backed and then the rough skin rubs the inner thighs raw and red. In June 1997 I had mounted an elephant in that fashion in Mudumalai Sanctuary. Sukumar and I were checking on an old female elephant that just seemed to be standing in the forests to die. She had a mysterious smooth hole in her wrinkled skin. Over the last few days, she had withered away like a giant grey fruit in a summer sale. A closer look was necessary for treatment, so we approached it on a captive elephant. The wild one remained still, a stoic resignation in her weary eyes. Three days later, she was dead. Cause unknown: Probably infection from the old wound. I had not forgotten the wild female, nor the captive one. As the captive elephant had lurched forward, strips of skin were rubbed away from my thigh by its motion. Reminded of the pain, I winced at Kamini.

'As we went through the grass, we saw only the calf on the right side of the elephant. It must have been six months old at the most.'

Rhino calves six months of age have their mothers standing by, for rare emergencies such as tigers trying to take them away or rhino counters coming on elephant back at the crack of dawn. The mahout, experienced as he was, forgot this cardinal principle and edged his charge between the hidden mother and the inquisitive calf. The mother was, all of a sudden, no longer hidden. She charged out with a snort that sounded like a steam engine with a piece of charcoal sticking up its chimney. The grass stalks parted hurriedly and the earth flew up in clods out of her way. The inexperienced she-elephant ran for dear life, trumpeting and screaming shrilly.

'You should have heard the sound,' reminisced Kamini, 'it was the call of the Ahom death goddess.'

There were plenty of sounds to be heard all right. The elephant was shrieking like a four-tonne banshee. The rhino was snorting in self-righteous maternal anger. The mahout was urging the elephant on in rather unchaste Assamese. And the guard who was slipping off the back of the elephant was shouting to the gods and his mother in ululating wails.

The rhino caught up with the elephant just as the guard had reached halfway down the elephant's back. He was hanging on with one arm clutching desperately at the four-inch-thick twisted coir rope that harnesses the beast. Both the elephant and the mother rhino were galloping at well over fifty kilometres an hour, an amazing speed for the two giants to be trotting at. The world spun in large green vertiginous circles for Kamini and the guard. All rhinos run at a speed that most people attribute to more graceful beasts. They are not able to keep up their track and field prowess for long periods, but in short spurts their speed can be terrifying. The one-horned rhino has a trick up its armoured sleeve to be one up on its African cousins. It bites viciously and does not use its horn as a weapon of offence or defence at all. This was exhibited to great effect as it put a cloven foot on the elephant's rump and bit out a chunk of flesh. The elephant screamed in pure agony. The guard was by now almost at the rhino's feet and in inspired terror, he extended his gun arm over his left shoulder, closed both eyes in prayer and shot the animal dead with a bullet through its heart. The elephant stopped half a mile down the track and the men fell off the beast in tired heaps. They were safe for the moment. The census was disrupted to count the dead rhino along with the living one.

A couple of years before this, I had had my own little adventure in Agratoli or the eastern range, which exists in a different world altogether. The other two ranges are predominantly grassland. Agratoli is largely a forested woodland. It is also the home of the Kaziranga elephant. Parag Hathibarua, a young tea planter, was posted for a couple of years to look after rhinos in a special programme that the teawallahs had come up with. He took me into Agratoli in 1993, in a bright red Tata Tea mini jeep. The elephants of the range did not particularly seem to like the colour and I saw the first few woodland elephants charging out of the forest, a fanatical gleam in their eyes mirroring the red of the vehicle. A few moments after a particularly menacing tusker had ended his charge, a fallen log barred the way. I cursed Tata Tea loudly and vociferously as we screeched to a halt. A neat end it would have been, had the tusker decided to continue his charge. Boro, the range officer in charge of the eastern range, bounded towards us in consolation. He was busy planning to use the elephants in a different way. He had just discovered six pits on the border of his range and the central range. None of them had a rhino in it as yet but it was disturbing that poachers could have dug so many without detection.

'I have five domestic elephants that I am using against these poachers, you know.' He pronounced them 'poashers', with a slight lisp. His brow was puckered in disbelief at the sheer wickedness of the poachers.

'I will line all of them up in the night,' a full moon was rising rapidly, promising night light, 'then we will go in after the poashers.'

It is difficult to catch poachers on elephant back. But it is incredibly effective as a strategy to scare the hell out of them. A line of trumpeting and shrieking pachyderms marching through a moonlit night. A line of burning flame-torches swishing malevolently in the breeze. A bunch of energetic guards, led by the irrepressible Boro, on elephant backs, shouting the most unprintable Assamese epithets at the fleeing men. Agratoli had a record year of stopping poaching.

Four years later, I took a group of American film-makers to Boro. He was now in charge of the central range but the fire was still burning bright in his anti-poaching eyes.

'So what if Talukdar and Pankaj are not here any more.' The two had only just been posted out. 'I will still fight the poashers.'

The poachers had just started using electrocution as a method to kill rhinos in Kaziranga and Boro was furious.

'I will just tie these naked wires of current for the poashers, you know. Naked wires.' He spoke of the wires with reverence, as if they were naked women. 'I will keep them in waters and *beels*, you know. These poashers, they will not know that the entire water is full of current, you know.'

A maniacal gleam lit up his tiny eyes.

'They will come into the park to current my rhinos. When they touch the waters . . . Haah!' He waved his hands to symbolize the magical whoosh. 'Pfoooshh! Burnt into ashesh! All these bloody poashers!'

The Americans huddled in a concentric circle, giggling nervously.

'Aw gee, man! Great sense of humour, eh!'

'He means it, buddy,' I assured them, 'just look into his eyes.'

The film was completed in record, silent time.

~

If Assam spelt action and anti-poaching, the pace at Jaldapara and Gorumara was far more leisurely. The West Bengal protected areas had largely succeeded in keeping rhino poachers out, despite Siliguri, the rhino horn trade centre, being next door. The adventures of Mohit Aggarwal and Esmond Bradley Martin started on a December morning with a letter announcing the arrival of the world's greatest expert on rhinos to India. He would arrive in India at Delhi and then proceed onwards to Jaldapara to attend the World Conservation Union, Rhino Specialist Group meeting. So would Mohit and I, as WWF representatives, and also as chaperones to the United Nations Special Envoy on Rhinos, the first man to hold a position so glorified for an animal. The trip involved a flight and a long car journey. We would have to make sure that Esmond was in good shape when he got to the venue. Over the next few years, Esmond and I became good friends but when he landed I hardly knew him.

'I had a big problem with visas, Vivek,' he confided at the airport.

He was tall, pencil thin, with startlingly clear blue eyes and a shock of white hair that lay over his head like an albino nest of an Indian crow-pheasant. Any moment and I expected to hear the deep 'Whoop-whoop-whoop' of the coucal coming from within. All I could hear was the machinations of a well oiled brain.

'I am sorry to hear that. What happened? Did the chap interrogate you?' I was all concern.

'Oh no, no. I had to fill in this visa form, you know. For India, you know. I needed a visa. What a bother!'

Esmond was an American citizen despite spending more than two decades in Africa.

'But Esmond, so do I to go to the US.' It had dawned on me that Esmond did not have certain basics clear.

'But you don't understand, Vivek. I am an American.'

'Does not make any difference to us, Esmond.' I knew that I had to be as frank as possible.

'But I don't need a visa to go into Pakistan.'

'That's why we have fought two wars with them.'

Esmond seemed to understand. Mohit snorted uneasily.

The flight was uneventful, except for the accompaniments that an old Tibetan lady sitting next to me provided during take-off and landing. It was clear that she was not a daily flier. Her eyes, perched nervously on top of her high cheekbones, flew wildly in all directions. Her hands flew to the rhythm of an old Tibetan mantra on a well-worn rosary. As the plane picked up speed, her chant grew shriller and shriller, finally coming to rest on the high-pitched whine of an African anopheles. It was refreshing to get down at Bagdogara and find the waiting Maruti van and driver all set to drive us through to Jaldapara. The drive would begin the next morning, so the night would have to be spent in Siliguri.

Siliguri is located in the armpit of India, the north-eastern limb starting from its joint. And the town is as chaotic as an unwashed, unshaven tramp's armpit. It is the gateway to the north-east, the crossover point to Nepal and Bhutan as well as the entry point to Sikkim. It is from this town that the paths to the three hill towns of Darjeeling, Gangtok and Kalimpong originate. In case that is not enough, it is also the headquarters of the Marwari brigade. Originally Rajasthani businessmen, the Marwaris had invaded the north-east with their business acumen and in the span of a few decades brought the easy-going, fun-loving tribes of the area completely under their pecuniary control. Siliguri became the town of grain hoarders, rhino horn traders, construction warlords and transporters. It was clear to Mohit and me that the night should be spent outside the town. Luckily the mess that is Siliguri lies abutting the Mahananda Sanctuary and within driving distance of Buxa Tiger Reserve and Jaldapara, our final destination. Sukhna Rest House, in Mahananda Sanctuary, lies a little away from the Siliguri-Darjeeling road. From its backyard, the forests of Mahananda begin stretching away into the alpine heights of the eastern Himalayas. An altitudinal marvel, Mahananda has the elephants and tigers of the lowlands and the pandas and mountain goats of the highlands within its boundaries. It reminded me of a school 'ecology of a mountain' illustration. Its layers were cut away neatly to draw in the various components of different altitudes. Escaping from Siliguri, the night was spent in the refreshingly cool arms of the forest.

'Couldn't sleep a wink last night,' Esmond confronted us at breakfast. 'Couldn't get any work done in the evening, either.'

He must have seen a look of blank astonishment on our faces.

'It was the noise,' he confided. 'Too much noise just outside the window.'

Mohit looked extremely puzzled, and like he always does when something bothers him more than it should, he started exhaling loudly and wheezing in all directions.

'Noise? Noise? There's no noise here, Esmond.'

Outside, a few dozen birds broke out into instant melody.

'It's the train,' Esmond was serious, 'the train clattering and puffing up the slope just outside the window. How can anyone get any writing done with all that, eh?'

Sukhna lies on the Siliguri-Darjeeling toy train line where a small vintage steam engine pulls a few miniature carriages up to the hilltop. Holidayers love to take it up to give their children an old-world steam engine experience.

'But it is one small train, Esmond and it goes by only once. Surely that's better than the cacophony of Siliguri.'

'What goes up must come down,' Esmond was Newton reborn with white hair, 'it has to go by twice at least.'

Mohit grunted like an annoyed rhino.

Through the three-hour drive upto Madarihat where the conference was being held, Esmond Bradley Martin took notes. His hand had suffered an injury of some kind in the past and he wrote with a peculiar, loping action like a marathon runner's motion. He took down names of places, distances between them, the religion and economy of the place, any and every bit of wildlife information that could be gleaned from us and the driver and a huge amount of miscellaneous titbits. It explained how the man could be so prolific and meticulous at the same time. Much later, when I sat down to write a report on rhinos, I found that Martin figured in more than half of my bibliography. He was the Wordsworth of rhino conservation.

At Jaldapara we were offered early morning rides on elephant back into the forest. The elephant lurched slower through the thicker tangles of Jaldapara than through the open grass of Kaziranga. Sambar snorted away and a jungle fowl jumped aside deftly. A large male rhino appeared out of nowhere. For a moment Kamini Barua came to mind. The beast was an ash mound, armour plated for good measure. The elephant stopped short and then let forth a trumpet of assurance. This is the difference between well trained elephants and novices. The trumpet versus the shrill scream. The rhino moved away, wheeling around rather nimbly for its bulk.

Esmond was waiting at the rest house. We were all staying in the same rest house as M.K. Nandy, the Chief Wildlife Warden of West Bengal. Lunch and dinner were provided at the venue but breakfast tended to be a large affair with the north Bengal staff in full attendance.

Divisional Forest Officers could be seen lurking in the verandas, range officers cavorted in the halls barking orders, and a team of foresters and guards in newly polished shoes and buckles went around serving breakfast to their chief. It is not unusual in India to see such a flurry of activity when the top man pays a visit to an out-of-the-way office. This, in addition, was an international conference and the staff did all that was possible to impress. The three of us were inadvertently basking in the service provided to the rest house and Esmond was hugely enjoying it. On the second day, he spread his arms expansively over an overladen breakfast table. From outside came the fluting whistle of the shama. In the distance a deer barked. Esmond was in full form.

'The thing that is nice about India,' he told Nandy as two range officers hovered like unsuccessful sunbirds behind him, 'the thing I like about India is the number of servants you have around you.'

Mohit had got the perfect opportunity and he did not waste a moment. A well placed kick under the table saw Esmond wincing slightly. The good thing about Esmond is that he picks up very fast. He kept quiet for the rest of the morning.

Unlike Esmond, the rhino does not seem to pick up things fast enough. It lives slowly, savouring the long years of its existence. It does not understand that by taking the same routes to its food and toilet, it is aiding the poacher. It does not realize that one day if it came the other way around, it might be able to surprise the poacher. The rhino plods on, armour-plated only superficially, waiting for the six-inch lead slug or the zipping volt of electricity to end its earthly existence. The species seems tired; almost resigned to its fate.

'So long as there are rhinos, we will have to protect them,' Talukdar had declared, trying to reverse a trend.

I am reminded of Trevor Bailey, a particularly dogged English cricketer. In the face of hostile Australian bowling, the then English captain was asked how he planned to save the Ashes.

'Put a Bailey at both ends,' was his clipped response.

Perhaps one should try it with Talukdar as well.

Blonde and Dying

A golden monkey leapt into my life from the pages of a childhood book and kept me fascinated for over a quarter of a century. My very first book was an animal picture book bought for me by my mother. At that time she would have had no inkling that as the years passed, I would become partially wild myself. Like a good doting mother, she had merely provided me with a book that would allow her time in the kitchen while I pored over the flashing brilliance of a parrot's wings and the incredible sadness of an elephant's eye. Many years later, my father lent me my first real wildlife book. It came from his vast library that contained tomes on everything from psychology to religion, cookery to medicine.

'I think you will like it,' he said. 'It is about a mad Scot.'

It was Iain and Oria Douglas-Hamiltons' *Among the Elephants*, a book that took me into equatorial Africa and the secret life of the Lake Manyara herd. I was all of twelve years of age and the image captivated me for life.

A few days passed and the daily post-dinner ramble on the open terrace brought forth two more books. Dad was smoking his favourite brier and looked upwards at the sky, puffing into infinity.

'I wish there were more mad Scots like him,' he said, without a preamble.

We both knew who he was talking about. From a man

The first impression of Eravikulam National Park is that of a massive football field folded up into hills and vales.

© VIVEK MENON

I wondered whether Rajesh intended to clobber his nemesis James at an opportune moment.

© VIVEK MENON

My companions, I decided, had a definitely weird dress sense; Mohit, Michael and Rajesh at Eravikulam.

© JAMES ZACCHARIAS

As a predator, the dhole is unmatched in India for achieving what it sets out to do.

'Are these egrets, egrets, egrets?' chanted Shailaja as plumes of white rose daintily from the wattles.

The most endangered stork in India rifling through Pepsi cans, buffalo entrails and a hundred plastic bags at a Guwahati dump.

'In other parks they say that only God can protect the rhino. Here we do the work ourselves.' Range Officers Pankaj, Talukdar and Boro.

The horn and the ridges on the back of the rhino were visible like a piece of flotsam in the waters.

Pushing through the uncut Manas grasslands is like swimming through a pool of green caramel custard. (inset) Golden langur eating a banana.

Marine turtles laying their eggs in the sand is an annual ritual and undoubtedly the biggest wildlife spectacle on Indian territory. (inset) An olive ridley turtle killed by trawler fishermen.

© VIVEK MENON

The old man with a wicker basket full of gaping orange hill mynah beaks.

© MOHIT AGGARWAL

The male musk deer has two large curved teeth that give his otherwise handsome face a rather frightful leer.

© VIVEK MENON

Bharati trying to cure her asthma at a sulphur spring near Kedarnath National Park.

Slowly, rising from their watery playground, twenty-six massive pachyderms formed a single file on the verdant shore across.

Ashok with a netted vest and an olive green trooper's cap as if he has just come in from a patrol at Halduparao.

What use elephants if their teeth cannot help the Japanese sign their cheques?

When wildlifers sit on an elephant they straddle it, letting the pelvis get stretched like in pre-natal exercises; Sukumar riding bareback in Mudumalai.

The saddest thing about the threat facing the tiger throughout the world is the fact that it is but a cat.

who did not like animals, that was a big compliment.

'How did you like it?'

I said I did and very much. In fact it had beaten Biggles and his flying adventures into a very distant second place.

'Try these then.'

He thrust two plastic-covered volumes into my hand. He is very careful with books, my dad. I was occasionally capable of tearing into the plastic before opening the books. These, I treated reverentially. They were E.P. Gees' *Wildlife of India*, and Jane Goodall's *In the Shadow of Man*. The three formed my wildlife religion's triumvirate for over a decade. While the Douglas-Hamiltons and Goodall carried me away from home into the dark heat of Africa and the secret world of the elephant and the chimpanzee, Gee told me about the wonders of India. The buffaloes of Kaziranga, the lions of Gir, the 'bison' of Bandipur, the pelicans of Andhra. And the golden langur of Manas. Not cream or grey or any of the other nondescript colours that decorate the normal langurs of India, but a glowing gold, a burnished blonde. Blondes have never been a particular fascination for me in the human form. But a blonde monkey! Now that was something to look at from close quarters!

The langurs are a group of five leaf-eating monkeys that spread across India. Biologists call them colobines only to distinguish them from the *bandars* or the macaques. The langurs are built to lead a leaf-loving existence and have evolved long intestines to digest the extra cellulose. To match the internal coils, on the exterior they have an equally long tail. This decoration is held in a graceful loop over the back at some times, let loose and fashion-free at others. The langurs are largely arboreal creatures that live in social groups. From what we know of them, they seem shyer than the macaques of the human form. Most humans would also shy away from the langurs if they are queasy about bashing babies on the head. Many langurs commit the fascinating social practice of male infanticide. For langur fathers it means fewer babies that will grow up into potential rivals. In India, the whole concept of killing male babies is a novelty. My matriarchal upbringing in a Nair household should have taught me better. In my case, the matriarch of the family, my great-grandmother, refused to come to the hospital to see me yowl because I was a boy. If she were a langur father, she would have surely picked me up by my vestigial tail bone and flung me to the floor, biting through the jugular for good measure.

The golden langur might also indulge in such sweet social niceties, only nobody knows much about it. It was the last big mammal to be discovered in India and was first popularized by Gee in the 1950s after an expedition to Assam. Six years later, it was dutifully (for in those days scientists still believed in duty and a code of honour) named *Presbytis geei* by an Indian zoologist, H. Khajuria. Latin for Gee's Langur.

The spell of the montane woodlands of Manas and the blonde monkey tempted me over many years. Gee tried to bribe me into going there sooner.

'This spot could well be described as the answer to the fisherman's prayer and the artist's dream, and the so-far-unrealized hope of the wild life conservationist. And I cannot think of a more engaging and wonderful wild creature than the "newly-discovered" golden langur, as it feeds, plays and leaps from branch to branch in the tree tops, making the silvery-green leaves quiver against an azure sky.'

I finally found my piece of paradise one morning in May. The year was 1995. I woke up with the deliberate pulsing sound of rain falling all over me. Around me, my bedclothes were dry with the warmth of being slept in but the insides of my ears were wet. It was the incessant swishing of water, the magnetic sound of the Indian monsoon. It was a thousand taps being left open by a careless husband. A million rivulets forcing water over a dry river bed. In fact, that was precisely it. My sleep-dead brain was being teased awake by the first shafts of a liquid dawn. As liquid as the river Manas. I stumbled to the window of unquestionably the finest rest house built on Indian soil. The Mothonguri rest house was atop a small hill, and below me heaven met earth in ear-shattering silence. The only sound was that of the river; a broad sapphire-blue band of water. The deafening rush of water was so constant that in moments it dissolved itself into the background silence. Only the foaming white crest erupting now and then from its midst told a story of motion. The blue band was otherwise stationary, pasted onto a golden land. Towards me stretched Manas National Park and Indian soil. On the opposite bank, stretched another Manas, also a protected area for wildlife. One ecosystem, two countries; divided by a swirling blue ribbon. The great Sunderban mangroves of West Bengal constitute the only other trans-boundary protected area that India shares with its neighbours. There, it is Bangladesh that lies across the swamps. In front of me was the mountain kingdom of Bhutan.

From the left corner of my eye, I caught the slow wing beats of one of India's most spectacular birds, the great Indian hornbill. The birds winged past the window, a line of them in military formation. Through the binoculars their heads looked absurd. The shadow of the Manas hills was falling onto their faces in a black patch. What should have been a white neck was distinctly tinged cream by the stain of an oil gland used by the bird to preen itself. Young Myanmarese girls, their faces smeared with the yellow paste of a native bark, came to mind. For the first time, the silence imposed by the waters was broken by the sound of a clump of bamboo creaking against the wind. It was the hornbill.

'Kre-ee-aak', and then 'Kr-ee-aa-aa-ak'.

To the untrained ear this would be a bird call. The hornbills actually have a short *tok* call and a longer grunting bark. This sound was the scraping of their flapping wings. I counted them against their flight path, an old trick of bird counters. Let the birds come into your sight and then go out of it, counting all the time. If your eyes fly with them, the numbers would be all wrong. It was in the still poise of the head, much the same as a batsman about to play his cover drive in a cricket match, that the secret of wildlife enumeration lay. Eight pied birds with grotesquely enlarged yellow beaks and a ruby red eye flashing in five of them. Males. The jaundiced yellow eyes were the females. An old hornbill sexing trick. I had learnt it, funnily enough, in the Delhi zoo many years ago when I was a student warden there. A big problem in the zoo was the bird house where breeding rates were abysmal. Not surprising, considering that in at least half a dozen cases the two birds expected to breed were of the same sex! In most birds, females are hugely duller and less flashy than males, and this makes the work of zoo men very easy. In others, God has been less kind and the two look absolutely alike and you need internal anatomical tests to tell them apart. In yet others, such as the hornbills and many parrots, eye colour is a way to sex birds. I had done this to the caged hornbills of the National Zoological Park. In Manas, the birds could now be sexed in the air. Eight of them. I remembered the veteran birdman Hamilton, in the early part of the century, writing of an evening in Bhutan and a flight of 200 hornbills. He would have had problems sleeping that night!

The hornbill is interesting to the Naga and Arunachal tribals and to the rest of humanity for two very different reasons. For most of us, it is because the two sexes play a very interesting breeding game. When the female wants to lay eggs, it chooses a large tree, in many cases a fig tree, and lays them in a hollow big enough for her to go in. Now, big trees with big hollows are rarer than big trees to hold up adjutant storks in Assam. (PCB would have had a heart attack if he had to study hornbills!) Presuming that such a tree is found and that the eggs are laid, the female will then begin a process of incubation. Totally unpredictably, this begins with her own self-incarceration as she shuts the hole up with dung and leftover food. The male then gets into his act and fetches wallops of fresh mud and plasters her shut in the hole. The hornbill is obviously not a great believer in women's liberation, for the bird stays shut up in her wooden tower for all of forty-five days, waiting for the chicks to hatch and then become old enough to stay on their own and not be afraid of the dark. Whether this is a trick to minimize predator risk or just a social strategy that males have developed to be one up on females, it is difficult to say. The male, for one must be fair to the man as well, hangs around waiting for the day that the female pronounces her intention of getting out with a loud croak. Till then, he feeds her with the choicest titbits through a slit in the plaster and then gets the hell away from the tree before the female can reverse and shower him with white ammoniac waste. The force of expulsion of both the female and the chicks is rather great and the ground beneath is splotched with the tell-tale stains of a month and a half. As soon as she is ready, the male proceeds to set his partner free by tearing away at the mud plaster with his beak.

The beak is a golden dagger, fifteen inches long and ten inches wide. On top of the dagger, a hollow golden casque perches precariously. A wind instrument that blows nasal overtones into the bird call and allows it a surround sound effect. In Hindi film music, it is known as the Saigal effect. Tribes in Arunachal Pradesh and Nagaland love the hornbill only for this piece of bone. They prize the casque as ceremonial headgear, two tail feathers of black and white adorning a male warrior. It is sad that the bird has to be killed for this. Very primitive and tribal. Much like another ancient tribe, the Parisian bourgeois, who killed egrets and stuck the white tail plumes of the birds into designer hats.

All over its range, the hornbill is getting scarce. The bird has a curious association with fig trees, the importance of which was shown by a promising young ornithologist called Raghupathy Kannan. Based in USA,

Kannan is today better known for circulating electronic mails on the arrival of Viagara and the positive effect that this might have on the rhinoceros, given that rhino horn is thought of as an aphrodisiac by many. Kannan falls into the trap that many better people have fallen into before him on the use of rhino horn. About the figs and the hornbills, though, he seems to be right, as the tree is big enough to be a nesting favourite of the bird and fruity enough as well. Although persecuted through its range, in Manas the bird is largely left alone. One of the few species that has had that advantage over the past decade or so.

Outside the Mothonguri rest house, a medley of human sounds broke cover. From the wooden balcony that hung out onto the river front, I could see an excited little figure. One arm steadied a small pair of binoculars onto a white-topped bush, the other pointed insistently in its wake. It was Maan Barua, his legs dancing a tribal beat, the victorious primal tap dance that binds the ornithological community together. From the balcony, I followed the pointed finger, with my binoculars scanning the grass green of the bush, its tangle of vegetative offshoots, a flower here, a bud there . . . The gentle sweep of the glasses through green was stopped abruptly by a small rainbow. It was a jewel of a bird, its colours ascribing new hues to the conventional rainbow. There was a glossy black, a deep dark green, a swathe of blue, a purplish hue, a line of copper and a touch of blood. On its cheek, it also had a perfect, fine-formed leaf of ruby. 'Ruby cheek, ruby-cheeked sunbird,' danced Maan.

Sunbirds are old world hummingbirds, tiny jewel-encrusted flitters that are a classic example of convergent evolution. Long-tubed flowers with nectar pots hidden inside their fleshy folds are common throughout the tropics. In South America, the hummingbirds took advantage of this, in Asia and Africa, the sunbirds did. Long tube-like beaks are ideal for inserting into flowers like a straw, small bodies are a must to hover helicopter-like on top of the flowers, and an extraordinary amount of energy is required to whirr the rotor wings at a frenetic pace. Both families evolved to fulfil these conditions. Both families painted themselves gaudy as well. The rubycheek is four inches of colour inhabiting only the north-east. Very little is known about its behaviour and habits. If the rubycheek is the tiny marvel of the avian world, Maan Barua fills the niche in the birdwatcher's world. In 1995 he was still fourteen years old, thrust into adolescence amidst a plethora of birds. In Manjuda he had as unconventional a father as he could have wished to have. Taking him away from conventional school, Manjuda first put him into a revolutionary school in the Nilgiris and then brought him to Assam to put him into the custody of a guru. Maan grew up with the golden langurs and the black-crested bazas of Kokrajhar. To me, he represented the future of birdwatching in India.

'Look, look, please,' he whispered, intent, as a red shadow whizzed owl-like across the path. Maan was an extraordinarily polite young man. He punctuated most sentences with a 'please'. The bird was equally polite and did not think it fit to make any sound. The flight was silent and fast; a sort of nightjar-frogmouth flight. When it found a perch, the bird was stiller than death. In the crook of a silk-cotton branch, its red body gleamed a bright crimson. A light white band separated neck from body. The tail was white from the front. The head was held upright as if staring at invisible stars above. I had never seen a bird of the sort before but there was no doubt in my mind about its identity. It was a trogon, a group of shy forest dwellers found only in the deep south and in the north-east. This particular one was a red-headed trogon. In ten minutes of absolute bliss, the forest had revealed three of Manas' amazing repertoire of birds, two of them being those that I had earlier thought existed only in the technicolour dreams of Salim Ali when he wrote his magnum opus on Indian birds. Now I knew where all those birds were. Ashok came to mind. He had a great fondness for *bade mian*, as I like to refer to the jewel of Indian ornithology, the teacher of my teacher. Never a great birdwatcher and with a known penchant for the larger elephant, Ashok had discovered a bird that he could not find in Salim Ali's *Indian Birds*.

'But, Salim sahib, I can't find this bird in your book,' he is reported to have complained.

Salim Ali had a sense of humour that was as short as it was radiant.

'You can't get every bird in India for hundred rupees,' he chided, 'buy the big book, no!'

The big book would have definitely given Ashok the rubycheeks and the trogons. And then he would have had to ask *bade mian* where to find them in real life!

~

Maan and I were on the trip with Goutam Narayan, an old friend and ornithologist. Goutam had done his doctorate on the highly endangered Bengal florican in 1987 in Manas. That was before the Bodos took over the park and biologists and conservation took a back seat. In fact we were the first biologists to go back in a very long time indeed. There were reports of burnt bridges and no roads, a hacked-up range officer and stolen arms and rhino horns. The militants had created havoc and opportunistic plunderers had taken advantage of the situation and made it worse. In less than five years the paradise that was Manas had been cut down and burnt. A rhino population of over one hundred was probably all gone. The equally endangered swamp deer was down to a handful and nobody knew anything of the golden langur, debatably the most endangered monkey in India. Manas was a National Park, a World Heritage Site, a Project Tiger Reserve and a Man and Biosphere Reserve. Also, a complete and utter wreck. I was officially on my rhino project. The Assam visit was a rhino visit and the wish to get into Manas an equally rhino one. The golden langur hung around in the back like a dissatisfied ghoul, preying on nights when wildlife dominated my dreams.

I first saw the creature in 1991 in a grimy alley in Patna, held apart like a stuffed toy by a pair of lungi-clad traders. The face was a light cream-blonde and the rest of the body was darker gold. Its arms twisted apart in the grip of his escorts, the paws upturned, dark and creased leathery, the tail limp in defeat. And from his eyes shone a quiet resignation, a knowledge of pain and bondage. Mir Shikar Toli is by far the largest live animal mart in India. The Muslims who control it are undoubtedly the biggest traders of live wildlife.

'Ten thousand rupees, sahib and if you want a female

as well then six thousand more,' said Hasan Ali, dark and unkempt, large balls of muscle shifting uneasily beneath a torn shirt.

'I want a snow leopard cub.' That was my mission. 'Ten thousand for that.'

'Two months for a cub.' His gaze shifted to my pockets, for money or for a hidden weapon, I was not quite sure.

The snow leopard, an elusive mythical mountain spirit. Unseen by most wildlifers who have trekked his snowy kingdom, visible only as a ghostly blur to those fortunate to have seen it at all.

'I will blindfold you and you must come with me on a four-hour drive. Then I will show you a snow leopard in the wild. Only for you.'

Four hours from Patna. I thought that got you nowhere in Bihar, where the main highways peter out into dust bowls. This was incredible. I was sure I would take up the offer some day.

In front of me the monkey was shifting around in his grip. His mouth opened for a second, a pink cavern, in a disquietingly silent scream. I had to leave the animal there till I got back to the enforcement staff. Later, I learnt that my information was not acted on. The langur probably never lived. My guilt lived on deep within me. I was keen to see the animal this time in the wild.

For Goutam, however, the trip was all pygmy hog, a creature that he was in charge of breeding in captivity and bringing back to the wild. The pygmy hog was one of three mammals in Manas that people knew very little of except for the fact that they were very endangered. Two of them were creatures of the grassland and one a denizen of the forest. Manas in its heyday had plenty of all three. In a peculiar dream that I had, prior to the visit, I saw the golden langurs swaying delectably on a large forest tree like forbidden fruit, while in the grass that grew tall and uncut below, an extra-small pig played with an extra-big rabbit. I was reminded of Alice in Wonderland. Giving some leeway for the stuff that dreams are made of, the creatures could have been the pygmy hog and the hispid hare, extraordinary residents of Manas. The hog is a miniature wild boar, true to form to the last bristle except that adults are no more than ten inches in height. The hare, for there are no rabbits in India, is a large, bristly, short-set animal that inhabits the same terai grasslands that the pygmy hog does. The militants had kept forest guards off their jobs for long enough and the grass in which the two skulked was long like a hippie's hair.

Pushing through the uncut Manas grassland is like swimming through a pool of green caramel custard. It is a slow and laborious process made bearable only by the desire to be there in the first place. The fact that we had a jeep to do the pushing helped. Goutam was driving and I sat in the front photographer-documentor seat. Wisps of grass cut by the motion of the vehicle and a few bushels of Manas dust were drip-fed to us through the half-open windscreen. Outside, a flock of red-breasted parakeets took noisily to wing, mutinous and militant in their protests.

The grasslands of Manas are geographically an extension of the terai savannahs, large stands of tall grass extending from the foothills of the Himalayas to the lowland grasslands. These grasslands then go all the way upto the Ganges and Brahmaputra river systems. The lowland grasslands are regulated by rain and waterlogging but the terai grasslands, home of the hog and the hare and the backyard of the langur, know only one great natural threat—fire. The fire that burns the grass could be either a natural one or a semi-controlled management tool for the rhino and the elephant, the swamp deer and the wild buffalo; creatures that have management plans and conservation initiatives to save them. The fire unfortunately is the worst thing that could happen for the pygmy hog and the hispid hare, the snakes and the tortoises; creatures that are not fast enough to escape the flames, those that are not cuddly enough to warrant alarm.

All around us, a number of grass species were obvious by their sheer height. The pygmy hog had taught Goutam all about grass although the florican should have done it way back in time. Now, it was grass collection time for him. He had to identify suitable grass stock from the original range of the pygmy hog and then transplant it into the enclosures being readied near Guwahati. The captive breeding project was a long-time dream of William Oliver, the current chairman of the Pigs and Peccaries Specialist Group of the World Conservation Union, and Goutam was the manager of the project in the country. A closer understanding of the species was in order. Goutam was enjoying teaching me the basic differences.

'*Ullu* is the slightly shorter, thinner one—see those there? This one around us is *ikora*.' *Ikora* spread like a curtain of green resistance all around.

'Can you see the slightly more rounded stalks? That's *khagori*. The one that looks like *khagori* and grows near the water, now that is *nal*.'

It was as plain as grass. I was taken back two years to a day at Wild Grass in Kaziranga. I had the day off from going into the park and had chosen to skulk around the compound, seeking shade and inspiration to write. I was caught off guard by a gaggle of schoolgirls from the nearby secondary school. The then park director was trying to give them a talk on Kaziranga. Would I oblige as well? I needed bespectacled schoolgirls like I needed a wisdom tooth eruption, but this was all part of the game and I obliged. My nemesis, the bespectacled one, rose from the front row as soon as I had finished.

'Sir! Sir, tell me, sir . . . what is the most important species in Kaziranga, sir, please?'

She was too polite for me to dodge. She had got too close to the central point of wildlife conservation for me to be comfortable. The answer, of course, was that there was no single species which was the most important. Kaziranga was rhino land but so was it wild water buffalo land and swamp deer land. It was also grass land. If the *ullu* and the *ikora*, the *nal* and the *khagori* went extinct, would the rhino survive? One thought of the confusion this would cause amidst the herbivores and then the panic among the carnivores made up my mind.

'It must be a grass species,' I replied, not entirely convincingly, 'but we do not know for sure.'

The girls giggled appreciatively at what they thought was a joke. Grass! And important! While rhinos and elephants and tigers still remained. What would this creature come up with next!

Each grass stalk of these four species rises as high as an elephant. Strangely enough, therefore, they are known collectively as elephant grass. This does not mean that they are all the same species. Scientifically, they have other names as well which nobody but the ilk of Rajesh Thadani bother to remember. *Saccharum, phragmites, themeda* and *arundo*, along with many others, cram into this thicket of life. The term thatch-grass is also not entirely correct for the lot of them as many of them are more reed than thatch. In the middle of this elephant grass, thatch-reed, live the rhino, the pygmy hog, the hispid hare and other endangered species, some seen, others largely unnoticed and hidden.

Around me small ginger-like plants grew in thick profusion with ridged leaves that looked like green potato crisps.

'*Lea crispa*,' announced Goutam. Of course crispa. Maybe lea meant potato in Latin.

Much taller were the wild cardamoms.

'*Alpinnia alugos*,' claimed Goutam from the driver's seat. I thought he was a birdman. It was only just about all right to accept his mammal credentials. The botany bit was getting a bit too much.

'You know why I like this grass bit . . .' Goutam never finished the sentence properly. From beneath the moving jeep slid a large length of reptile, which then stood up to glance him in the eye.

'Shit!' breathed the biologist, eye to eye with a king cobra. I needed photographs and started to zoom out the lens. Maan was observing the spectacle dispassionately.

'Shit! Shit!' heaved Goutam and accelerated quickly out of the way. The cobra slid five feet down. Cobras have a habit of lifting up to a third of their bodies in a threat display. That made our friend up to fifteen feet long. He certainly looked it. As far as I was concerned it was sheer curiosity, not threat. Surely a king cobra had not seen biologists around in Manas for quite some time as well. It is likely that I would have had much the same reaction were a king cobra to suddenly pay a call at my house through uncut grass, after five years of social ostracism. Stand up and have a good, bloody look at the visitor. Made capital sense. Goutam Narayan did not think of it that way.

'Want to take photographs with the thing staring in my face, eh? Why don't you do the driving, now?'

'You know I don't drive, Goutam.' This was a convenient lack of skill for wildlife photographers and biologists. As long as there were others to drive them around. And get the cobra calls.

Behind us, the cobra was slowly winding itself into the *ikora*. As we looked back we saw the actual reason for the snake's posture. Stretched out on the jeep tracks was a four and a half foot monitor lizard lying on its back. It was a Bengal monitor even though we were in Assam. Obviously he was unaware of the ongoing agitation in the state. He had all his four legs in the air and on his neck a little below his stupid death grin was a blue bite mark. The cobra had just finished preparing his dinner. We had driven into the kitchen and over the frying pan, so to speak. No wonder he had raised himself to his full height. Come to think of it, it was good that he had not raised himself to his full capability. It would have been very difficult to photograph it that way.

The next morning we got into the moist deciduous forest of Manas. I was keen to see my first golden langur.

A dirt road was being widened on the Bhutan side

using European aid bulldozers and earth moving equipment.

'This place is going to go, Goutam.' I was sad. 'Where does the road lead to?'

'Connects a small village with the Indian side. Once the road comes up there will be traffic through here as well.' Goutam looked equally pained.

He had seen the park ten years before me. He was now watching the start of its decline. I could sympathize. The bright yellow bulldozer raked up an iron fistful of cream earth and threw it into the forest. World Heritage Site. On the opposite side was the picturesquely situated wooden hunting lodge where the Bhutanese king used to stay. In the old days he had to hunt a rhino to become a man and then king. Hopefully, now that both were established facts, the rhino could be left alone.

A small dirt track skirted the king's hunting lodge and went into the forest. Even five hundred yards inside, the forest was much more dense and tall. This was the moist deciduous sal forest of Manas. Sal dominates Indian forests like no other tree. Even teak is restricted to the peninsula. Sal is India just as the wattle is Africa. In Manas, they form a closed canopy with their large wavering leaves. Large-boled trees swam into a vertical abyss. When you craned your neck you could see the ripples formed by their leaves in the sky. Every now and then a squirrel attempted to jump the gap between two trees, splashing through the placid air.

From somewhere in the tangles of the aerial pool, I heard the first tentative hoots of the langur. They were not the call of the common langur, nor the loud persistence of the hoolock. There was a musical quality in the notes. A soft cough set in rhapsody. One moment there were only the notes from the trees. The next moment four wild golden langurs crashed into my life, overhead. It was tiring to look up at them at such an angle. I felt infinitely sorry for the coyotes who had to howl with similar neck positions. Above me, the langurs were swinging from tree to tree, not particularly bothered about concealing themselves nor seemingly anxious to share their privacy with us. At first glance, the langurs were white, not golden. Pale cream like a good cream of mushroom soup in Chung Wa restaurant. They are reputed to turn coppery-golden in the winters and pale during the Indian summers. It is good to turn copper when the leaves around you are a burnt bronze and the grass a bold brass. Good for camouflage. These ones were distinctly cream. Long strands of hair hung from around the face onto the leather-black of their facial skin. Their noses were puckered in disbelief, their eyes shining with intent. Like all other monkeys they lived in social groups. This is perhaps why monkeys and elephants have fascinated me in larger measure than other mammals. In watching them, we watch a strangely human life being played out by marionettes of a different kind. As a mother langur gathered up an errant baby that had swung too close to me, I empathized. In her maternal scoop, the tight hug of affection and the almost careless ruffling of baby hair, she turned human; and I anthropomorphic. A cardinal sin for a scientist. A momentary must for my soul.

~

The golden langur is a taxidermist's blessing. For a while it was considered a sub-species of the capped langur, then later given a new species ranking. The taxidermists worked hard at giving it a biological positioning. They shuffled and arranged, changed and re-arranged. Meanwhile, most Indians decided that it was a golden langur anyway. The similarity between the two monkeys has always struck me as odd. Especially when watching capped langurs which can be far more golden than the golden langurs. Two instances came to mind.

On the main Kaziranga highway, Pankaj Sarma and I ran into a troop of capped langurs one summer evening. It was the Kanchenjhuri area and we were out looking for hoolocks. Kanchenjhuri, like Panbari, is an evergreen patch in the midst of the Kaziranga grasslands. Tourists avoid it because of the poor visibility, all the big herbivores avoid it because of the lack of grass, and conservationists and park officials avoid it because of the leeches.

'*Jok ase,*' Pankaj warned. 'There are leeches.'

And so there were, creeping up onto our ankles with the slyness of a Central Park mugger. One of them was hanging tenaciously from the rotten rim of a purple fungus, waving its head at me in eager, bloodthirsty friendliness. The leeches are the sad part of the wet evergreen forests. As Mohit discovered in Eravikulam. But there were compensatory factors in the verdancy of this wet evergreen as well. There were hoolocks and emerald doves, pied hornbills and the capped langur. Animals of the moist, damp, dark forest. Creatures that you would normally not find cavorting in the grass with the rhinos and swamp deer that every tourist tries to see on his first outing. The hidden world of Kanchenjhuri and Panbari remains only for the very interested connoisseur to discover and the capped langurs broke cover from out of this mystery world without so much as a whoop.

Compared to the incessant hooting of the hoolocks, the capped langurs are quiet and peaceable monkeys. The Kaziranga ones were definitely very pale cream. The cream was tinged rufous towards the back and near the shoulders. The face, like all langur faces, was pitch black with coal diamonds shining from the eyes. An imperceptible band of black hair defined a neat cap on the head. Not the swirling whorl of the bonnet macaque of southern India but a French beret. The inside of the thighs was a light cobalt-blue. This was a naked skin patch, a startling colour in a mammal. There are so very few mammals that show a touch of the colour blue that it takes some time for it to sink in. The langurs were feeding peaceably, not making eye contact with us but slowly and deliberately pulling leaves from overhanging branches and munching them with quiet contentment.

In direct contrast were the capped langurs of Cachar. On the Bangladesh border I hitched a ride with an Indo-US Primate Project Survey Team. I was actually looking for elephants but the team members were welcome companions. Arun Srivastava, quietly stern and sternly funny in parts, who led the team. Joydeep, corpulent yet handsome, laughing readily and singing even more readily. There were four other quieter members. The night had been spent listening to the Bangladeshis celebrating Id across the border. The neighbouring Indian village blasted '*Pardesi, Pardesi*', a hugely popular Hindi film hit, a few dozen times through the night. Early morning found us trekking the border, large areas with seven-foot-high barbed wire fences. The boundary was only notional, for in many places convenient entry and exit gates had been torn by villagers on both sides. The Border Security Force kept vigil at certain points, but, like everywhere else, the border was too long to be manned effectively. The BSF were suffering in their own quiet way as well. As we drove into BSF territory, we were stopped by an armed guard.

'The Company Commander wants to see you.' He seemed uncertain whether to welcome us or arrest us.

The CO was a Haryanvi Jat, tall in height and loose in the limb. It was his last posting before retirement and his grey hair spoke of the years he had spent at the border.

'How dare you pass this place,' he barked stentorially, 'without stopping by for a cup of tea?'

He had heard that a Delhiite was in the area and badly wanted to speak Hindi to someone from nearer home. He chatted with me for well over an hour over several steaming cups of tea. Black without milk. *Lal sa*, as the Assamese say. Literally, red tea. Black or red, the CO was not amused.

'Milk!' he snorted, the man from the buffalo state of India, where milk and dairy products gained precedence over wealth.

'Milk! Hah! You think these chappies have milk in these areas? Hah! No milk! And I am supposed to keep my men in fighting condition. You know, in all other places we have a ration of two full glasses of milk a day.'

If I know a Haryanvi Jat farmer, his glass holds a litre and a half of buffalo's milk. North-eastern India mostly does without milk. As you go further east into Myanmar, they keep cows only for the meat. Milk is neither wanted nor common, except for babies and expectant mothers.

'Guard the border! Hah!' The CO had found someone before whom he could vent thirty years of service frustration and he was not going to let go.

'No milk. And I tell you what. Look at this. Just look at this and tell me now . . . Do you think we can guard borders eating this stuff, eh?'

He was holding up a bunch of small bananas, each the size of a swollen thumb.

'Look at the size. Can you guard the border on these? Only fit for monkeys . . .'

'And about the monkeys of this area . . .' I began.

'There are no monkeys here, only the occasional Bangladeshi.'

The CO was not a spare-time primatologist.

Four kilometres from the camp, through a particularly large tear on the border fence, I spied my first spectacled leaf monkey looking at us from a large jamun tree in Bangladesh. The species, also called the Phayre's leaf monkey, is an ash-black monkey with a black-black face. Unlike any other Indian monkey, it has the most unusual facial markings. Around its eyes and lips are the marks left by the rims of cups of pale cream. White leprosy markings, offset brilliantly by glowing black eyes. The white spectacle frame gives it the first name. There were twenty-five of them and we slowly crept in towards Bangladesh. Shy at first to do the voyage without a visa, and then moving on in bold joy at seeing this very rare primate. As Joydeep got ready to take his behavioural notes, I proceeded further with his colleagues. From the left side of the road a large golden monkey leapt into the middle of the path, bounded on steaming pads and leapt into the right void. Somewhere below me, a tangle of vegetation cushioned its descent. Suddenly there were capped langurs everywhere. These were a different sub-species. Larger and distinctly more golden. There was no blue on the thighs.

'Blue? On a monkey? You must be seeing things.' Joydeep did not believe the Kaziranga story.

The capped seemed to know how to confuse people. While we were there, there were reports from a few hundred kilometres west in the Garo hills about golden langurs and their rediscovery in Meghalaya. If there is one thing that gets the whole government system behind you, it is the discovery in a state of a species which hitherto has existed only in a neighbouring state. Just as Gujarat is possessive about its lions, Assam is parochial about its rhinos and golden langurs. There have been allegations in the past that both states have stymied attempts by neighbours to translocate lions and rhinos respectively into adjoining habitats. 'The animal is ours, how can we give it to them?' seems to be the general refrain.

If there is one state without its very own mammal it is Punjab. At a Chief Wildlife Wardens' meeting a few years ago, the portly Gurmeet Singh, a friend of mine for long sought out his Gujarati counterpart.

'Give me some of your lions for our Chat Bir zoo,' requested the genial sardar.

'And what can you give me in exchange?' Gujaratis tend to be good traders.

The Sardar was flummoxed and sat down heavily, tending to his unruly beard in the hope of coming up with a home-grown species. The idea of offering butter chicken must not have come to mind or else he would have done so without batting an eyelid.

'From Punjab? What can I offer, *praji*? *Gehoon*? Wheat?'

I later heard the lions were sent anyway, before bushels of wheat landed up in Gandhinagar.

Meghalaya, which is relatively a new state, had similar Punjabi problems. The land of clouds did not have a large number of endemic and yet charismatic species that it could boast of. Naturally, then, the news that the golden langur had been rediscovered in the Garo hills of Meghalaya was being made much of in the media and by the government. Arun Srivastava tore his hair out in sheaves.

'How stupid they are! The creature has never been recorded from the south bank of the Brahmaputra, let alone from the Garos. The golden are almost completely bound by the two rivers Sankosh and Manas. A more or less rectangular distribution.'

'What's all the fuss about then?' I was to go to the hills just after Cachar and was interested.

'Capped. Obviously capped.'

He rushed to Turra, the district headquarters of the Garo hills to explain this to the Meghalayans. I suggested that he make a poster explaining to the layman that the golden monkey is the capped langur and the cream one the golden langur. It is only that in winter the golden actually gets golden and in three out of the five races the capped is not golden any more. Such simple things and people get confused!

I needed to follow Arun to the Garo hills, although with an official Meghalayan delegation. The Meghalayan government was having some problems with Balphakram National Park, their premier protected area.

Balphakram lies high up in the Garo hills, part of the tripartite range that makes up Meghalaya. They had just lost a hundred square kilometres of it. It was evident that there had been a mistake in calculating the area in the first place.

'Must be the way we calculated it when we declared it you know, sometimes mistakes are made,' a senior official was trying to make amends.

'A hundred-square-kilometre mistake?' I was astounded .

'The land is all up and down, here, no. Sometimes you count it like that and then it is not the same when it is flat.'

A few honest officials were trying to set things right. Their only happiness was that the government exchequer had not lost very much because of the sudden decrease in the land owned by them. When the land was purchased, it was done at the rate of a lakh of rupees a square kilometre. An absurd real estate value. However, it was still a loss to the government and senior officials were rushed to the spot to re-survey and re-assess. I was to go with them to have a look at the elephant situation in the Garo hills. They did not ask me to look for the golden langur in the state. This was just as well, as I found no evidence of it in my travails. Brushing aside the ecstatic memories of a troop of the highly endangered stump-tailed macaques at Balphakram and the agonizingly shocking sight of a gibbon arm draped across a clothesline, I happened to stumble on some interesting evidence. Droppings of the *safai dalgopa* or the big hare. Cylindrical in shape instead of the one with pointed ends.

It just might be that I had found the scientific evidence for the existence of the hispid hare in the state. Last known only from Assam. A new species for the state! Next time I reach there, I might well be a state hero.

The flight back to Delhi was delayed, as usual. The airline was Indian Airlines, as usual. The sufferer was me, as usual. I sat back and thought deeply on the hog, the hare and the blonde monkey.

'What do you want to do with the two hours that you have extra?'

Kamini Barua had a cigarette dangling from his fingers, as usual.

It was, as you might have guessed, a usual morning. Or so I thought.

'I suppose one could laze around Barua Bhawan.'

'Or see some golden langurs.'

'Or see some golden langurs.'

There never was a problem in agreeing with a madman.

Kamini had a very serious air about him, though. He returned, ready to leave in five minutes.

'You ready? Let's go, eh?'

'Where to?' I had not believed a single word that he had said earlier.

'Umanando Island, to see the langurs.'

Umanando is a temple on a small island in the Brahmaputra, visible from the Guwahati banks and about a twenty-minute boat ride away. The nearest known golden langur population was more then a hundred kilometres away.

'You must be joking!'

Kamini still did not seem to be joking.

'You are not talking of common langurs, are you?'

'But there are no common langurs here. They don't extend up to here.' Kamini looked a little hurt that I was not taking him seriously. Twenty minutes later I was climbing a dozen steps up the island bank to the Shiva temple. Shiv Shankar temple in Hindi. Or as the Assamese pronounce it, Khibokhonkhor. On the opposite bank a dozen boats, some large and some small, were tied up in sullen silence. I had once talked to Manjuda about converting them into floating restaurants and opening up a new trend in India. A European idea. On many occasions I had been happy that he had not taken me seriously. Sometimes the lack of certain kinds of tourism is a good thing.

There were a few devotees who had come to pay respects at Umanando but by and large we were left alone. Kamini was climbing up slowly behind me, his face writhing with the short pants of a chain smoker. He caught up with me at the top. His eyes were on a mango tree that grew ten metres below and the branches of which, laden with unripe fruit, climbed to eye level. The green fruit was moving slowly, tantalisingly. From the middle of the tree a pale shadow was detaching itself. There was no doubt about it. It was a langur. But which one?

'The golden.' Kamini speaks softly at the best of times.

The trees parted a bit more and the shadows re-aligned. It was a mother, with an infant clutched tightly to its heart. Some distance away, another adult separated itself from the foliage.

Silver-gold, long cheek whiskers and tasselled tail. No cap of the capped langur, no cobalt inner thighs.

There was no doubt now. These were golden langurs. Kamini looked elated. He lit another cigarette.

Slowly, with the art of a practiced magician, he took a packet of bananas from his pocket and laid it out on the stone ledge running around the temple. I was learning something every minute. The most arboreal of Indian monkeys, the creature that never comes to the ground, the golden shadow that one saw from a peculiar crick of the neck, was slowly climbing down from its perch and heading towards the forbidden fruit. A golden creeping figure, two golden offerings and a change in the known behaviour of a species.

It was a wild chance. I picked up a banana and held it up. Slowly, very slowly, the monkey came to me and reaching out, took my offering. This could not be a wild animal.

I turned suspiciously to Kamini.

The usual lazy smile played on his lips.

'From Manas area originally, the pundit says. Two trappers caught the adults. Bihari trappers. Then the monkeys were babies too. They gave the pair as an atonement of their sins to the temple.'

Slowly, realization was dawning. Indian religious conservation at its best.

I went back a full ten years. It was Delhi and the posh drawing room of Satyapal Malik, a minister in the Janata government in the South Avenue area. The interior of the house was all Iqbal Malik. Dr Iqbal Malik, the primatologist. Iqbal, the designer. Walls choc-a-bloc with pottery and mirrors, cushions in the most ethnic Rajasthani colours, plants creeping up painted tiles and drooping on lacquer-work furniture. On the shelf was a rhesus skull with a red vermilion mark on its forehead. Indians worship their monkeys. On the wall was the photo of a rhesus in the vice-clamp of a pharmaceutical laboratory torture rack. Indians kill their monkeys.

We sat on the carpet writing out a management plan for the rhesus in Delhi. We had earlier written a paper on the effects of captivity on monkeys. It was my first full-length scientific paper. She was already a veteran. For over ten years she had been the rhesus lady of India. Today she has branched out into other environmental issues, leading the crusade with élan.

'The Tughlaqabad monkeys, Vivek, what can we do to stop them from entering the air force base?'

An old politician was waiting for her husband in a rocking chair. His starched white creaked with effort as he listened in on the conversation.

'If translocation is tried, will the locals like it?'

The truth was that the local villagers fed the monkeys as gods. The monkeys forsook traditional foraging and moved closer to humans. One of their babies then went and broke a windscreen wiper. Or a dominant male displayed by rattling the electricity transmission lines to the neighbourhood and a two-hour blackout resulted. Now they were no longer gods. Only pests. But come the time to take them away and a section of the society would protest. We discussed long and hard. The politician could no longer bear it.

'Iqbal ji,' he was sagacity revealed, 'as I understand, you want to protect *bandar* ji, no?'

Yes, we demurred. *Bandar* ji, the monkey god, was to be protected.

'But then, just build a temple there, no. Of Hanuman,

the monkey god. Who will dare disturb your monkeys then?'

Clear conservation solution. Religion and the preservation of species. Now extended to the banks of the Brahmaputra and to the golden langur.

The pundit in this case had let the animals go wild. Now the langurs had mated and given birth to a baby. Technically, a wild baby. Or was it feral? The langurs seemed reasonably tame. As I went closer, though, they scampered up the trees. Not totally tame either. For the first time, I saw wildlife trade as having benefited a species. Given adequate protection, this could well become an alternate population. Every one of them would count in an unsecured future.

As the boat pulled away from Umanando, I saw the monkeys come down to where I had scattered biscuit crumbs on the ledge. A golden morning. Not the usual one.

Turtles and an Olive Soup

'Never trust a reptile,' I said.

'Okay,' said Mangesh, and thrusting his forefinger towards me, added, 'but I have just one question . . .'

'No!' I was as sharp as I could be. 'No!'

The only sound that remained was the gentle swooshing of the tide as it taunted our weary feet with false, cool promises. A pair of grey-headed fishing eagles circled lazily overhead, afraid to break the silence with their mewling calls. In the distance, a couple of Oriya fishing boats spun with the incoming tide laden with a hastily bundled fish catch. Further away, closer to the horizon, three battleship-shaped trawlers broke the mirage of unbroken water. The sand was clear gold, marred only by the stump of a washed up boat-rafter and three winking fishing floats. Strangely, there were no washed-up shells; neither of scallops and periwinkles that God has created solely for children to collect nor of the highly endangered olive ridley turtle that we were looking for. As the tide swished in and sucked away, the sand opened up into long, deep tubes and the delicate feathers of a tube worm colony waved in the breeze.

The turtles had not come in for two years now and it was beginning to be a bit of a nuisance. For almost all of ten years, I had wanted to see these marine reptiles lay their eggs in the sand. It is an annual ritual and undoubtedly the biggest wildlife spectacle on Indian territory. In Africa, wildebeest stampeding across the Serengeti is the image that brings to mind the teeming of wildlife. In India, where a mysterious forest cloaks most of its residents and numbers are never hugely apparent, the turtles constitute an anomaly. For a few weeks, annually, the olive ridleys swim in from all over the world to Gahirmatha and the associated coastline of Orissa. Keeping up with the Indian tradition of comfort in numbers, half a million normally turn up. The Spanish call it the great coming or the *arribadas*. The language is common to the other two large turtle nesting grounds in Mexico and Costa Rica. I had in the past seen the green turtle, a closely allied species, nest on the beaches off Karachi in Pakistan, but Orissa was in India and I wanted to see it in my country. For ten years something would turn up just when I was ready to pack my bags for Orissa—a sudden bout of malaria, an absolutely crucial deadline for sending a proposal to save all the elephants and rhinos in the world, an old flame . . . And now that I had come in, the turtles were not turning up—dead or alive!

I looked over my shoulder at my two companions, straggling aimlessly behind. Mangesh was a thin, hollow reed of a man, broken, it would seem, in many places, by many events. His hose-pipe trousers glinted with shining acrylic. A shirt hung loose on his torso, open strategically to reveal a stubborn tuft of hair poking out at the world. His face was dominated by two dark hollows that formed recesses for his eyes to hide in and peer disconcertingly at the imperfect world around him. His hair was 1970s' Telegu movie stuff combed at intervals by a singing yellow comb. The singing was produced by thumb and forefinger in an attempt to clean the comb, usually next to the ear of the nearest human being. A pair of Hawaii chappals flopped in tune to the singing of the comb. Keeping close to him, indeed observing him with more unabashed interest than my surreptitious over-the-shoulder glances, was a Telegu fisherman picked up a few moments before on the coast. His only attire was a blue checked *lungi* and a three-cornered hat made of white thermocol that had been salvaged from the sea. Crusts of sea salt clung to his body; flaking peels of white on a sun-burned wood sculpture. His face was wreathed in a moronic smile that was either a birth defect or the complete bliss of a man unaware of his current purpose but fully aware that he was happily unaware.

'*Enni unnai?*' asked Mangesh. 'How many?'

'*Em ledu,*' grinned the fisherman. 'None.'

Peace prevailed once more on the coasts of Ganjam.

~

Biswajit Mohanty, chartered accountant, wildlife enthusiast and scion of an old Cuttack family, had been a friend and host in my Oriya travels.

'Orissa is the only mainland state that I have not set foot in,' I had complained when I first got to know him.

'Not surprising,' he had said, 'even the government has forgotten it. Doesn't matter. Come and I'll show you.'

He had been true to his word and had looked after me and pointed me in many a right direction for the past couple of years. This time around it was the turn, it seemed, of Mangesh to do the chaperoning. I had never met Mangesh, only heard of him from a few friends. Till now, I trusted Biswajit. Now, I was beginning to have my doubts.

'Don't worry,' he said with classical Biswajit brevity, 'he is quite a character.'

He must have seen a cloud of worry passing over my face.

'He'll keep you entertained,' he clarified, giving me a bottle of a bilious new soft drink released in the Oriya markets to promote sports and poison the local populace. We were standing outside Cure Aids, a small chemist shop owned by his friend Bibhu—dog breeder, Oriya dance promoter and a recent convert to the Orissa Wildlife Society ethos of Biswajit. On the streets, a brisk sunshine lit up the crawling traffic of the Orissa capital.

'Mangesh will take you around for the next two days. Don't worry, Bhibhu will take over then.'

I was getting extremely worried about the number of don't worries when Mangesh wheeled in dramatically on a sports bike; a dusty apparition with a rucksack, two plastic bags and a rolled up quilt. Slung across his body.

'Hello,' he introduced himself, not bothering to dismount immediately from the comforts of his cycle. 'My name is Mangesh and I am an idealist.'

The brand new ambassador car that had been hired specially for my travels in the state, was driven by a boyish-looking man with spectacles. Usually a Mahindra jeep is the first item on the wish list when jungles are to be negotiated, but Biswajit had laughed away the small possibility of forest roads not being good enough for a car. Besides, it was election time and every fool knew that it was disastrous to travel in a jeep during elections in

India. Any political party, election commission or other minor district functionary had the right to requisition the vehicle for official government duty, usually leaving the traveller with his bags on the highway. Orissa is considered to be a poor state but its highways are among the best in India. Biju babu, politician, pilot and the Oriya equivalent of Winston Churchill had left this as a bequest to his state. The driver was proving the quality of the road. We passed at a fair clip across a verdant countryside. I learnt quickly that Mangesh was an idealist. Also, that he was actually the son of a rich Telegu landlord, who had migrated to Orissa to pursue his idealism. To marry a girl that his parents did not approve of, I later learnt, but is that not idealism as well? Then came the knowledge of the several jobs which he had chucked up.

'Birla is only interested in making money, so I left him,' he said.

I was surprised. I thought Birla built temples and fed the father of the nation. By the time we had got to the edge of the large saltwater expanse of Chilika Lake, I had greatly broadened my knowledge base with which I could face the world.

'Now, animal rights. Did you hear about thousands, perhaps millions of chicken killed in Hong Kong because they suspected a virus might spread from them to human beings?'

I confessed that I had.

'What about the Mad Cow Disease? How many cows have been killed so that man is safe from eating contaminated beef?'

Thousands. Probably tens of thousands, I agreed.

'Ah!' said Mangesh delighted at my knowledge of world affairs. 'Now what I want to ask them is one small question.'

I was soon to learn that he had one small question to ask of everyone. I was also to learn that they were mostly painful and embarrassing questions, based on his high occupation of being an idealist.

'One small question. Why don't we just round up and shoot all the people who have AIDS? Eh? Do you know the risk of their spreading the disease? More than chicks and cows, eh?'

I hastily agreed.

There was little to do but think of the reptiles that had drawn me to Orissa in the first place. The true turtles are a 200-million-year-old clan. Old enough, one would think, to have evolved means of avoiding and evading the half-a-million-year old human being. Yet, year after year, the chelonians (for that is the term by which scientists call their pet turtles and tortoises) face persecution from a variety of man-invented tortures. In the sea, a large number are caught in trawler nets and drown or struggle desperately in the mesh, tearing large turtle-shaped holes in them. This then leads to them being clubbed to death by irate fishermen who see their catch disappearing as a result. If they make it to the shore to nest, they find minor irritants such as cities and human dwellings already taking up their nesting grounds. One of the largest obstacles in the subcontinent is Karachi city which is certainly no more than a few thousand years old, built by man years after the turtles first used the beach for nesting. When they do manage to nest, the eggs are dug out and sold in village bazaars. As if the whole ignominy of being an unwanted customer in the human environment is not sad enough, they are also specific targets of man in his excitement to get hawksbill shell to make tortoiseshell spectacle rims or its fat to make soup. India is particularly rich in turtle fauna. There are twenty-six tortoises and turtles found on land and in fresh water. And then, there are the five highly endangered species of marine turtles.

It was on the Karachi coastline that I first saw the phenomenon of mass turtle nestings. The year was 1990 and I was in the capital of Sind to attend a waterfowl conference.

'*Bhaisaheb, yeh Filmistan ka rasta kaun sa hai?*' I asked a pedestrian, trying to find my way to a predetermined meeting place.

'How do you speak such good Urdu?' asked the incredulous Sindhi, his question drowned by a blast of Hindi film music from a passing Karachi minibus.

'I don't, I speak Hindi.'

'Hah!' he exploded rubbing his hands in unconcealed glee at having caught out my joke. '*Kahe ko kali peeli bum marela hain, sain!*' (Why are you jokin', man!) he said in Bombaiyya road slang.

His pure uncorrupted Bombay Hindi lifted out of an Andheri chawl and deposited a few hundred kilometres west, caught me unawares.

This was Pakistan but for all practical purposes we were in the same land. What he called Urdu was what I called Hindi. What I thought was Urdu turned out to be Bombaiyya. Around us, a million colourful people crammed into scores of colourful buses and went from streets of hue to black and white homes. I was luckier. I was bound for the beaches of Hawkesbay, a small belt of white sand, a reminder that the megalopolis had not always been there. I was luckier that as friend and guide I had the vivacious Fahmida Firdaus, a gutsy young Sind Wildlife official who had an official title that completely slips my mind and a popular pseudonym that translates as turtle lady. It was time for the green turtles to come out of the sea and begin their phenomenal nesting and I was at the right place at the right time.

The sea was pea green and the waves rose in crisp attendance. Behind us, the skyline of Karachi was rapidly getting swallowed up by the dusk. The beach turned a deep golden, then dark, then as the sky lit up once briefly just before sundown, a burnished copper. Then it was dark and as we lay on our stomachs side-by-side, the only sound was that of the greedy water lapping up the sand at the edge of the land. Slowly and laboriously, the moon rose out of the dark. It was almost full moon, a good night for the turtles to come. Beside me, Prakash Rao, a fellow Indian ornithologist who was studying birds at a rocket centre in southern India, breathed deeply and steadily.

'Keep awake, Prakash.' I was afraid that the sudden peace would make him fall asleep.

Fahmida was suddenly a very quiet girl and did nothing much to help keep him awake. Her eyes were on the distant horizon and I let myself fall into that easy, somnambulistic peace that is often a prelude to an event of great significance.

'They're coming out. See that shape there.' Fahmida was pointing into the sea. The little light that the moon provided lit up the water with a milky glow and a huge black shadow rose out of it rather laboriously. Our eyes took some time to get adjusted to the turtle. Meanwhile, there were more turtles to our right and then more to our left. They were coming out of the marine woodwork, crawling out of the primeval slime that oozed on the sea bed.

'Good God!' Prakash breathed more heavily. So it was not sleep. Just a natural heavy breathing. 'There are so many of them.'

And so there were. Twenty-six on the beach. More, probably, breaking out of their marine slumber elsewhere. In front of our supine bodies these two dozen and two monsters were slowly invading the land. This was an old science fiction movie that I had forgotten the name of, in which aliens invade in reptilian forms from the sea. It had to be sci-fi. What else could it be!

If you are not a fisherman on the high seas or Fahmida Firdaus in Karachi, then it is quite possible that you may miss the most part of a sea turtle's life. Females, and only females, come ashore once every three or four years. If she is very successful the female turtle may come once in ten days, as many as ten times, to lay her eggs in different beach nests. Each time she may spend a few hours on the land. Males on the other hand almost never come to land. The amazing story of the reproduction of these turtles begins in the ocean, with the males and the females swimming a slow courtship crawl in the waters. Males are forever looking for different females and turtle watchers often see the lady rising up vertically in the water in a classic refusal position. Successful males leave their sperms inside the females and these will remain there for months on end. The female, meanwhile, starts the long swim to the coast, braving trawlers and gill-nets, to find that rising mound of sand to build her sand castle. The two common sea turtles of India take up different parts of the coast. While the olive ridley prefers the eastern coast, the green takes up the Andamans and the western shoreline of the subcontinent.

The turtles were now coming up closer and we dug ourselves deeper into the sand to avoid detection.

'Don't disturb them now or they will go back,' instructed the turtle lady.

I did not want to do that at any cost. To make a mother wait another five years was cruel beyond belief. It was like a hospital offering maternity ward services five years down the line to a mother in labour. Also, if we spoiled the occasion, it would be a long wait before I got an opportunity like this again.

Once on the shore, the greens began to quickly dig shallow body pits with their front flippers. The flip-flop of soft sand was a mesmerizing lullaby. Like a hundred beach-bums walking in line. A single Mangesh flopping along. The turtle nearest me was only ten yards away. It had not got my smell or heard the sound of my heart beating against my rib-cage. The beast started to let itself into the half-dug pit.

'Now she will make the main nest hole with her back flippers,' explained the shadowy figure on my left. 'Still. No sound.'

The turtle looked around warily but still perceived nothing. A crow flew over the moon and the turtle glanced up briefly. Then back to work. Huge shovelfuls of sand were now being sprayed in all directions. Some of it clogged my nose and mouth.

'Bhen do dey stad laying?' I was breathing through the sand.

'Just a few more minutes. Patience.'

The turtle seemed to have stopped short. Its derrière, green and pointed, was lifting slowly and then descending again. Around her, the others were still digging away, throwing sand into the night. Slowly, the back lifted for the fifth time. This time, at the very rear, a pearly white golf ball made its appearance.

'A hundred and more white eggs are laid, before the mother covers it up to avoid detection by the predators.' Fahmida was very instructive. 'On the eastern coasts, the ridley does not bother to make the body-hole but straightaway gets down to making the nest-hole. After an equal number of eggs are laid into the hole she covers it up with sand, often adding bits of nearby fronds and plants to hide it completely.'

She had got up and was approaching the turtle.

'Careful. Don't frighten it away.' I was the cautious biologist, aware of animal rights and welfare.

She smiled an experienced smile.

'Come. Now that she has started laying she will complete her job. In fact, we can pick her up and see the whole process up close, if you want.'

Fahmida had picked up the ancient reptile by her cloaca, a most disrespectful way to treat an ancestor of sorts. From up close, we could see the slimy bubble of an egg emerging from her motherly innards, blossoming into a full sphere and then plopping away from the body, enveloped in protective ooze. There was a slight smell of fish and this I thought strange.

In front of us, deep in labour in an open-air maternity ward was this million-year-old creature, least bothered about the mid-wifely attentions being given by a totally different species. If I were a human woman, I would most definitely protest if a turtle were to come and pick up my legs just at the time of my giving birth. I wanted to ask Fahmida if she felt the same way but decorum made me stop short.

Sea turtles, like all other turtles, have evolved to fit plan C of the basic reptilian plan that exists today. Plan A is that of the lizards and crocodiles; short, low-slung bodies on fat, short legs and a powerful tail. Plan B is that of the skinks and the snakes, which is to get as low down as possible to the ground. This involves giving up limbs altogether and adopting that drunkenly graceful movement that biologists and poets call serpentine. Plan C is the turtle plan. A roughly oval body plan, which the terribly romantic call heart-shaped, with bony plates growing out from the ribs outwards and encasing the body in a bulletproof vest. The plates below the body are covered with a thick yellow skin called the plastron and the plates above are covered with a horny material that is called the carapace. The horny part is missing in species such as the leatherback which is the largest turtle in the world. Like all persons entitled to having a bulletproof vest, the turtles also go in for designer wear. Each species has a different combination of plates and different colours of shields, making it easy to tell them apart. Out of this armour, four legs and a head stick out to negotiate the world. Snakes and lizards need to be able to move their bodies like supple gymnasts, as their movements are dependent on body flows. Turtles, instead, have a rigid body with only the head and legs being flexible and even these cannot be fully withdrawn into the shell as in their freshwater cousins. At sea, the legs are not required for walking and become paddles, designed to thrust water away from the body in a strangely bird-like motion. Once the turtles come to land they are all at sea, and females labour across the sands, swimming without any water.

The moon was now completely out of sight and our eyes were lit by the aspirations of the night. A little further down the beach, a collection of turtle eggs had started pulsing with life. This was not a natural nest but a rescued collection of eggs from predator-struck sites. A rare human helping hand. This sort of exercise has two very important contributions for conservation. Like bird counts. Turtle watches or egg collections are as much a meeting ground and developing school for conservationists as they are life-savers for the reptiles. B.C. Choudhary, an old friend and one of India's most respected aquatic life scientists, started his career with a turtle watch. Now at the Wildlife Institute of India, BC has done more combined work on turtles and crocodiles, dolphins and otters than any one else in the country. He often talks of the sheer fatigue of daubing the shells with a little paint as the turtles came onto Gahirmatha to nest. The mark of human kindness.

The warmth maintained by the kindness in Karachi had allowed the nest to develop just that little bit faster. Fahmeeda hurried to it and we prepared to witness another adventure. Under normal circumstances, the mother turtle goes back to sea not very bothered about parenting the young. She depends largely on the natural forces of heat and light to do the job for her. As the sun burrows into the sand, tiny creatures start forming inside the eggs. The control panel inside the children informs them that twenty-eight degrees is right for hatching. If the temperature goes below twenty-seven or above thirty, the eggs will not hatch. This biological trick ensures that they hatch in the cool evenings when the temperature is just right and there are less predators around than in the day time. Strangely enough, almost until hatching the eggs contain foetuses of indeterminate sex. Between twenty-seven and twenty-eight degrees more males than females come out, while between twenty-eight and thirty degrees more females appear than males. The sex of the turtle child is determined by the temperature. A situation like this in the human race would most definitely cause many an Indian man to refrigerate his pregnant wife!

Prakash produced a small metallic torch and I used it to illuminate the path being taken by the turtles. The temperature had done its job and the eggs were cracking unevenly, exposing the tentative heads of their inmates. Like most other turtles, the green had used its single egg-tooth to break open the shell from inside. Adult sea turtles lose this soon after, to lead a toothless existence for the rest of their lives. As the young turtles crawled out into the open world, the light from the sea lit up their way. The moon shone softly on the water, illuminating it more than the land. The ocean was neon-lit for the young ones to head towards. Prakash shone the torch directly behind a young turtle. In a moment, the youngster was lost. The artificial light was stronger than the light of the moon and by now a thoroughly confused turtle had turned around and was climbing up my trouser leg, looking for the sea. In a larger version of this drama, man has built coastal roads lined, inexplicably, with street lights, attracting young and impressionable turtles away from the sea and towards the wheels of oncoming traffic.

~

On the Palur beach, Mangesh was walking behind me, his flip-flops ascribing new vermicultural patterns in the intertidal zone. The expanse of the beach was unbroken by turtle shells, alive or dead. This was all very strange, as only a few weeks earlier Mangesh and an artist friend had trekked many a kilometre on the coastline, documenting hundreds of dead turtles being washed ashore. I was in Bhittarkanika at the time and had received an urgent message to check out the disaster. Most of them, Mangesh reported, had been trapped in the nets of deep-sea trawlers, many of them clubbed to death, others suffocated and drowned. Trawler owners rarely heed the ten-kilometres from land restriction placed on them and come closer to the shore to get better catches. This is just the area where turtles come out of water to look up at the land. They get enmeshed in a rather fatal controversy instead.

'Count the trawlers that you can see,' the Telegu fisherman spat a blotch of wet spittle at the sand. 'All rich foreigners. They have paid off all the officials.'

Foreigners meant foreign to the coast, in most parts, but there were uneasy rumours of Thai or Indonesian boats in the Indian waters as well. The Telegu guide spat a few more times on the beach, overtly spiteful of the rich trawler owners. The small traditional fisherman is no competition at all for the well-oiled hinges of big time business.

'Two men come and mark the turtles and bury them,' said a wandering Oriya man whom we stopped on the beach to query about the large number of missing corpses. 'Just yesterday they came, sir, buried all the things in a cycle, sir.'

Difficult to bury in a cycle. Only slightly less difficult would be the task of burying the fifty kilogram adults in damp sand. Laborious work. Mangesh and I exchanged glances. Who would toil to bury dead turtles? A forest department that wanted to tally their dead and not allow for a re-count? A fisheries department that did not want the true tally to be known? A people's department that wanted to spare the fishermen rotting corpses near their homesteads? The last one was absurdly considerate. Totally ruled out. The second one was a distinct possibility.

At a top-level meeting a past fisheries secretary of Orissa had wanted to know the economic value of turtles to the nation.

'What can I answer?' Biswajit had asked me in desperation.

'Tell him our country does not traditionally put a price to all things,' I had to think of some answer to counter such rampant ignorance. 'Not to our wives, not to our mothers and not to wildlife!'

But I knew he would not be strong enough to say such a thing to an Indian Administrative Service man, one of those civil servants who run the country like a personal fiefdom. Perhaps Mangesh was a better person to send for such meetings. My faith in his directness had been strengthened the day after the Palur trek.

Sitting in the newly-built rest house in the Lakhari Valley was a peaceful experience. Mangesh had stretched out on the chair nearest to a fountain and was intently telling Bibhu of life in the back-streets of New York. I had just ordered cups of tea when I noticed a solitary foreigner hanging around in embarrassed silence.

'Want to join us for a cup of tea?' I asked him.

The man readily agreed. He was young, white and looked as if a dose of inter-cultural talk was what he needed most with his cup of tea.

'Hello . . . Pierre,' he introduced himself to the group. 'I am from France.'

Mangesh who was reclining in his chair till then sat up with the alacrity of a cat who had spied a lame mouse sauntering by, on his off-day.

'France, did you say, France?' he had closed his eyes and I was steeling myself to the inevitable. 'I read *Le Monde* whenever I get the chance, you know. Sartre, croissants, Champs de Elysee.'

I wondered whether *Le Monde* was distributed from Bhubhaneswar or Vizag.

Bhibhu winced visibly as the dreaded finger was produced.

'Ah, my friend, you are just the person I wanted to ask one small question about France.'

'Sure,' agreed the Frenchman, unaware of the intentions of the ideal idealist.

'Your ex-President Mitterand, you know who I mean . . . Mitter-rand?'

It took Pierre two minutes to understand the name. He nodded his head vigorously.

Mangesh came forward with a gleam in his eye.

'Now, Mitterand . . . did he or did he not have a mistress? And if he did, how did you as self-respecting French people tolerate him as your President?'

'Sorrrry?' asked the pole-axed Pierre.

'That's right. Did he or did he not commit adultery?'

'Aah! meestresss,' agreed the Frenchman, 'many, many meestreeses. Not one, no, no. Many. Many.'

'And your law tolerated it! What sort of law do you have anyway?'   .

'Aw, come off it, Mangesh,' Bibhu interrupted, 'let the poor chap have his tea. What's it to you anyway if Mitterand had his mistresses or not?'

Mangesh had gone back to his semi-reclining sulk.

'Just the law!' he sulked, 'I was just interested to know French law. I don't care if he has mistresses. But if bigamy is not allowed how can you keep a mistress? Is that fair . . . is it . . . is it?'

Monsieur Pierre withdrew after a few apologetic comments.

~

My search for turtles had started earlier in the month at Bhittarkanika, a jewel in Orissa's collection of wild places. Gahirmatha was the turtle beach at Bhittarkanika. The area was also the training ground of BC. From his richly accented accounts of the state, my vision of Bhittarkanika had taken shape. Its flavours came back vividly as I coursed the mangrove waters. Wide blue-green lagoons and inland waterways stretch placidly, kilometres on end, linking the hot, dusty mainland with the sea. When it does reach the seashore it broadens spectacularly into golden-white beaches of burnished sand. In between, tangled roots of mangrove frame the waterways—silent sentinels of a mystical world. On an arched root, rising three feet and more out of the water and then dipping humbly back again, a black-capped kingfisher glittered like an unfinished gem. As our boat passed, it stretched its black head out, red bill pointed accusingly, and rattled a loud protest.

'All this is ours to protect,' waved Chadda expansively at the flashing reams of water. Lolling on a leather-finished bunk of a luxury boat owned by the forest department, I nodded. It was better to agree with Chadda than to philosophize. There was perhaps not a better officer in the Orissa forest department than Sanjiv Chadda, nor one who had fought harder for the cause of the fast vanishing forests of the state. There is also perhaps no one as stubborn or mentally tough as him. Far better to agree, than disagree.

Chadda is a Jammu Pandit and somehow, his montane toughness brought back memories of childhood and a school friend. Vikram Nanda was in school in Chandigarh what Sanjiv Chadda was in Bhittarkanika. His ruddy vitality led most of us into believing that mountains could be climbed and hills run over in record time. Trekking was a sport encouraged in school and the Himalayas beckoned from close by, a land of white and green to be explored come autumn. In the mountains night fell very early and dawn arrived a few hours too early. I was usually up before any one else. No toughness there . . . I had forgotten my sleeping bag. Frozen in borrowed blankets, I had soon found out that the best way of keeping warm was to circulate outside the blanket. On such horribly early morning perambulations, I would run into the redoubtable Vikram getting ready for the morning trek. He would be up and bathed by four o'clock, looking scrubbed and rosy like the apples that hung all around the Kulu valley. His favourite perch was a strategic boulder outside the campsite where as darkness gave way to the first morning vistas of snowy magnificence, he would polish his three-ton army boots into an alternate mirror. Looking at his face in the black glow of his boots, he would whistle merrily. Many of us would have strangled him for free.

Chadda shared a place of birth with Vikram and by all accounts the robust outlook to life as well that Nanda had shown when very young. Accompanying us were Biswajit and Bibhu, the idealist Mangesh a vacuum in my wild life. We had spent two days in the mangrove forests, not venturing out into the golden sands of Gahirmatha—the place of the arribadas. The range officer was certain that the turtles had still not come ashore. It was frustrating to wait for the crackle of his wireless that would bring the glad tidings, it was more prudent to accept that it would not happen during the time we were there. Bhittarkanika in Orissa and the Sunderbans in West Bengal are the two important mangrove swamps of eastern India. The turtles of Gahirmatha are ecologically only a bonus to Bhittarkanika, so rich is the area. As we cruised along, small herds of shy spotted deer stumbled across the swamp fringes. These were the first wild mammals that I had seen clearly in the daytime in Orissa. Otherwise one would think that wildlife is nightlife in the state. On a previous visit to Simlipal, the state's best known protected area, Biswajit and I had spent two days without a glimpse of a mammal. Suddenly, two feet in front of us a wild boar shot across the road as if fired from a twelve-bore gun. It broke all previous speed records held by wild swines.

'Look, look, wildlife,' shouted an excited Biswajit.

I informed him that in other parts of the country you could watch wild boar for a few hours more at a time.

'You have to come in the night to see animals like that in Orissa,' he told me confidently. Later I came to know that they were shot into becoming shy and excitable. At the very sight of man they would sprint into cover and hardy diurnal animals had started taking the night shift with the owls. Orissa the land of night life. The red-light wildlife state.

Not so in Bhittarkanika, however. The chital were happy in the knowledge that an expanse of water separated the boat and them. In the grass beyond, a four-foot water monitor lizard slunk away into the forest. A sinuous, yellow splotched reptilian, complete with a forked tongue. A miniature dinosaurian in a pre-historic land. There were signs of the elusive fishing cat, sandy-golden in colour, which like a good eastern Indian lives on the offerings of the river. The cat would wait, its long-furred body hunched in anticipation, and catch a moving ripple in the water, slap a fish out of the creek with amazing exactitude. Small mud-skippers, the only fish in the country with rudimentary lungs, were gasping for air in the inter-tidal zone between the huge breathing roots of the mangroves. The fish had two sacs of air on their cheeks and these ballooned in and out as they breathed. The mangroves, trees that look like victims of erosion, stood all along the fringe with their exposed roots. The whole area seemed bursting at its seams with wildlife. All except turtles that is.

In 1974 an intrepid American biologist, H.R. Bustard discovered Gahirmatha. That is almost as absurd a statement as saying that Livingstone discovered the Victoria Falls in Zimbabwe. Standing before the awesome rush of white water cleaving through the black continent, I was amazed at the supreme arrogance of the discoverer. It was unlikely that a natural spectacle of that magnitude would have gone unnoticed by people around it before an explorer who could communicate in a European language had discovered it. In any case, the Smoke that Thunders, the Shona version of the falls, is a far more poetic rendering of nature's fury, than Victoria. Luckily for Indian conservation, Bustard did not name the Orissa beach Carter Sands or Reagan Rookery or anything as commemorative. He had merely pointed out the importance of the beach as an international site for turtle nesting and then badgered the respective governments at the state and centre for protecting it. To give Orissa its due share of credit, Gahirmatha was declared a sanctuary in 1985, eleven years after its discovery.

Gahirmatha has weathered many a storm in its thirteen long years of protection. A disastrous natural one struck the beach in 1989, leaving only a part of the northern area suitable for turtle nesting. A four kilometre sand spit north of the river Maipura's mouth was all that remained of the original fifteen kilometre nesting ground. The Ekakulanasi rookery was the result of a cyclone wrought by God. The cyclone wrought by man has literally brought Gahirmatha to its knees. Poaching and construction have both left the sanctuary a virtual cripple. If it is not jetties that spring up in the vicinity spawning boats and catamarans, trawlers and dhingies in their wake, it is a proposed missile test range for test firing onto the nesting turtles at Gahirmatha. The woes of the ancient creature seem endless. BC and the tireless C.S. Kar fight through science. Raj Panjwani, the lawyer with a wild heart, tries litigation.

'The problem with you wildlife-wallahs is that you do not have a martyr for your cause.' Raj has always been provocative, especially over a plastic cup of coffee on the lawns of the Delhi High court. I silently wondered if he could be the first one. Or then again, he could have been trying to tell me something very personal.

A million storms have come and blown over. The one today is the absence of female turtles on our beaches. After an exhausting wait, a few hundred turtles nested in Rushikulia, a few kilometres south of the Palur beach. The Indian coastline is long and varied enough to always provide the intrepid turtle with a few spots of sand. The poaching of turtles and their incidental catch in fishing nets, however, may still stop their nesting en masse. There is a silver lining to the marine cloud—TED, an American who can fit onto fishing nets in a number of different ways depending on the net shape and size. TED, of course, is nickname. The expanded Christian name is the Turtle Excluder Device. It works on the simple principle that turtles and commercially caught fish are of different sizes. Openings that allow the fish to be channelled into a separate chamber will not allow the turtle to reach that part of the net. The turtle, meanwhile, has a secret hatch through which it can escape back into the welcoming arms of the sea. A fantastic option. If the Indian government can be convinced that it is not a secret CIA plan hatched by the Americans, peeved at the nuclear tests. The fate of the turtles and the small fisherman hangs in balance. In a world where it is increasingly being portrayed that the pay-off for saving wildlife is being borne by the common man, turtles are a happy exception. The small fishermen only benefit from turtles and almost never are a cause for their death. It is the man who can afford a trawler, who can flout the coastal fishing regulations and harden his heart against these ancients who causes the biggest damage.

The olive ridleys did not like me enough to appear on the trip. But the splendours of the Lakhari Valley Elephant Sanctuary and the wide Chilika lagoon more than made up for the reptilian disappointments. And then there was always Mangesh. Berbera was our last stop before returning to the urbane safety of Biswajit Mohanty's Cuttack. Teak trees stood tall and welcomed us into their sparse shade. At Berbera itself, the Commandant of the Central Reserve Police Force had made splendid arrangements to receive the saab from Delhi. His men were on parade and he had got them to line up behind the rest house. He was wandering up and down in a smart uniform after having given instructions for an elaborate dinner and a morning trip to see the famous teak trees of Berbera. The teaks were planted by the British when they were ruling the country, ostensibly to enrich Indian nature. Some were giants. The CO planned the reception perfectly. Sadly for him, he had not completely anticipated Mangesh.

'CRPF! CRPF! Ah, I have one small question to ask

you,' he said as soon as we were done with the preliminary introductions. His finger was pointing ominously at the middle of the Commandant.

The teak trees bent their leaves towards us, straining to catch the gem. The CO waited with bated breath.

'Tell me one thing. Why are all of you known as lathi-wielding goons? I mean, your image, why don't you change your image?'

The Commandant's face fell visibly but he was an intrepid man.

'I suppose sir, it is because we are lathi-wielding, you know,' proffered the military man stroking his chin thoughtfully.

'Ah! I thought so!'

Mangesh was content for the time being. He spent time distributing handfuls of wild lentil seeds amongst the men standing at attention in parade formation. He came into his own during dinner once again. The Commandant's house had few utensils and so we were sharing a fish and rice meal out of many tiffin-box canisters, some serving as serving dishes and others as plates.

'I don't eat fish,' declared Mangesh. 'Gave it up many years ago.' He started eating the rice with a small portion of lentils that was also available.

The CO probably wanted to avert any further conversational mishap and switched on his radio set so that we could catch the ten o'clock news.

'You may put it off,' ordered Mangesh. 'Don't worry. Put it off.'

'But...' sputtered the officer, 'the news... the election

results.' He was visibly shaken at being ordered around in his own tent.

'I know, I know,' nodded the idealist wisely, '. . . the election results. I know it already. In fact I have known it for the last twelve years. It is the BJP.'

He whispered the last bit conspiratorially, as if Sonia Gandhi was waiting behind the kitchen tent to catch his pearls of wisdom.

'How do you know?'

'Two hundred years ago there was a wise Telegu astrologer who had predicted it.'

'You were not alive two hundred years ago, Mangesh.'

I was trying to save the CO.

'Yes, but I got it by word of mouth in Vizag. The astrologer has predicted everything accurately. The BJP is going to start the golden age for India. First the Guptas, now the BJP.'

'How did he know of the golden or saffron or whatever-colour BJP two hundred years ago?'

'He was very, very wise.' Mangesh leaned forward as always when about to deliver a real gem. 'Do you think I am a fool, eh, a fool?'

The CO was vehement in his denial. Of course, he did not think so. How ever could he? Meanwhile the rice was getting cold.

Mynah Talk

It was on a dusty Meerut road that I got my first lesson in plucking a bird from the skies. My tutor was a young lad who virtually ran the illegal bird market of the small northern Indian town. The sky was a deep spring blue, virginal and aquamarine with a few wisps of white floating across its face. The quarry was a sleek little brown dove that ornithologists have imaginatively named the little brown dove. It sat hunched in thought, its feathers ruffled and puffed with effort, on an electricity line. We were approaching it from the back and all that was visible were its grey flanks and the back of a pleasantly brown head.

'Keep a low profile.'

The boy was carrying a long, supple pole with a snake's tongue at the end, a pliable green twig cut to form a forked protuberance. A fishing line for the day. The celestial waters rippled in expectation.

Between the two forked ends spun white strands of *lhasa*, the natural milk of the fig tree that oozes out of a cut made in the bark. The bait was ready, the die was cast.

As we approached, the dove shifted uneasily, murmuring deep within its breast.

'Now, absolutely quiet, please.'

The pole inched forward, seeking flesh or feather. The line was taut with hope. The skin on the boy's cheeks was stretched in concentration.

The dove turned slowly around and saw death coming on a gilded line. Gathering up its mournful notes it chattered into a take-off. The sky splashed apart for the bird.

'Now!'

The pole shot forward and the dove was enmeshed in minute strands of *lhasa*. Fishing in the skies.

'All that remains is to draw the stick in.' His face was wreathed in the smiles of a successful predator.

The bird was reeled in from the skies. The waters above closed in silence. The lesson was complete.

Two years later, in the north-east, I learnt lesson number two. My teacher this time was twenty years senior to the Meerut lad. Asim led me to him on the back of a trembling scooter that took the twenty-odd kilometres from Guwahati rather badly. The road wound up a hill and past a row of shanties that marks the boundary of Meghalaya. Twenty-five liquor booths and chemist's shops, both selling their brand of contraband. Cough syrups with two per cent codeine in them are hot favourites. A life-long addiction to Fensidryl results in a bloated, glassy-eyed, hallucinogenic, cough-free existence. If salvation is required, it is at hand. On the left side of the road is the state of Assam. Glittering litter along the roadside marks the temple of Ganesha. Passing motorists roll down their windows and throw their small change onto the road, ringing a knell on the hard tarmac and clogging the drains with coins. Good luck would then be with them for the entire journey. On the way back they would have to do it again. Ganesha does not believe in return fares. Four kilometres to the right, along a raw red earth track, is the village of Killing. The killing is not done here, nor the catching. Killing only controls the collection and disbursal of live animals and birds for the illegal trade. The actual catching is done by people like Philip Sangma.

'The Garos don't believe in capturing the hill mynah. They raise a crop of babies instead,' Asim said, smiling at my puzzlement, as we approached Philip Sangma's village.

The Garo village was neat and clean, stilted houses raised high over hard, swept ground. Chickens and dogs squabbled ineffectively under the houses. Large porkers, pink flesh freshly anointed with a mud plaster, acted as impartial referees. Little children swung sultrily on improvised hammocks in the warm breeze of a May afternoon. Old gnarled crones and full-breasted young women were bending together over a heap of golden grain that had to be dried before the monsoon rot set in. Philip Sangma and his father welcomed us with fresh betel nuts and glasses of cold water. Philip was in his thirties, the father an old man. As the green betel nut is chewed a sensuous wave of dizziness sweeps through the body. I felt it almost at once. The coloured posters of Juhi Chawla and Jesus Christ that adorned the walls of the Sangma household were also taken in by the wave. They swam and merged, met briefly in an unholy alliance and then swam back to their respective ends.

'*Tamul* got to you, eh, my boy?' The old man held up a glass of water. A chicken clucked hilariously.

'Come, I'll take you and show you my mynah nests, Okay?' Philip liked to refer to the nests as his and not the mynahs' and in this he was justified. The mynah is only a tenant, a temporary occupant of the lovingly constructed home.

Like all villages in the Garos, the surroundings were a succession of small hills and vales, and as we walked, the path climbed and dipped. I leaned against a large silk cotton tree, careful not to let its incipient barbs stick into the back. The tree grows the barbs on the bottom-third of the trunk to prevent goats and cattle from grazing on its infancy. I needed to lean on it, though. There is nothing of the bovine in me, I just needed to wait to allow my breath to catch up with me. Fifteen metres ahead grew a Terminalia, a noble forest tree with its upraised branches a full thirty metres from the ground. On the topmost branch sat a spindle of straw.

The hill mynah is the most uncommon of one of the most common Indian bird families. The Sturnidae are a family of perching birds that include mynahs, starlings and grackles. The mynahs are common city birds with at least four species being found almost throughout India. The most common of them, the common mynah, is the average Indian's concept of what a bird must look like. Mynahs and bulbuls are the easiest Indian bird names on any romantic's tongue. Not the black commonality of the crow or the chirruping garrulousness of the sparrow, not the screech of a pea-green parakeet nor the gaudy opulence of a peacock. In the mynah and the bulbul the Indian has built his crystal world of romance and song, yin and yang. The common mynahs that flit around cities are counted eagerly by pimpled schoolgirls. 'One for sorrow,' they chant, looking furtively for its companion to make that 'Two for joy'. Arithmetic was never learnt faster.

Unlike the common mynah, the hill mynah is more a forest bird and is strictly speaking a grackle. The Assamese fondly call the bird Sonali, the beautiful one. The mellifluity of the name notwithstanding, Sonali is one of the most favoured birds in the world pet bird trade. In the Hathibagan Sunday bazaar of Calcutta or the Crawford market shanties of Bombay, which are the country's premier illegal bird marts, the black-and-yellow bird is reserved for the connoisseurs. Its soot-black body breaks out into a golden-orange beak. Fleshy orange wattles on its head crown it, laurel-like. The grackle gains its popularity both on account of its resplendent looks as well as its penchant for talking. Hindu epics glorify the rose-ringed and the alexandrine parakeets as talkers par-compare, but the hill mynah with its fluty notes and an ability to mimic the owner's speech is reputed to learn faster and have a larger vocabulary. So popular is the bird that traders catch the common 'one for sorrow' mynah and dye it with lamp black to sell it as its more illustrious cousin.

Under the Terminalia we looked up into the branches for its curious offering. The spindle was much the same as what hung from a dozen or so trees in the vicinity. Philip was not being original, merely a carrier of tradition. Like many of the other residents of his village, he painstakingly constructs the three-foot long oblong nest from dry grass and straw and places it on a convenient fork of the looming Terminalia tree long before the nesting season begins. His architectural expertise guarantees occupancy and a few weeks after he hangs up his offering, a pair of gaudy mynahs, their eyes presumably weary with home-hunting, move into the nest. Philip does not disturb the duo through the nervous days that precede egg-laying and the wary ones that follows it. He leaves them strictly alone till the eggs hatch. Years of experience has taught him that once disturbed prior to the hatching of the eggs, the birds abandon the nests. On a fine summer morning, he hears the first chirps of the two nestlings. A pre-fabricated bamboo ladder tied to the trunk of the tree acts as a lift taking him the thirty-odd metres to the brim of the nest. Peering into the nest from his vantage point and unheeding of the piteous cries of the hovering parent birds, he slinks a wiry hand into the nest and brings out the chicks. Carefully, he lowers his precious cargo into the wicker basket that he has carried up between his teeth and returns to the ground with approximately a hundred rupees worth of cargo. At the poacher's level, this compares with forty or fifty rupees for a parakeet, which makes it a far better option. The mynah makes it even better with utter biological idiocy. If the nest had been disturbed early on, the mynah would have abandoned it thinking the site to be unsuitable. At this stage, however, the disturbance only causes in the bird a return of the reproductive hormones and soon the female lays another clutch. Philip Sangma repeats his operation three times a year for every nest, capitalizing on the simple biological principle that compels the bird to lay again. Six to nine birds per nest. Fifty nests in the area can produce four hundred and more chicks for the trade. A small mynah factory in the middle of nowhere.

The old man was bent over a wicker basket full of three gaping orange beaks; hungry offspring wanting satiation. A plate of betel nuts lay beside the basket with a wickedly curving knife stained red with betel juice next to it. His granddaughter, all of seven years of age, stood swaying her young hips to an unheard melody, a short blouse baring the midriff over a loosely tied wraparound. The old man was chewing a mouthful of maize meal with complete concentration.

'This is their secret,' Asim woke up with a start. 'Watch this carefully, few people get to see this. The chicks will not survive until two things are done. This is the most important of them.'

The old man picked up a chick from the basket and brought it lovingly at level with his lips. Slowly, his pointed tongue protruded out with a small capsule of maize meal balanced neatly on it. The bird gaped larger, cheeping with frenetic hunger. Its stiff birdie tongue stuck out like an arrow head. Slowly, lovingly, the old man inserted his tongue into the bird's mouth, transferring with his kiss of life the morsel of food. The bird gulped hurriedly and gaped.

Feeding birds is a tricky business and some particularly finicky ones can leave the caretaker an exhausted, sleepless, mental wreck. Hill mynahs are bad enough, needing to be fed with a lifeguard mouth-to-mouth action, but ask me and the black tern would certainly rank very high on the list of impossible birds to feed. I found one under the armpits of a fisherman one wet and windy day in 1989, on the beaches of Point Calimere. At one glance he recognized me as belonging to the Bombay Natural History Society (BNHS) research centre and held the bird out to me.

'I was just getting it along to the *kuruvi apees*, saar.' Guilt was written on his face in large, curving creases.

Kuruvi apees or sparrow office was the fond nickname given to the BNHS by a populace that was alternately amused and astonished by the nature of work done by the centre.

'Where did you get it from, Appa?' I knew that he had originally meant to take it home for his dinner.

'The storm from the sea, saar. It was lying on the waterfront. See how ragged and wet its wings are.'

They were tattered and glued together by the salt of the sea.

At first glance it was only clear that it was a tern. In two days the assembled crowd of scientists had identified that it was a black tern, that it was only a second record from India and that it was a juvenile and had to be fed. Now, the last finding was particularly disturbing to me. Not all scientists like animal care even if they study animals. Even fewer are good at it. The bird landed up with me and I had a twenty-four-hour schedule pretending to be a mother tern. It was a lesson in biology that terns are continuous feeders, eating only small morsels, a little at a time. Fresh fish had to be bought every morning, cut into bite size morsels with a pair of paper scissors and fed lengthways to the little one who would be chewing hungrily on my toes in the meantime. Two morsels later the stomach would be full and the bird satisfied. Five minutes gone by and an incessant cheeping would break out and the bird would find a vantage point on my body to let loose a full and coordinated display of a hungry offspring meeting a parent. Fish were cut up and the tern fed for over two weeks until one day it tried to take off into the wilds across the beach and ran into a brahminy kite a few kilometres down the line. The kites were my primary study objective and so I could not even be angry with it for claiming its rightful meal.

Chlidoe, the tern, came to mind that day. The old man was still feeding his black-and-orange wards. The little child was still swaying seductively. Philip and Asim were smoking grass in the corner of the courtyard. The Garo hills around abound with households like Philip's. The area supplies the trade with an estimated 20,000-25,000 birds annually which are fed into a bird-trade monster machine that consumes at least twenty-five million birds a year. One that requires a raw material of a fifth of the world's bird species. At least 500 of the 1200 Indian birds. Most of our endangered species. Why do birds fascinate man so much? It could be the flight. The capability to wing above humanity in a demonstration of utter contempt. In their propensity to whirl around in the air in simple *joie de vivre*, to chase rainbows with a wing-beat and to climb on top of clouds in a bid to escape daily humdrum. Or it could be the colours.

'Look at the yellow and the black and the red,' my mother once marvelled at a photograph of a blackheaded oriole held firmly in my grasp as I force-fed it water. 'It must be God's own creation.'

'God's own,' shrilled Shaila, the sister-creature, 'that's why it is so gaudy.' She went off into one of her raucous, high-pitched laughs.

'No, no, not gaudy. It is so beautiful, so soothing.'

The golden of the body shone brightly forth. The soot of the head was coal-black. The red gape of the beak was coralline.

'So beautiful,' my mother marvelled, 'just like the cushions on my sofa.'

The cushions were as unfortunate as her comparison. It could still be the colours though.

Mynahs are a colourful lot of birds despite the predominant body colour being black. My early study of the birds of the Delhi Ridge forest gave me an insight into their family. There were four residents and two migrants, a large enough representation of the family. The most common was the common mynah, glossy black-brown with a yellow beak, dandified and strutting. It was the one found nearest humans, and built a variety of nests, most resembling a conventional untidy bird's nest. The bank mynah, slightly smaller and with an orange beak and wattle, frequented the wetter areas near streams, canals and drains. It lived in holes in the bank of the river, or if man had given it an artificial bank hole, like drainpipes that were unused, it adapted to those. The pied mynah was a black-and-white garden bird with a much larger old-ball shaped nest built higher on the trees than that of the common mynahs. Finally, there was the slightly rarer brahminy mynah, with a glossy black crest and a cinnamon body, that lived in holes in trees. What a wonderful partitioning of the habitat by a related group of birds. When the starlings and the rosy pastors arrived during migration, they had their own niches, all carefully partitioned by, what I would, were I not a biologist, have called a clever divine hand. As I am a biologist I am forced to call the mynahs an adaptive taxon displaying optimum utilization of available habitat niches. Luckily for the mynahs, their adaptive nature has been complemented by the fact that by and large, they are not threatened by the bird trade This is another reason why they have been able to flourish evolutionarily. The hill mynah is perhaps the only member of this family that faces an immediate and very direct threat by the trade.

~

The 1990 waterfowl conference in Pakistan, on hindsight, introduced me to a number of things. North-eastern India, the idiosyncratic world of waterfowl enumeration and the money-muscle of the conservation world were some of them. Also, international trade in live wild birds. Despite my childhood acquaintance with the old world bird marts of Jama Masjid in Delhi and Lal Kurti in Meerut, the international aspect of the trade was quite unknown to me. Like the hill mynah, the shaheen falcon is also a bird almost exclusively destined for the international trade. I met my first two shaheens on an Air Malaysia flight from Karachi to Kuala Lumpur.

It was with a great sense of relief that I greeted the Karachi airport. I hurried through the formalities eager to leave a country that had been so unfriendly to me in large bits and pieces. As I neared customs I noticed the sheikhs. There were two of them, dressed as sheikhs should be; head-gears haloing around their necks and shoulders, no moustaches, pointed beards, white cloaks around the rest of their bodies. Both had a brown leather glove on one hand. On each, hooded and jessed, perched the finest shaheen falcons that I have ever set my eyes upon. Shaheens are Indian peregrines. A sub-species of a falcon king. The bird that has ruled the world of falconry with its stunning good looks and extraordinary speed of the swoop. On the sheikhs' hands, the birds sat regally. Perhaps it was the proximity. The birds shone like pieces of the Arabian sun. The dark slate of their backs was set off by the gold-red of their undersides that came to the throat in a piece of russet and then split into a three-rayed brilliance radiating onto their neck and face. Through the underside, dark bars rippled across the background, creating waves of red on a lean, muscled body. There was something of a prize fighter in the birds, a restrained power and elegance that shone through.

Two years later I saw an adult bird swoop down vertically across the Chikaldhara plateau in central India. It was a moment of suspended time, waiting breathlessly silent, as the bird ripped the air around it effortlessly. A few hundred feet below there could have been the traces of an unwary prey. The bobbing back of a black-naped hare, the springy gait of a rodent. Spied from up above by exacting eyes, clutched at the very last moment by claws of steel. The sheer power and precision of the bird caused a shiver to run the length of my body.

'Can I have a closer look?' I asked one of the sheikhs rather uncharacteristically, for I normally tend to leave co-passengers severely alone.

He undid the hood with paternal pride. A dark head peeped through, dazzled for a moment by the lights outside. Through the yellow rim around the eyes, a coal-black jewel surveyed the surroundings. There was no panic.

'Ten thousand dollars . . . from Iran,' the Sheikh boasted.

Shaheens are caught from India as well and are smuggled across to Pakistan to feed the burgeoning falconry business in the country. In Pakistan, locals are not allowed to practise the sport. Falconry is the sole preserve of the Arab gentry who choose the country to indulge in an ancient orgy—the hunting of the houbara. If a rhino horn dagger handle is the symbol of masculinity to the Yemenese or a penis-gourd the choice of a Polynesian, the Arab has to houbara hunt. The houbara is a small bustard with a West Asian distribution. The bird is the colour of earth for camouflage and has the speed of the wind and the soul of a prize fighter. Attributes that make it a favourite prey for an Arab sportsman and his hooded falcon. A prey whose stringy, slightly salty meat has no gourmet value except for mildly enhancing the endurance power of the diner in his desert tent. A prey in whose quest the Arab sheikh brings parties of scores of falconers and attendants, the paraphernelia of a mini township, land rovers and deluxe tents, and, on his hand, the apple of the Arab eye—a trained falcon. For whose comfort and his own, the wealthy falconer sponsors roads to be built before he flies in. For the comfort of his hosts, the local villagers, the sheikh sponsors schools and hospitals. The country welcomes him with open arms. The locals smile with the warmth of a million suns. The houbara hurries towards its desert doom.

The sheikh walked leisurely through customs with the bird on one hand.

'Don't the authorities check you? CITES and all that?' The sheikh looked surprised at my impertinence and shook his head.

Shaheen was an Appendix I bird, listed on the Convention on International Trade in Endangered Species of Wild Fauna and Flora. No international trade absolutely. Totally contraband.

'Does it bite?' the Pakistani customs man was wary, moving away as the gloved hand approached.

The sheikh smiled and shook his head. As we passed through unchecked and unhindered, he waved an imperious hand about. The shaheen took momentary fright and flapped its wings but calmed down as its owner patted the hood.

'Nobody has stopped me till now,' the Sheikh claimed, 'and if they do, I will buy this plane of theirs. After all, he is my son.'

On the plane the hood was silkenly slid down over the eyes of his prize charge. The falcon was at peace with his surroundings in seat 14B. Next to him, a Malaysian businessman snoozed, a pair of sleep-goggles drawn over his eyes. The ghost of CITES floated around the cabin behind the air hostess. Oil had once again bought an international treaty rather cheaply.

~

Back in the Garos, the old man smiled as he set his trap. Two small leg traps slipped under a bed of brown leaves.

'Will this be enough to get a leopard, then?'

The traps seemed very small and ineffective.

'Leopard! Hah! No! This is food! Dinner!'

The forests of the Garos parted a path in deference to his years. Trees stood dank and silent. Leaf mulch piled up, rotting. A barking deer coughed in the distance. From over his left shoulder, a stream of red-breasted parakeets screamed at the skies. The man looked up at their flight with a tinge of remorse.

'Not time as yet for them to lay eggs. Not like mynah,

this *tota*, no! We need to climb up to its nest hole and check for chicks every week or so.'

His trade was a tough one and Philip seemed to bow down under the burden his father carried. His nose was now almost touching the ground and he quickly parted his lungi with a deft hand and crouched down on the trail.

'Leopard!' he said excitedly. 'Leopard!'

The track was a cat's with no sign of a claw mark. The completely retractable claws of the cats makes it easy to distinguish cats from the dog families in the field. This track was smaller than a tiger's. Even smaller, perhaps, than a leopard's. More elongated as well. It fitted a Reynolds pen-length very well.

'Could it be a clouded leopard?' The biologist in me was waking up to the challenge. The old man and his son were now interested in me. It was worth hanging on to my words if the prey turned out to be five to ten times more valuable than a common leopard. I could not be sure.

'I will come back in a short while.' The old man was enveloped by forest clouds that had appeared all of a sudden.

Philip turned back to check the previous small traps. Asim and I followed.

There was already a scuffling in both the traps, a desperate attempt to break free as we approached. Small puffs of red earth flew about, obscuring the identity of our captives. Philip held them up for me.

Two martens. Yellow-throated martens. Their golden throats gleamed softly, contrasting with a rich velvet brown back. Sharp teeth gathered around the half open stoat-mouth.

'Dinner!' sighed Philip.

'Can you let me have one skin for my house?' I needed evidence and this was as good a chance as any.

Philip smiled approval and hurried away towards his hut with his two captives. His father replaced him in the forest. He held a larger leg-hold trap. Much more of a leopard one. He smiled as he reached a fork on the track.

'It is good to place a trap on a fork. Then you get the big one that comes this way and the one that comes that way.' He looked down into the valley at the river. 'Even better to have water nearby. Then animals are sure to come.'

There was precision in his laying of the trap, his smoothening of the leaves over the cold metal, his test-springing the rusty clamp with a piece of twig acting as the leopard's foot.

'Look at this very carefully, Vivek. This is a trap laid specially for the clouded one.' Asim was crouching low as well, his dark shadow falling across the trap.

The bait was a piece of rotting carp. Fish for the clouded leopard. I would have expected it to be meat.

'No! No! Not meat for the clouded one,' the old man whispered into the ground. 'Meat for the normal one and the tiger, rotting pumpkins and jackfruit for the bear, but fish for the clouded one and the small wild cats.'

He could have meant the leopard cat, the fishing cat, the marbled cat or any other smaller being.

As I was observing the bait, a masterstroke was under way. Years of Garo experience, inflamed by the act of performing before a stranger from faraway lands. The trap was camouflaged so well that my knowledge of it was solely due to my not having taken my eyes off the spot even for a moment. Just shy of the trap, a foot length away, the old man was placing a round bamboo pole across the tracks. Strands of moss were piled on top of this, not quite camouflaging it but lending it a natural, fallen-over look.

'A speed-breaker, see?' Asim enlightened me.

'A cat. It will never step on a slippery pole.' This is true of the common tabby as well.

A leopard on the path could technically step completely over the trap and miss it even if he did come along. But the speed-breaker would ensure his capture. The cat would see the log and step carefully over it . . . into the waiting jaws of a metal monster.

We reached the hamlet after an hour's trek. I was keen to retrieve the skins of the martens. To try and assuage my guilt at having been party to their slaughter. To make amends by laying my own little leg-hold trap.

'The skins, Philip,' I reminded him.

He hurried into the hut. Loud voices of dissent floated through the doorway over a sleeping dog and a child with flies around her nostrils. Philip emerged holding one badly charred skin.

'I am sorry,' he explained sheepishly, 'this is all I could save from the fire. My wife, she was hungry, you see. She ate the other one too fast.'

She had eaten the marten, skin and all. Chomped on its yellow throat. Shredded the black, velvet ears. There was disbelief and horror in the camp through the evening.

Philip and his father supplied the village of Killing. The hill mynahs went there, as did the live bear cubs and leopard cats, the gibbons and the slow, slow loris. And so did Kamini Barua and I. Kamini was briefed by me after my first trip to the area with Asim. The road wound up past the medicine shops for four kilometres. I stopped short as an arrow thwanged through the air in front of my nose.

We were in an archery ground. The sport is a favourite with Meghalayans. Young men, stripped bare-brown to the waist, were shooting at five targets set thirty metres away. Betting men clustered around the players, bottles of booze spilling over in the excitement of the game. Kamini joined a small drinking party.

'Where does the big man live?' I asked a lean, muscular body. The name I was given was well known in the area and small sparks of fear ignited in eyes that heard it.

'He is in bad mood today. No meet anybody. Broken wall of neighbour today.'

The way he said it, the deed seemed to have been done with bare, angry hands. Part of the folklore that surrounded the big man. The king of the live animal trade and also of the live woman trade, of militancy and gun-running. A giant of a being with arms the size of an average full-grown man. He welcomed me into his home, stooping to get past a low six-foot threshold. We were to discuss guns, not animals, and so he had no hesitation in taking me into the animal room. There was little else I could call his drawing room. Four clouded leopards growled softly in two large cages by the front door. A few fishing cats and jungle cats lay sulkily in corner cages. Three large wire meshes held a pair of hoolocks, hooting softly in distress, their soft eyes seeking the visitor with an unsaid plea. All around were three kinds of parakeets and at least a dozen other species of birds. A good thousand or so beings, crammed into wicker baskets and mesh cages. The birds in the foreground were all Alexandrine parakeet chicks, two to three months in age. They lay linking pink beaks with each other, the soft red patches on their wings flashing in distress. The big man pulled up a chair in front of the show and beckoned me to sit down beside him. A pair of hill mynahs called out a name and a child served us cold water and then colder beer.

'Where are the mynahs from?' I was trying to be only casually interested.

'These are from Assam but different ones come from Orissa as well.' He had unfastened the clasp of a guncase and was now assembling a semi-automatic with a practiced air.

'Don't you export them as well?'

'Only through Myanmar to Thailand. That is done by road.'

I knew the Myanmar border slightly. In towns like Tuensang and Mokokchong there was a brisk trade in almost anything you wanted. Spices for salt, timber for rhino horns, drugs for guns, hill mynahs for women. It was all barter with very little money being exchanged. The big man controlled that area rather well, I had been told. He had finished assembling the gun and was now cleaning it out with a piece of flannel and a cleaning rod. The gun oil came out blue-black onto the flannelled rod. With the air of a nonchalant worker he stretched out and rubbed it onto the backs of a pair of common mynahs. The birds chirruped in alarm.

'Don't worry, babas,' he assured them with a smile

stuttering across his face, 'one step closer to becoming a hill mynah. Sonali. Much more value, na.'

The Scent of Extinction

I have no second thoughts about the fact that smell runs the world more than heart and mind put together. The animal world bears ample testimony. The male moon moth smells the love of his life even if she is five kilometres away. Dogs and cats release their vaporous love secretions into the air and establish individuality in a world of the hoi polloi. The female boomslang snake coils on an African wattle and signals to her mate enveloped in an aura of serpentine scents. Civets, especially the stars of the family, the skunks, have gained immortality with a certain unpleasant smell. Mohit signals the end to a conversation by taking off his trekking shoes. There can be no doubt about the power of smell.

Two Indian smells have propelled me through childhood into smelly adulthood. The first summer showers on a thirst-cracked earth and the night air sweet-scented by the pale *raat ki raani*. Evocative and irrepressible smells; an unforgettable aura of the past. Two other Indian smells have captivated the world in equal measure and these have little to do with childhood. Strong, sensual and sexual, musk and agar have been perennial favourites with Parisian and Arabian high society. In the quest to smell better, they have endangered a Himalayan deer and a tropical tree.

Both are essentials in the guide book to fashionable

aromas but originate in two very different smelly spots of the country. One lies nestled in the Himalayas, a hamlet at nearly 10,000 feet. The other is a boil on the skin of the sultry Brahmaputra valley in Assam. Both dubious headquarters of an international trade in perfumery ingredients from India. Musk comes from a small tennis-ball sized abdominal gland that the elusive Himalayan musk deer possesses. Agar is a dark infestation in the wood of the agarwood tree that is being mercilessly felled in eastern India. Back in 1991, when I joined WWF, there was a need to find out a bit more about the two species. At the nascent TRAFFIC-India office, assigning work depended as much on skill and aptitude as on the part of the country one liked to be in. I got the rhino and the elephant, Ashok kept the big striped pussycat for himself. I also shared musk and bear bile with Mohit and agarwood with Ashok and a genial Bengali forester called Kalyan Chakraborty. Asim was at that time a general guide into parts of Assam that angels avoided. As a part-time job he caught wild cats that came into homesteads in Assam, trained wild dogs to mate with domestic Alsatians in a deep pit dug in his home, and helped the Guwahati zoo with leopards that needed to be caught and treated.

Before TRAFFIC-India came into being, trade studies were not done by biologists. Now the Wildlife Protection Society of India has added some much-needed verve and punch to this sort of a work. As a specialized anti-poaching and trade monitoring NGO, the organization created by Ashok and Belinda Wright has done a great deal of work at the cutting edge of conservation. In those days, however, the magnitude of work that had to be done was staggering. There needed to be a hundred trade studies done in India, but we were not going to be fazed by the lack of people.

'And what about your landscape of commitments?' Thomas Mathew, the soft-spoken Secretary General of WWF-India, would query at staff meetings. We never found a shortage of things to tell. The musk study was part of the landscape that was getting perennially postponed. Mohit had done some preliminary work in northern India but more information was needed.

'We need a trip into the Valley of Gods,' Mohit approached me one morning.

I had just received an anonymous phone call. The caller had wanted to send me personally to the gods for helping bust a tiger-bone gang.

'I think I will go to hell in any case.'

'Be serious. We need to go next week to Kanchula Kharak. Bharati will come with us.'

My date with Lucifer seemed all planned and well set. After Sariska, I should have realized that Mohit and Bharati together produced some sort of strange chemical reaction in a wilderness area. Meet the two of them in the city, with a glass of beer or vodka, and you might even be taken in by the peace that emanates from the combination. Put them together on a field trip and things happen all by themselves. It is the elements, without a doubt, finding an outlet. Prometheus getting unbound. Atlas shrugging. The world tilting a little, giving those around a new perspective.

Kanchula Kharak near Kedarnath peak in the Garhwal Himalayas is as peaceful a place as you will find in India. It nestles in the Valley of Gods, beyond which tower the five peaks that claimed the lives of the five epic Pandava brothers. A little beyond Kanchula Kharak, the ground levels out into the magnificent *bhugiyals* at Chopta. These are alpine pastures, kilometres of rolling green that receive the first monsoon with a parched throat and then break into a floral song. There can be no better display of wild flowers in India than the *bhugiyal* one. A few hundred wild species carpeting the plateaus and vales. A patchwork quilt of reds, yellows and blues drawn up to the chin of a quivering mountain, a light drizzle and a thin mist adding to the mystery of the moment. A little away lies the famous Valley of Flowers, but Chopta, next to the musk deer farm, is no less spectacular. There is nothing to disturb the peace there except the musk deer that live in a small breeding farm run by the state health department, a few hundred birds and a few million flowers. None of these living beings knew of Bharati or Mohit. The trip to get some musk deer data came therefore at a very opportune moment. It was time to produce a little bit of the magic in the Valley of Gods.

'Chiranjeev from Goyal Taxi Stand, sir,' announced a four-foot, scrawny, hen-plucked, squint-eyed apparition. He looked like something that the cat had brought in the tumultuous night before.

'Just like a weasel,' confided Doracs. 'Weasel. Weasel.'

I had never heard of a cat dragging in a weasel before but the name was better than anything else we could come up with. It stuck. Weasel crept into the white Ambassador car and slunk his way through the utter insanity of Uttar Pradesh towns to drive into Roorkee. If there is sanity in western Uttar Pradesh it must lie somewhere in the Roorkee-Dehradun belt. For the most part, the state is an assemblage of old roads in a shambles after the last monsoon, eleven months earlier. Connecting these aimless tangles are clusters of humanity, a few million at a time. Most of them lead their lives bang in the middle of the road. '*Nadu* centre' as a Tamilian might put it, using the same word twice in two languages to make a point. Centre Centre. This is the world of the philosophical traffic warden performing private ballets for complacent cows. Donkeys bray out the frustration of an entire population only because they have the better voice. Veiled women in black lead dust moulds of little children home. A well-built muscle-man does push-ups on the divider, his head jerking out onto the fast lane. He has nothing to fear, for the fast lane is clogged with a long-winding bullock cart trail, four kilometres of sugarcane laden madness that ends up via a sugar factory in a cup of tea. Cars squeeze their way through, folding in side mirrors and removing hub-caps to take the least space. Japanese designed Maruti Suzukis fare the best here, drawing in their tiny frames well within themselves and weaving through the maze.

Ashok and I have developed a routine in our million trips through the crazed small-town world of the Gangetic plains where each town is worse than the other. As we pass Muzzaffarnagar, an epitome of all that could be and is not, I shake myself out of shock and whisper hoarsely, 'For God's sake. How the hell did we get into this mess?'

Ashok consoles me instantly.

'We could turn back, you know. Back to Delhi via . . . say . . . Hapur.'

Instantly Muzzaffarnagar is Paradise revisited. The rest of the trip passes uneventfully.

The Ambassador progressed ponderously, a million brakes with a couple of accelerators. It pushed itself out of the air thick with people and shook itself clear onto the broad university boulevards of Roorkee. To welcome us to a night's halt at the Hotel Polaris was Diwakar Sharma. Diwakarji is a Brahmin first, a wildlife enthusiast second, an Ayurvedic doctor third and, finally, a winner of two Red and White Bravery awards. You would think he has something going with the cigarette manufacturers, only he does not smoke. He does not drink or go near women either and this makes him braver than ever. His shunning both is done pointedly and astutely.

Diwakarji rans an NGO, Prakriti Mitr, out of a duplex room lined with Ayurvedic medicine bottles and a few dusty tomes on the importance of breath control in treating diabetes. He sat in a corner of the room all evening, lecturing to the three of us on Ayurveda.

'Do you have an Ayurvedic substitute for musk?' I knew that the Indian medicine system was as much a consumer of the substance as the perfumeries of France. Diwakarji produced four volumes that were ostensibly written 2000 years before man learnt the art of writing, seven medicine bottles full of exotic Himalayan herbs, and stone tablets that the archaeological department had ignored but which actually charted and plotted the history of mankind and musk a few thousand years ago.

As is the case with most traditional medicine systems, there is always an alternative for ingredients. Certain Himalayan herbs may be used in the absence of musk. The deer could, in theory, get a reprieve.

Back at Polaris, Mohit crawled into his favourite posture and fell asleep almost immediately. Doracs slept soon after, tired after a day of unsuccessfully trying to get Diwakarji to talk. I lay awake with many alternative smells and substitute substances permeating my thoughts.

The morning dawned bright and car-less. For hours we waited for Weasel and Bharati chanted a thousand alternative names that may be used for him. Finally, in the forenoon, he appeared, more ragged and dishevelled than ever, more furtive in the eye and slimy in the mouth.

'There has been an accident, sahib. In Rishikesh, sahib. I had gone there in the night to visit my sister, sahib.'

Rishikesh is more than fifty kilometres from Roorkee. Visiting sisters in the night is a common Indian term for whoring. The antecedents of his sister were suspect to say the least. The fact that he was touring the countryside while we slept, comfortable in the knowledge that the car was in the parking lot, brought Mohit to boiling point. It all took a full day to sort out. A new car was provided by the taxi owners and a shame-faced Weasel swore by a few more non-existent sisters and mothers his will to reform.

'Of course he will, the brother of a she-weasel,' chanted Bharati. We moved onwards to Haridwar. Haridwar is as unwashed and unrepentant as the modern brand of Hindutva that swamps the land. As souls float down the slimy ghats, past unclean minds and grimy beings, they attain nirvana. On the banks of the river, a cripple, a saint and a traditional medicine man sat in cross-legged concentration. They were hawking their wares silently. In a place as holy as Haridwar you do not need to shout to be heard. The cripple displayed an astonishing contortion of his limbs, broken in childhood by kidnapping gangs of *hijras*. The saint was covered in holy ash that dripped off his forehead onto a saffron cloth covered with the name of the lord in multi-colour. The medicine man had a curious assortment of wares in front of him. With the herbs and roots, gnarled shoots and dried leaves, he had a boiling pot of spiny tail lizard oil on display. In front of it three specimens of the lizard, earth-brown in colour and backs humped, lay helplessly. They had been collected in Rajasthan and their backs broken so that they could not escape. They were not fed any food or given any water as lizards and snakes don't need these things. They live off the fat stored in their tails and much before that runs out, find their way into a red-brown cauldron of boiling oil. They scream silently, gaping pink, cavernous mouths at the floating souls of the Ganga. The souls wink back nonchalantly in the light of the lamps that float alongside them.

Two shy youths were bargaining with the man for a quart of the oil, to be applied daily on disobedient organs. The scalded soul of the lizard would swell in anger, the mendicant assured the men, for a very long time. This in turn would turn tumescent even the most moistly flaccid of phalluses. 'But only so-so-much, not more,' the man hastened to add. 'If more-more then you need to cut it open so that it goes down.' The youths nodded, mesmerized by the diabolic promise. Beside the pink-mouthed lizards, on a dirt-brown cloth, lay ten oval testicles of the langur monkey. The medicine man sold them to unsuspecting buyers as musk pods. The actual musk pods are far bigger and have on them a coating of thick, hollow hair that trap air within them to insulate the musk deer. These are the only mammalian hair that can be bent backwards and stay in that shape without springing back with the spirited vengeance of a dog tail. The testicles are poor substitutes, coated in any aromatic substance that is readily available, sometimes filled with damp earth and two drops of incense. The science of identification is not easily understood by the majority of the population who go back with a quart of spiny tail lizard oil and a monkey testicle in secretive glee.

Musk in India is a medicine used in a large number of ingenious ways to cure a thousand ailments. Musk to the Western world is a fixative in the perfume industry, a substance that can take in a few dozen smells and give out a single lingering aroma. An amazing feat for a small tennis-ball that smells like urine. So strong is the smell of raw musk that it is one of the only chemicals in the world that can mask the smell of asafoetida or *hing*. Rub a little asafoetida on a string and then rub musk on it and the smell of a town urinal will take over. An easy way to test real musk in the field.

To get this musk, the easiest way is to kill a musk deer and then slit open its abdomen for removing the pod. Musk can also be extracted from a living deer, using a syringe extraction technique. The principle is that of a biopsy with a probe inserted carefully to draw out the needed portion from the animal. Bears are milked in China for their gall-bladder extracts in much the same way. In India there are two major problems with this sort of functioning. First, it goes against the Indian ethics of conservation. In India wildlife is not looked upon as a money-making proposition. This is no Western concept of keeping Third World wildlife as a natural history museum, as the Africans have often alleged. Neither is it a view harboured only by intellectuals and the elite. The common man of India has traditionally had a tolerance, even sympathy for wildlife, and will thus conserve a species as long as he is not directly affected by the animal. There is no doubt, of course, that in a country like India, given all the problems that plague it, wildlife conservation is far from the common man's mind. But, so also is wildlife utilization.

Secondly, the greed that exists in that minority which controls the illegal market is such that a systematic milking programme would just not work. In the cold Himalayan winters whole villages march off to hunt the bear and the musk deer, simple ways of keeping themselves occupied. The money that comes in from the trade is a great extra. This has been capitalized extremely well by one Punjabi family based in Hong Kong and Nepal that has controlled the musk trade from India and indeed the world for nearly a quarter of a century. Smuggling the substance across the borders is easy and at its final destination it is worth three to five times the price of gold. So to hell with the possibilities of sustainable utilization. Killing the animal is so much more easy and profitable.

Weaving through holy crowds at Haridwar and Rishikesh, artfully avoiding the holiness of the Gangetic basin, we reached God's own confluence for the night. The rest-house at Deoprayag is situated just above the confluence of the Alaknanda and the Bhagirathi. Five minutes down a cobbled pathway between hill houses planked with a red-rust wood, and the waters opened up to the eyes in amazing splendour. From behind, the sweep of the Bhagirathi glistened with the light of a million undiscovered gold guilders. As it rounded the corner, the Alaknanda reared its placid blues and the river seemed to stop on its heels, screeching in huge white froth. As the waters met, waves of white turned to quiescent blue-greens. Around them, a whole village clattered to the last great sounds of the day. At the rest house, Mohit was already asleep in an awkward jumble. He lay half on his side and half on his stomach, one arm bent at the elbow and one leg at the knee. The corresponding limbs stretched in a sort of rigor mortis.

'The seventh most comfortable position in the world to sleep in,' giggled Bharati.

I was not sure I wanted to know the other six.

There was only one large double bed and the three of us had to cram in. It seemed unlikely I would get any sleep, caught between rumbles of snores and slivers of giggles, but when it did come it was a long, deep mountain sleep. Till, suddenly, a shout through the window ruptured the peace.

'Ummm? Ummmmm? Ummmmmmm?' queried Mohit intelligently.

'What the hell!' Bharati jerked awake.

Half-shaking unspent dreams away, we watched a curious assemblage outside the window. It looked as if half the village had got into the compound of the rest house. All of them seemed to be pointing to a dark, secret bush in the corner of the compound. The shout was the only loud sound. Now, the entire gathering was shrieking in whispers. Nobody could make out what was happening.

'What are they looking at? Tell me, tell me.'

'Will you keep quiet, Doracs, so we can hear what they are saying?'

Suddenly, the bush erupted with the loud sound of a man sawing wood.

Kreeshew, krreeshew, krishew. A leopard.

'*Guldar*,' Mohit used the hill name for the big cat.

It is a strange coincidence that in the hills where the mighty *tendu* trees do not grow, the leopard is called *guldar*. In peninsular India, where the *tendu*, which yields the bidi leaf, does hold sway, the leopard is called a *tendua*. It gets further complicated as one goes eastwards into Orissa. In Oriya, the *tendu* tree is called the *kendu*. The leopard is, but of course, the *kendua*.

Outside, the group had seen the leopard slinking away. There was no evidence of this one having taken a local dog but everyone knew that was the reason leopards came to the locality.

'Give it a chance and it will pick up a child.' An old wizened leader had started the ball of discontent rolling.

I knew that this could well happen. The leopard, less afraid of man than the tiger and cleverer, is more responsible for attacks on humans than the striped cat. In most parts of India the two are confused because of the similar names used for them. In Hindi *bagh* could be either, in Malayalam so could *puli*. The tiger is the more spectacular of the two and so gets more blame. It is difficult to convince people that the leopard is more responsible. Though, come to think of it, I do not particularly want to do that either. In my three years with TRAFFIC-India nearly fifty tiger skins had been recovered in covert operations and raids. At least three hundred leopard skins were recovered during the

the same period. The work of professional poachers, disgruntled villagers and the ever-present opportunist. The leopard is easily the most underestimated carnivore that is threatened in India today. Because of the ease with which it lives near human settlements, people see more leopards. Because they see the animal more often and because it takes the occasional dog, calf or even human child, it is feared and hated. Because it is hated, it is killed. Mercilessly.

'It is the bastards, the forest department,' the old man had to get rid of the vapours of the evening half-bottle. 'Yes! It's they who are releasing leopards in our village.'

The rumble of discontent grew louder. This was a crowd of sleepy village folk, bones aching with the weight of a full day's work, minds clouded over by the fear of an animal taking away their children. The leader sounded convincing.

'Why, in heaven's name, would they want to do that?' I knew I had to intervene and talk to someone.

'You don't know the department, *shaab*, they just want to terrorize small people like us, that's all.'

'But what proof do you have? This is a very serious allegation.'

His face grew sullen like the darkness around him.

'In my childhood, *shaab*, there were no departments in these parts and there were no leopards in the villages. Now the forestwallahs, they have come and with them the leopards.'

His arguments were as clear as the waters of the Alaknanda.

'But, baba, in your days there were forests on the

mountains, no?' I pointed at the bare earth clothing the hills above him. The water around the confluence had given rise to some green. More green around the humans than above. That was ironic. 'Now where are the forests?'

He could sense his hold on the crowd growing weak. He puffed on his bidi a little and watched the proceedings restlessly.

'If the leopard does not have his forest, where would he go then? Into your main streets, no? The forests have gone down your *chulhas*, where can wildlife go then?'

I may have won the night but I knew the rumble was only readying to become a quake of a magnitude that the species might find difficult to deal with. It is easy to save a cuddly beast or a soaring bird, but to conserve animals who prey on your livestock and your children requires both a luxury and a sagacity that I do not see in the Indian populace.

Kanchula Kharak itself turned out to be more zoo than sanctuary. A health department project, the musk deer were initially brought in there from various parts of the western Himalayas. The idea was to commercially produce musk to satisfy the needs of the Ayurveda and Unani brands of domestic medicine that swear by *kasturi*.

The deer stood glaring at us from the confines of the large mesh enclosure. The few males in the distance flashed their vampirical smiles. Musk deer possess no antlers like normal deer. The male has two large curving teeth that give his otherwise handsome face a fearful leer. The large velvet-brown body is perched on equally large rabbit legs. The knees are perennially bent with the anticipation of a jump. Progress closer and they demonstrate their capability, leaping off into the unknown.

Several logistical problems had made the Kanchula Kharak project a small, failed dream. The three of us entered into the large enclosure through a padlocked gate. Small alpine butterflies fluttered away in alarm. A brown hunched shape leapt away from the corner.

'Rabbit! Rabbit!' screamed Doracs.

Mohit bent into the tall grass trying to focus at infinity.

'It is the deer, silly!' I could not actually blame her. The musk deer did jump in a rather rabbit-like, or in the Indian context, hare-like, fashion.

The animal had retreated to the far corner and now peered out of the grass uncertainly. Mohit was fast this time with the experience gained with the tahr. His photographs had even made it to *National Geographic* and *Time*; the days of Eravikulam seemed over.

'Why does it stand so close to the wire-mesh?' he grimaced.

Those were still days when the computer did not scan away the background of pictures. A wire-mesh behind one of the world's most endangered deer could entirely spoil the photograph.

'Look! Look! There are more of them, and not near the mesh either,' Doracs was helpful.

There were two males and three females crouching in the grass and staring at us with brown almond eyes liquid with fright.

There were less than twenty of them at Kanchula Kharak. The total number in the country was anybody's guess but probably numbered in the low thousands. There were only two known studies on the deer and both were around the hills of Uttar Pradesh. Michael Green, now a Cambridge-based researcher, and Satyakumar, a scholar at the Wildlife Institute of India, had only dented the cloak of ignorance that lay around the velvet deer. It is extremely rare to sight the musk deer in the wild in India. Just once after Kanchula Kharak have I seen it and then too only for the most fleeting of moments in the high forests of Arunachal Pradesh. It fled into the woods at the sound of human footsteps, uncannily seeming to scent the fetid smell of its own extinction.

At the musk deer farm, however, the deer were still at close quarters.

'I will go around and make it come towards you, sir,' the assistant at the farm was looking for a tip.

The three of us chorused our refusal synchronously. The worst thing that can be done to a captive animal is to herd it. Even if done for emergency exigencies, it scares the animal greatly. To do it for a photograph is a complete taboo with any conservationist.

'I'll take it with the wire mesh,' Mohit said. 'No point letting him chase it all over the bloody place.'

'Yaa, yaa,' Doracs concurred. 'Much better, very much better.'

A large male, as if to repay this small debt, leaped into the small space in front of the camera. For a moment my eyes captured the athletic freeze-frame. Knotted pine-brown muscles tensed in its hind legs; the forefeet danced prettily ahead in the air. Stretched over its precious booty of musk, its velvet skin rippled across its abdomen. The ears were pricked up, rather dog-like, and the face half-turned to me. It was a perfect leap and I wished that it was one that would land it back safely on the ground and not catapult it over the brink into the chasm of extinction.

~

Somewhere between the Himalayas and the riverine plains, the smell of musk mingled with a waft of agar perfume. Ashok briefed me on the Ajmals at the India International Centre. In the cosy confines of the bar we discussed a family that controlled the agar trade from faraway Dubai. The similarities with musk were striking. A perfume that sends cognoscenti into raptures of dollar notes. Headquartered in two of the big trading capitals of Asia. Drawing with octopussian ease the raw material from India. Controlled tightly by an Indian family that had made good by crook or by crook.

Historically agar was known as the Otto of roses from India. An oil that embraces and imbibes a thousand French perfumes into its greasy heart and then releases them subtly. The Arabs prize it even more. It is used in the incense sticks they light in discreet corners of their ladies' baths—a smell that would permeate their pores and at the same time drive away lice from their armpits. The Indian joss stick has retained the name agarbatti or wick of agar, though the prohibitively priced perfume is no longer used. Arab ladies have continued their oil-induced practises and for their caprices a tree is being cut all over its restricted range in south-east Asia. In some parts helicopters whirr over the forests looking for the tree. In others, like India, people walk on foot, searching for a prize that grows up into the skies.

A winter's day in February found me accompanying three agar poachers to the forests of Meghalaya. We were on the edge of Assam and the forest served as the inter-state boundary. Marak was a Garo tribal, the chief agar hunter, and Lyngdong his Khasi helper. The third man, Markotia, was a Marwari businessman from neighbouring Guwahati.

Agarwood is the eagle among trees. Its Latin name, *Aquilaria* or eagle wood, may have come from its towering bole. The stand before us had at least fifty fifteen- to thirty-metre high trees. They rose straight and strong with a sharp-cut fluted edge. High above, where the leaves touched the rim of the sky, a cluster of white blooms sprayed upwards. Marak leaned heavily on the stem.

'A good strong tree. No agar.'

Agar is a pathological product in the heartwood of the trees. It is the dark, decaying soul of a tree infected with a fungal growth. More often than not, it is linked to a past injury that the tree has borne. A fungus of the soul that gets in through hurt. The fifteenth tree was a weakling. The stem was curved and weak, the crown of leaves sparse, the branches decaying at the fingertips. The wood was a sickened yellow under the bark which raised itself every now and then into ugly cankers.

'Ants! Agar!' Marak had found his tree.

A column of marching ants plodded out of a deep fissure, walking steadily towards the base of the tree. They were coming from deep within, from agar country. The skill required to locate the right agar tree was obviously a very rare one. Around this one infected tree was a forest of a few thousand uninfected trees.

'You will get two kilos from this, maybe three if you are lucky.' Marak displayed consummate skill. Three kilos was a large amount from one tree. The tree would have to be at least fifty years old for this. Young trees rarely have much agar. The soul decays with age, with the gradual attrition of being. In rare cases, the entire tree would be agar. One seething mass of black under the skin. The Marwari was happy. His skin laughed the high laugh of an excited child. It was not every time that he got a good diagnosis like this. In most cases, he had to fell trees, split them open and discover that the black treasure was not within. A complete waste of the tree and utter disappointment for the men. In this carnage of agar-hunting, the species is being slowly pushed to extinction in the wild. More sad, when considering the fact that as a tree agar grows readily and well. In silvicultural plots and social forestry plantations, agarwood has grown under human care and supervision. The problem has always been how to get unhealthy trees. Scientists have inoculated healthy trees with fungi extracts, cut deep gashes into pink healthy wood and tried a host of other methods. If only the ruddy tree would grow sickly and ant-ridden! The secret of agar production is closely guarded by nature.

Man too has followed nature by guarding the material with his life once he has laid his hands on it. Assam is the centre of the agar trade and I was there with Asim to try and get into the secret family-run operation.

Nilbagan near Hojai is a small Muslim dominated town in the Brahmaputra valley. As we approached the town outskirts, a glint of metal in the sun flashed onto the eye. A *vakba*, an oil still. It lay by the roadside like a brand new toy yet to be used by the owners.

Asim jumped out of the car like an adolescent tiger who has spotted a lame wild boar.

An old man in a chequered blue lungi and a skullcap welcomed him.

'Vikram sahib is a representative of a Dubai trading company,' I was introduced. My false card with the false name did not have the desired effect. The man in the lungi was still standing with his legs spread out and arms planted heavily on his hips. He was smiling, a traditional welcome for a stranger, but from behind the smile seeped a cold, yellow distrust. The Ajmal card had to be produced. It had a startling effect. The legs came together, arms folded back and his body moved aside to let us enter a low doorway that arched over an unkempt courtyard.

'He's my nephew. Such a big man. Just my nephew.' His teeth flashed yellow and crooked. Son of the scented soil. The Ajmals may have originated in Assam but today rule the agar market throughout the world. The centre of the trade in eastern India shifted to Nilbagan after Partition. Earlier Dakhsinbagh, Sylhet was the agar *adda*. Now nearly 200 oil *vakbas* were operating in just Nilbagan.

The samples were coming out now. Small vials like those used in a laboratory with grades of agar oil. Muddy brown to a rich red blood brown. Each weighed by the *tola*, a traditional measure also used for gold. Only the most precious of all items is weighed in so minute a measure. There were agarwood blocks too, greenish with age and only used as samples.

'Can I see the oil being made?' I was innocent.

The distrust came on again just as the tea and biscuits

were also brought in.

'This is a family secret, no.' He was making no attempt to move.

His sons had now entered the room and were definitely more hostile. With age a certain mellowing of suspicion takes place that is overshadowed by the brashness of youth. We had been there for a few hours in any case. All the important facts were stored neatly into my memory. To attempt taking down notes in such a situation would be suicidal. Two vials of oil were procured as samples and they were already staining my breast pocket a light cream-yellow. It was time to move on to Naogaon where a senior district official had promised us help in curbing the illegal trade.

The roads of Naogaon at the best of times do not have the traffic that one is used to in the rest of India. At eleven in the night it had petered out to a few odd vehicles and the perennial drunkard. The traffic policeman in the middle of town was having a tough time of it with a rather beaten down old Ambassador car.

'Binoyda! Oh, that's Binoyda!'

Asim's face lit up slightly at the prospect of meeting an old friend. Binoyda was a high ranking administrative official of Naogaon. Everyone in the small town knew Binoyda's car. So did the policeman. He was smiling half apologetically, hands sunk into khaki pockets. Binoyda was alternately reversing and moving his car forward as the lights changed. He would wait for the light to become red and then inch the car slowly forward, six inches ahead of the yellow line that traffic in Assam is meant to follow. When the light turned green, he would reverse back to his original position. He was waiting for the cop to tell him that he had violated the rules. That would be a good occasion for him to get out of the car, stretch to his full five-foot-three-inch height and tell him exactly who he was. That would settle him once and for all, Binoyda had decided. The policeman, who was just finishing a harassing day, was not in a mood to oblige. He just stood by and watched the highest ranking civil servant of the area play the fool with the car and the dignity of office.

'Binoyda,' shouted Asim. 'Isn't it time you went home?'

Binoyda looked around angrily at the intrusion. The next moment his face was wreathed in a most beatific smile. Asim was still wearing his. A temporary warmth of camaraderie swept Naogaon chowk.

'Asim! My friend, where have you been? Who is this you have brought along? Come home and have a drink with me.'

Whole sentences followed each other like the waves from the wave making machine at Sun City in South Africa. This was what happened when man thought he could create an ocean in the middle of a land-locked area or when he has had the odd two dozen too many. Insanity prevailed.

Two hours later we were still ensconced in his bedroom drinking Patiala pegs of Indian malt whisky. Patiala pegs are the usual three fingers of drinks poured with the fingers in a vertical position. The name comes from the original patronage that came from the city of Patiala in Punjab. Today a good Bengali IAS officer was demonstrating his capability to match the Punjabis. His feet were piled high on the sofa and his paan-chewing mouth was open in full-throated song. Rabindra Sangeet sung by the bard of Bengal.

'Vivekda, this agarwood business is very disturbing what you tell me, *haan*?' Binoyda was exuberant one moment and melancholy the next. 'Just give me a note tomorrow morning and we will sort it all out. But tell me, are you married, now, *hain*?'

'No, no. And as for Hojai, can I just give you a one-pager or do you want . . .'

'Any pager, Vivekda, any pager.' His eyes seemed to light up with a new light. 'But this marriage-sharriage business. Now . . . it is time, no?'

I tried to get back into the burning solace of the Patiala. Asim was grinning wryly.

'*Arre shuno to*,' Binoyda called out to his wife, 'bring a *gamocha to*.'

The *gamocha* is a well-known accessory in Assam. It is a small piece of white cotton cloth that can be used as a cotton towel or as a measure of respect. The *gamochas* with a red border are Ahom, the ones with yellow borders, Bodo. I remembered PCB. He had put one on my neck the first time I met him.

This one was red and gold. Definitely much more respect. It landed with a soft swoosh around the neck.

'Bring Vivekda some tea *to*, baby, and our biscuits, the coconut ones.'

Baby came out shyly with a tray. She was a six foot by four foot construction.

Drinking tea with scotch was not entirely pleasurable, but I knew that tea was the ultimate welcome. What was happening to Binoyda? Asim's grin had widened to a savage slash of pleasure.

'The agarwood papers . . .' I began.

'Bring one more *gamocha to, chotti* baby.' The smaller baby was two inches taller than her elder sister. Both seemed to be in their mid twenties. They stood by the bed, arms folded demurely in front of them and eyes cast mysteriously on a spot six inches in front of their toes.

'I think we should go, Asim.' I was beginning to get the drift. No agarwood work would get done this way. I had stumbled on to a middle-aged man and his unmarried daughters. The biggest curse in traditional India. The heaviest burden. The one nightmare for a retiring father.

I was halfway down the steps. Asim followed reluctantly like a boy who has been refused the last act at a local circus show. From behind, Binoyda's stentorian voice boomed drunkenly.

'Teenu baby, bring out a *gamocha* for Vivekda *to*. The full gold one.'

I escaped into an unperfumed night.

The Voice of Ganesha

Twenty-five kilometres east of the sprawling east Indian town of Siliguri, a strange offering was being made to the elephant god, Ganesha. It was dusk and the paddy fields, ripe with a bumper crop, silhouetted a group of thirty able-bodied men of the village of Hathi Doonga. Literally translated, a village called Elephant Knocked Down. An apt name for a small cluster of shanties and huts scattered in the path of a hundred and fifty traditionally migrating elephants. The houses are in the shadow of the Mahananda hills in north Bengal. If the protected area system of India is taken seriously then the elephants are legitimately allowed to move in and around the Mahananda and Buxa sanctuaries and slightly further afield. Hathi Doonga is not mentioned in any official elephant document of the state or central governments and is shown, on paper, to be outside the elephant's range. Despite this, on a cold night in December, twenty-six animals marched from the forests through the narrow Sukhna corridor into the village to pay it a surprise visit. The range officer was told of the unusual incursion as the sun was reluctantly deciding to set. The news reached the Sukhna guest house, where I was staying, an hour later, courtesy two watchmen and one forest grass cutter. Both the range officer and I were at the scene within an hour.

The fields around the village were full of men, a few hundred of them arrayed in ragaband battle formation. The only sources of illumination at the scene were a dozen-odd rag-and-wood torches that the men carried. Two men were beating improvised cymbals which at one time were aluminium cooking utensils. The leader of the party was shrilling a popular religious chant to the Lord in a high-pitched voice. The remaining members of the party had their hands full of what looked like paddy balls and long sticks. A motley village crew, trying to fight sleep and the possible destruction of all they owned.

I remembered the much more colourful rendering of an elephant drive by the grand old man of the pachyderms, Dhritikanto Lahiri-Choudhury. Then, the incursion was taken much more seriously by the government. A herd of wild elephants had placidly walked through the town of Hoogly and was threatening to enter Calcutta! Not a decrepit north Bengal village, but Calcutta, the pride of the Bengalis! Lahiri-Choudhury, Professor of English at Jadhavpur University and an elephant hunter of yore, was called upon urgently.

'Everybody wanted an immediate solution. There was a *minister* out on the scene as well. Hah!' mused a reminiscing Lahiri-Choudhury, a burnished scotch changing levels in his glass. If Dada had a story to tell, he would do so in impeccable language and with adequate emphasis. The emphasis placed on the minister expressed what he normally thought of politicians.

An old photograph of a hundred men and women huddled on Hoogly rooftops was brought out. Underneath the gawking humanity, a single file of elegant elephants marched resolutely. In no particular hurry or bother.

'There was no other way. I had all the trucks in the region brought out and facing the herd, with instructions that the drivers were all to act together.' As Dada went back into the past, his fleshy countenance wrinkled with memories and the gentleness of an elephant's profile played upon his own.

As the lead elephant came round a bend, all the trucks and lorries switched on their headlights simultaneously and blared their air horns into the night.

'The elephants just turned back and went towards the forest. As gracefully as they had come in. No panic. No vengeance.'

The Calcuttans must have thanked Lahiri-Choudhury for saving them the embarrassment of sharing Chowringhee with a wild elephant herd.

In northern Bengal, however, there were neither ministers nor lorries.

'Stand well back, sir,' the range officer who had invited me to be part of the joint forest-village committee elephant drive was careful. Bengal had always been bold enough to experiment. With *sandesh*, *hilsa* and communism. Or participatory forest management for that matter. In North Bengal, the elephant drive teams were doing a good job. Co-operating clusters of forest staff and villagers were keeping the migrating elephants within limits far better than either had been able to do alone. These were 'conflict populations' of elephants according to Project Elephant—not elephants that were a priority for conservation; just a nuisance herd that needed to be tackled.

The elephant problem in Bengal is not a new one. Year after year the state has faced the wrath of herds that found traditional routes blocked by human settlements or the joy of herds that found the temptation of ripening paddy or an illicit liquor brewery too strong. Elephants love raw alcohol and the fumes from a still in the forest can easily draw them from a few dozen kilometres. The night before, the same herd had smelt alcohol in the village and had come looking for the evening quota. Panic-stricken humanity fled into the shadow of the hills. The elephants went house to house looking for booze. It was like an absent-minded man looking for an important fax message on a paper-strewn desk. The elephants knocked off all that stood in their way with sheer impatience. By daybreak they had gone through twenty-four houses that lay clumsily opened like shelled pea-pods. There was no room for a repeat performance.

The bunch of us crouched shuddering with nervous chill, at the edge of the forest. Suddenly, with an eerie cry, somewhat reminiscent of an angry child, an elephant standing at least ten feet at the shoulder broke cover from a nearby grove of trees. Ten feet at the shoulder is very large for an Asian elephant which usually does not reach African elephant shirt sizes. With a war whoop, the men lit putty balls and flung them towards the creature and within moments, the entire dimly-lit scene was transformed into a rural interpretation of Guy Fawkes Day. Jagmag Chocolates, which was the brand name of the putty balls, were actually powerful crackers which brightly illuminated the scene and drove the angry pachyderm, and the rest of the herd following him, back to the safety of the forests. All through, the men chanted

'Jai Ganesh' —'Hail to thee, O Elephant God'—while at the same time throwing lighted fire-balls at the elephants. The pull of religion was definitely weakening. From within the forests a few terrified trumpets came from the fleeing elephants: 'Let's go back! They are gone today.' The range officer was clearly tired.

'What about tomorrow?' I asked.

In reply, it seemed, a young village boy threw a few more Jagmag Chocolates into the forest.

~

Hindus do not practise nature worship. Yet, while most Hindu deities have been bestowed the human form, there are also animal-gods, and animals who are associated with gods and are considered sacred. A complex situation indeed, as the Hindu preserver of the world or Lord Vishnu has as many as ten forms or avatars. The first is a fish, the second a turtle and the third a wild boar. In his fourth avatar, Lord Vishnu takes a transitionary form, for Narasimha literally translated means man-lion. The remaining avatars are human but still helped greatly by semi-divine animal forms such as Hanuman. And just as the monkey is worshipped as Hanuman, the bull is worshipped for being Nandi, the carrier of Shiva, and the brahminy kite as Garuda, the vehicle of Vishnu.

What caused the wise men of early Hinduism to designate certain animals as gods and others as mere beasts? Scientific or rational speculation is today possible. Glance down the avenues of early religious beliefs, and the nature worshippers of the pre-Hinduism era are seen to worship animals that were needed for daily living or those that were admired or feared for certain characteristics. And so, the cow became sacred for its contribution to man's life and the tiger and the lion found their way into mythology due to their fearsome reputation. What better vehicle could a fiery Shakti or mother goddess have than a tiger? What better form could Lord Vishnu take to slay dreaded demons than that of Narasimha? The peacock got its sacred position presumably because of its glittering train, while the snake was assigned to Shiva, the destroyer, because it was feared and respected.

In giving these beasts exalted positions instead of merely admiring or avoiding them, the ancients had sounded out a message. In today's parlance the message would be an ecological one, or what could be called a conservation blueprint, but for our ancestors it was a way of life. In central India certain tribals still regard elephants as their elder brothers. To talk of the mighty beasts in any other form is considered degrading and a personal insult. Elephants are given their own tracks to walk on, which go different ways from the human ones. In these parts, the term conflict is not known as yet. When there is any transgression or aggression there is immediate forgiveness, tolerance and respect, characteristics that one would expect from siblings. Respect is a key word when dealing with elephants, whether wild or captive.

The elephant should never be trifled with. It was from Johnsingh that I had learnt my first lesson. During his work on the wild dogs at Bandipur, Johnsingh was part of a terrible tragedy. A long-time forester and head of the Kerala Forest Research Institute, Dr Nair, had accompanied him into the forest. Accosted by a male tusker, Johnsigh had found his favourite rosewood and climbed it. Nair, who knew elephants for many a decade, chose to photograph the charging animal. The elephant killed him outright and Johnsingh could not go back into the forest for many a month.

'He said that he knew elephants,' he would later muse reflectively, 'but the elephant, he did not know him.'

During the last ten years I have been charged at a hundred times by elephants. Most of them have been mock charges, the 'I-am-sorry-but-will-you-please-get-the hell-out-of-here' charge. Some of them have been more serious. Charges that required fleetness of foot and a slice of luck bigger than the slice of pizza dished out by the new Italian restaurant that has just opened up next door. A very few have been really dangerous, like the one that happened at Dholkhand.

The rest house at Dholkhand in Rajaji National Park is raised on an earthen mound, overlooking a dry riverbed that coils like a protective mother snake around its base. The riverbeds are called *rokads* by the locals; dry water courses, covered by sparrow-egg pebbles and dinosaur-egg rocks, round and oval, white and red, bold and burning, smooth and pitted. The gravel in a river's stomach, the grinding of its innards. The *rokads* break up Rajaji National Park into bite-sized forest bits. During the dry months it is rare to find water in them. Wherever water holds up, animals pay daily visits. Mad men and women like us crouch around them in uncomfortable machaans, behind thorny bushes or crammed into vehicles, waiting for the golden moment that would reveal a part of their secret lives. The rest house at Dholkand is a good place in which to sit and wait for animals. Forest rest houses usually are, with their generous verandas and high ceilings. The British, who built these structures, are to be commended for something after all.

It was a hot afternoon in June 1995, as hot as it gets at Dholkhand. Ashok and Shaila were both asleep inside; emulating the Romans. The arjun in the courtyard wept with a listless breeze and I sat in its shade, letting the remnants of the breeze filter down from the leaves onto my upturned face. From down below, a pebble crashed against a rock. I woke to it, like a lover in waiting. The first sounds made by approaching wildlife are a stimulus that our tribe waits for and lives by. From a corner of the *rokad*, a lead bull made its way to the river bed. It walked indolently, swaying with the magic intoxication of a summer afternoon. The massive thighs rolled to the lilt of an unheard music.

'Shaila! Elephants!' I shouted to wake her. Ashok needed no waking up. The first crash of a bamboo clump had brought him out in long under-pants and netted vest. His olive-green troopers cap was perched neatly on his head as if he had just come in from patrol.

Shaila came out just as a small trickle of elephants broke through the protective foliage at the edge of the *rokad* and wound down into the stream bed. Ashok was already revving up the jeep. Shaila clambered in at the back. I took up my usual naturalist-navigator seat on the left. The jeep left, lurching unerringly towards a possible crossing point for the mammoths, three kilometres diagonally through the forest. Ashok is by far the best jungle driver I have been with in India. His anticipation of elephant movement is as wonderful as the soft, silken approach to a crouching nightjar in the middle of his road. Four years earlier, in an associated forest, he had driven like a stalking panther, silently inching on the feline pads of the jeep. The jungle nightjar, its eyes pink rubies frozen in the headlights of the jeep, crouched deeper and deeper into the track. Mohit leaned out of the window, arm extended, zoom lens whirring softly, and got his portrait. The nightjar got its moment of flashing fame. Ashok got the accolades.

At Dholkhand, he had calculated his approach to perfection. The track wound between thickets of lantana and to our right we heard the elephants parting their way through. The deliberate crunching of offending stems in their way, the ripping of roots by a stubbing toe. Sounds of gentle giants. Reassuring, not threatening, but to the uninitiated a whole wave of animal noises. The herd was very close. Ashok brought the jeep to a standstill, the ignition running softly.

'Tusker!' breathed Shaila in my ear. Her face was pressing, cool yet throbbing, against the back of my neck.

The first elephant that emerged from the shrubbery had a magnificent pair of tusks, curving downwards, upwards and then outwards; a perfect balance. Slowly, with the passing of every breath, a new elephant broke from the right. They would emerge onto the track, turn around to face the jeep, sniff the air delicately and move to the cover on the left.

'Six bloody tuskers!' Ashok was ecstatic. This was rare. Something that could be toasted to at the Tollygunj Club in Calcutta with the grand old tusker of Indian wildlife, Dhritikanto Lahiri-Choudhury. Normally tuskers move solitarily. Occasionally they form small bachelor parties.

Six of them together was extremely rare. Suddenly a seventh one was onto the track. It loomed huge, a clear foot or two above the others. The eye was cold and unforgiving. The left tusk was broken off in half. Its trunk was curled and upraised.

'A perfect Ganesh,' Ashok breathed.

'I don't like the look of it. Let's move back slowly.' I had decided early on in my jungle career that discretion was most definitely the better part of valour. A bull tusker could make a disbeliever into an ardent devotee in the matter of a few minutes.

'Coward,' taunted Shaila. 'Animal-lover! Let's wait for a few more moments.'

Ashok is easily swayed by a woman's wisdom. The Ganesh had turned away and was walking off like the rest of the troop.

'No problem at all!' Ashok chanted. 'He was not even starting a mock charge.'

Elephants should first do a mock charge, warn and then do the real one. Most of them end it in the mock one, a display good enough to drive away pesky humans. A real charge should begin with the ears floating outwards and then stiffening like outstretched punkahs in the breeze. The trunk should snake outwards and gulp tentatively at an air scented with the distasteful sweat of nervously perspiring humans. The trunk should then curl back into the mouth seeking the olfactory area high on the roof of the mouth. And then with a nervous scream and a few tentative shuffles the elephant should begin giving Flo Jo a run for her money. This is exactly how an elephant must behave. Every once in a while, though, you meet one which has not read his rule books carefully enough. The Ganesha suddenly charged through the left cover, tearing a huge clump of lantana as he turned around abruptly.

'Back! Back!' I yelled.

Ashok had the jeep into reverse in seconds. Shaila braced herself tightly against the leather of the back seat. The elephant came at us in a cloud of dust.

The animal should have normally stopped its charge within a few hundred metres, perhaps as much as half a kilometre. Anything more was very serious.

'Turn the jeep around, Ashok!' I knew that the vehicle in reverse could not beat the charge of an angry elephant. Ashok knew this far better. The animal was distinctly closer and gaining. I could see the first flashes of panic glint through the complete self-control mask on Shaila's face. I turned around and pressed her hand into mine. Ashok could use his own for steering. Just as Ganesha would will, the thick vegetation on both sides parted just that little bit to allow Ashok to squeeze his vehicle around for turning. The elephant was now within fifty yards of the vehicle.

The Gypsy spun in Ashok's hands as he twisted it around. Ganesha followed the screeching tyres with an earth-shattering trumpet of his own. As the jeep gained a lead, I looked back at the hump of malevolence. Back in the safety of the rest house, Ashok and Shaila headed off into the solace of large gins. I walked downhill tentatively to look for the tusker. Halfway down I saw him through the parted leaves. He had reached the bottom of the hills more than three kilometres from where he had begun his charge. His trunk was still waving around uncertainly. He stomped the ground uneasily. The chase was not successful or satisfactory for him. He had to vent his ire elsewhere.

Almost exactly one year later we met another Ganesha in the nearby Halduparao forests. This time Ashok was not with us and Shaila had used the best of her judgements to be alone with me. Halduparao, Mothonguri in Manas and Thaanikkudi in Periyar are my perennial favourites for the rest house of the subcontinent award. The Halduparao rest house was built in the late 1800s, a hundred years of solid solitude. Around the very basic constructions, the *rokads* and jungles of Sonanadi Wildlife Sanctuary have laid siege. The forests link up to Corbett in the south and to Lansdowne forest divisions in the north. Birds frolic in the trees like restless nymphs; elephants are the migrant monarchs of the kingdom.

Reading the entries in an age-old forest rest house register ranks very high amongst principal personal hobbies to be indulged on a summer's afternoon in a forest. The Halduparao register stretches all the way back to its construction, with a conscientious forester noting in the register that the building had cost all of two hundred rupees to erect. 'One hundred years later, a wildlifer testifies,' I entered in my own handwriting, 'that it was money well spent.'

I was put in my place on my next visit. Divisional Forest Officers still read rest house registers, I discovered. At least some of them. 'Two thousand, not two hundred, please!' screamed an indignant entry and I was abashed into trying to recalculate whether it was worth it after all. Halduparao won once again, all hands down.

The evening light confirmed my decision. It filtered clear and pale yellow onto a herd of elephants bathing in the stream. Slaps of mud packs were being applied rather vigorously, and the thwacks sounded through the forest. These are insect repellant strategies that may be used by humans when they run out of Odomos and when they are sleeping all by themselves. We were on foot, having left the jeep near by. Shaila picked her way gingerly but rather expertly through the mud wallows. There was still plenty of cover and then an open ground between the elephants and us. Most importantly, the wind was in our favour, blowing towards us and bringing in the rank odour of fresh dung. For nearly an hour we hung around the edges of the forest, changing position only to take photographs from a different angle. Night started creeping in as we made our way back to the vehicle.

'That was divine.' Shaila was ecstatic and that made it all look worthwhile to me. The *rokad* at the edge of the hill bearing the rest house was flowing fast and furious with a low stream. A Himalayan pied kingfisher screamed deliriously, rattling its crests at us menacingly. As the jeep rolled downwards into the *rokad*, the engine shut off suddenly. In a jiffy, the driver had it back on but the vehicle had lost its momentum. The jeep we were in, a Tata Sumo, sank with a whisper into the soft mud of the *rokad*. For an hour we struggled with the vehicle. It was doing nothing more than churning the mud deeper. We would need more people. Out of the forest fringe, a torch glared balefully. A small procession of forest guards who were out to search for us. They came like saviours out of the primeval ooze, grumbling softly to themselves as they came forward. They were soon groaning loudly as sweat lathered their heaving hands. The vehicle only sunk in further into the mud. It had a large steel bar welded to its underside to make its weight that of a commercial vehicle and therefore to save tax. Not the best industrial decision, we concurred. The situation seemed absolutely hopeless. From all around, as if to celebrate this human failure, a herd of elephants surrounded the night.

'Let's abandon the vehicle. C'mon. Back. Back to the rest house.' Somehow, the absurdly tragic story of Johnsingh and Nair kept coming back in short hallucinogenic doses.

But the forest staff were determined to save the vehicle. They bent to the task once again, sweat pouring small rivulets into the *rokad*.

'What if the elephants damage your vehicle, saab,' the most innocent of them appealed, 'you will lose at least ten thousand rupees won't you?'

The vehicle cost three hundred thousand. The naïveté of the guard made me bend my back just once more. No go. The vehicle had to be abandoned. The night was spent furtively and restlessly in the rest house. Below us we could hear the herd and I anticipated the crunch of freshly mangled steel any moment. It never happened. Once during the night a tusker wandered into the compound making the two of us bolt ourselves in with much of the furniture stacked against the door in preparation. Only a few months earlier an elephant had broken in and chewed up the mattresses.

In the morning, I ventured out tentatively downhill. A strange sight met my eyes. A few of the guards who had attempted an early morning rescue were seated on top of the vehicle. All around, a herd reluctant to leave but nonchalant about the human presence, grazed ruminantly. Sudddenly the bushes sprang apart and our visitor of the night before charged up the hillside. I ran with the the tusker close behind. My bathroom slippers, rough slabs of rubber, fell to the mercy of the marauder. This may have slowed him up just that little bit and I reached the rest house trench with the elephant just a foot behind me.

'Can you not come in more quietly when I am sleeping?' Shaila demanded, sleep blurring her face into a palette of tenderness.

It took half a day and a lorry with tow ropes to retrieve the vehicle. This was after the herd had decided to move on, leaving vehicle and man untouched. After having gently reminded us of that which could have been.

~

A biologist would blanch at clubbing an elephant with a rhino. In size, the two mega-herbivores are both capable of turning a Tata Sumo on its head. Nevertheless, the two are totally unrelated, with the rhinos being more closely related to horses. The nearest living relative of the elephant might well have been the rock hyrax, a rabbit-sized African mammal which evolved along with proboscideans nearly fifty million years ago. In loose colloquial language, the rhino and the elephant are both pachyderms. Pachyderm is Latin, merely a physical description meaning tough skin; unscientific, illogical but convenient. In India, the giants are linked by much more than a name. Both are mega-herbivores, both require space and both are killed for parts of their bodies that are high value commodities in the wildlife trade markets of the Far East. In trying to conserve them, these similarities are therefore paramount. Another area where similarities come up in a big way are the political battles that are fought in the international arena when either species comes up for a special hearing.

'Every species must pay for itself,' exhorted Robert Mugabe, the President of Zimbabwe, as he opened the 1997 Convention on International Trade in Endangered Species of Wild Flora and Fauna (CITES). Philosophically, ecologically and ethically, a retrogressive call set in prehistory when a dinosaur on the prowl only meant dinner. New scientific proof is gathering that will probably make even the most primitive of our ancestors sound a far more cultured lot. Meanwhile, centuries of civilization has allowed *Homo Sapiens* the gall to put a monetary and utilitarian value to creatures who have evolved alongside them. During the week that followed the CITES conference, the wheels of this very same progressive chariot of man had spun further, opening, albeit in a limited fashion, the international trade in ivory which has been banned for nearly a decade. Sixty tonnes of ivory from three southern African nations was to be sold to the Japanese. More than half, perhaps even three quarters of it would go into making hankos—cylindrical name seals that the Japanese use on official documents. Lacking a signature, in the strict Western sense, the Japanese use this seal as a mark of their individuality. What use elephants, if their teeth cannot help the Japanese sign their cheques? This question has been around for quite some time now.

A small group of people have been gathering once in two years for more than a decade to debate on the merits of allowing international trade in ivory. Without a single exception these meetings have ended in a resounding negative vote. Elephants in the wild, they concurred, are too threatened, the use of ivory is not essential and the economics of the trade not relevant enough to necessitate the re-opening of the 1989 ban on international trade in ivory. Yet, as another two years pass and the next biannual conference of the parties of CITES draws near, the pressure falls back on these scientists, conservationists and activists to meet all over again to defend the elephant against a pecuniary lobby. Attending the 1997 reiteration at Johannesburg, South Africa, I was struck by the fact that this was probably a very unique event. It is difficult to recall repeated gatherings of people debating on whether the economics of growing marijuana is crucial for boosting health care in developing nations or whether high velocity rifles should be made available to the children of the world. No other group of people have vocalized for so long and so repeatedly the futility of the consumptive use of the elephant without the global community recognizing the very anti-social nature of the trade. In this the Indian judiciary has been forthright about its philosophy. 'The ivory trade is pernicious in nature,' it notes in a landmark judgement against the trade in 1997, 'and is anti-social in nature, much like prostitution, gambling and the printing of counterfeit currency.' The judges in India are taking over conservation and people like me can happily become obsolete and jobless.

The Indian perception to the use of our *gajatma* for its incisors has been governed by a millennia of tradition, religion and conservation ethic. India, at one point of time, had the highest number of ivory carvers in the world but consciously decided that artistic excellence must find an alternative medium given the precarious existence of our wildlife. How much of a precipice is it, then, on which the elephants and other wildlife of India are sitting? In comparison to 1500 rhinos or 4000 tigers, the elephants seem to be sitting pretty at 25000. Yet, it is crucial to understand three overriding factors that will decide the fate of the species. First, only male elephants have tusks in Asia. Poaching for ivory would therefore remove only the males and that too preferably the older breeding males with larger tusks. This is much like killing only the male heads of families in the human race and not worrying about the numbers game as the number of women and children seem sufficient (ironically, in the elephant it is the female who is a matriarchal head of the herd and not the male!). The resultant skewed sex ratios of male to female or tusker to the rest of the population can have very deleterious effects on the population dynamics of the species. Already one southern Indian population is left with only one adult tusker for 400 females. There are various estimates of the number of tuskers in India but all agree that this is unlikely to exceed 2000 by very much. The elephants are facing what can definitely be termed a male-drought coupled with a tusker-deprivation syndrome.

Secondly, elephants are large, space-consuming mega-herbivores which are increasingly coming into conflict with a human population that is already bursting at its seams. India has only four per cent of the country under the protected area network (i.e. sanctuaries and national parks) and elephants as a rule do not seem to respect this paper-noting too much. The tragedy is that people or their livestock do not either, and the resultant clash of dubitably the most successful species on earth and the largest land mammals has left a number of casualties on either side. Poaching comes as the proverbial last straw.

Thirdly, there are a number of new angles to the poaching story that give cause for worry. Elephants in the north-eastern part of the country are being killed for their meat, which is partly smuggled to neighbouring states and partly used to supply the needs of a meat-eating militia hiding in the jungles. The semi-processed nature of the meat which because of the long fibers lasts long in the wild without refrigeration, indicates an organized slaughter and trade far removed from subsistence hunting by tribals for food.

The resurgence of poaching for tusks which has claimed at least a hundred elephants in the country in 1997, the highest toll for over a decade, represents a growing malaise. The trade seems to be increasingly in need of the lustrous material. Surprisingly most of it does not go into making art forms but rough blocks with Japanese names engraved on them that serve as name seals for the nouveau-riche Japanese. Hundreds of thousands of hankos—chops, in China—are churned out annually. Not so many elephants left to provide the ivory, though. Of what ivory is left after the name seal onslaught, a significant percentage goes into the bead-at-the-end-of-a-kimono drawstring industry. The Japanese who are the world's largest consumers of ivory are fuelling the demise of elephants in Africa and Asia for the *hanko* and the *netsuke*, trivial signs of affluence with little bearing on their own traditions. It is surprising, therefore, that a large segment of the wildlife intelligentsia still considers it a case for debate.

~

Masayuki Sakamoto is a rare Japanese. He heads the Japanese Wildlife Conservation Society which tells the Japanese that all wildlife is not to be eaten, turned into pretty artefacts, used as signature chops or stuck into the hair as hairpins. That is almost as suicidal as forming a Uganda-Against-Cannibalism association when Idi Amin still ate power in Africa. Yuki *san*, as he is popularly known, is a slight, young lawyer with an almond-shaped face. He is forever late, hurrying in a rushed-looking suit, crumpled in a thousand places by the stress of handling two occupations. In India to attend a meeting as the Secretary General of the Asian Conservation Alliance set up by six Asian countries that wanted to combat the utilization policies of others, he had a secret desire. He had to see an elephant. What better place to see it than at Mudumalai and what better company than that of Raman Sukumar, the chairman of the Asian Elephant Specialist Group. When Sukumar began his research in the early eighties on elephants, he was sent to Sathyamangalam division, a forest outside the protected area network. More than fifteen years later, I would tour the area in a coracle, fighting shy of the biggest forest brigand in southern India, Veerappan, and count fifteen carcasses littering the forest. Much before the Veerappan phenomenon claimed Sathyamangalam and the adjoining divisions of Chamrajnagar and Kollegal, Sukumar set out to study elephant-human conflict in a battered self-repaired diesel jeep. The hard-drinking and eccentric Rauf Ali was one of his first guides. An initial worker on bonnet macaques, Rauf is part of the great Salim Ali family and shares both the genius and the eccentricities of its chaotic heritage.

'You sent poor young Sukumar into the forests with Rauf?' an incredulous co-worker asked Madhav Gadgil, the head of the Centre for Ecological Sciences and one of the country's great green brains. 'In a month's time, the poor Brahmin will be completely corrupted by Rauf.'

Madhav is said to have smiled long and deep into his hunched shoulders. 'If I know anything of Sukumar, they will come out a month later with Rauf a confirmed drinker of buttermilk!' he quipped.

Neither happened but Sukumar did emerge with a doctorate on elephants, one of the first field studies on the animal in India, and a reputation which grew rather alarmingly for his age and catapulted him onto the centre stage of world conservation politics in the early nineties. I was still in TRAFFIC at that time, and struggling with a longish article on elephant poaching. Ivory was finding its way into the northern Indian markets by the bushel and I was determined to write long and hard about it. At the time WWF rarely encouraged 'live research', as they called my brand of work, in contrast to the library-based desk research that went into most of their writings. I was reasonably proud of my piece done for their quarterly. What I had not reckoned with was a new commercial newspaper editor who had just been hired by the NGO. Like a good journalist he referred the article to experts and took their quotes. When it finally did appear, it did so considerably hacked and chopped although still retaining my original 'look out for poaching' message. After the last line of my article a double space added weight to what followed. 'An eminent elephant expert, Dr R. Sukumar of the Indian Institute of Sciences, Bangalore, however, thinks that this is not true,' it read and I exploded both within and without. In one line an editorial buffoon had debunked my entire article. And who was this Raman Sukumar anyway?

I met him an year later in Delhi. He was pole-shaped, with a neat dark mop of oiled hair balanced on top of scholarly spectacles. He walked with the lope of a hungry giraffe and he talked with his sinuous fingers twisting strange molecular patterns in front of you. He did research on elephants, tropical vegetation and climate change in the Nilgiris. He was an exciting ecologist who along with Johnsingh and Ulhas Karanth made up the triumvirate of Indian mammalology. He was also honest for a scientist, soft-spoken for an activist and seemed a decent person. He stoutly denied he had said things exactly the way they were printed. Even better, he admitted that poaching was indeed a problem and wanted me to be a consultant to find out how and why. Good man . . . and to think that I had doubted him!

When Sakamoto and I went down to Masinagudi, the small Nilgiri townlet that passes off for a forest village, I was already two years into my study on poaching and ivory trade. By then TRAFFIC was well established and WWF itself was growing too big for my liking. A little too much at odds with its *raison d'être* as well. I was part of a large exodus from a new-look WWF. The Asian Elephant Research and Conservation Centre welcomed me into its folds. I took Yuki *san* into the Masinagudi research station that Sukumar ran for the Indian Institute of Science. The accent there was on bare essentials for the body, large vegetarian meals and a 'let's-get-into-the-field-now' attitude. Usually watching a species with an expert is not very easy in India. This is a jinx that is very hard to explain but with the exception of Arun's dogs and a Bengal florican with Goutam Narayan in Assam, I have been singularly unlucky with experts. Sukumar is a rare exception. I have never gone into the field with him and not run into herds of females or a few solitary tuskers eyeing us warily from the corners of their eyes. One good reason for this is that much of his work is within the Nilgiri Biosphere Reserve, an area that contains more elephants in it than any other Asian country. Another must be infrasonic communication—long proven in the elephant but not yet tested in Sukumar.

Mudumalai is a complex of mixed deciduous and scrub forest. Dry to the east, wetter to the west. Joined to Karnataka by the interstate boundary and the infamous Moyar gorge that poachers and smugglers frequent. In Mudumalai and the adjoining Bandipur elephants are not uncommon. Early in my field outings with Sukumar came a young bull elephant called Cross Tusks Junior. His more illustrious cousin, Cross Tusks Senior, had been killed by poachers and now Junior had the biggest pair of ivory around. A little above Theppakadu a water tank rises out of a dirt track. Sukumar and I were crouched on it, two rather large outlines ineffectively trying to blend into the concrete of the tank. Cross Tusks Junior came out of the lantana scrub scattering yellow and orange flowers like a ritual offering. Wine-coloured berries plonked around him as he gathered the surrounding vegetation and draped himself with it. He was playful, still only twenty years or so. Not a child but still a child-man. There was no intention to feed for the moment and food was for splattering around himself. As he did it he raised his trunk half a dozen times, showing the yellowing bases of his magnificent tusks that curved down to below his knees and then crossed. The crossing over of tusks has become a great rarity in times when poachers target anything that gleams above the lip line. In one case, a pair of tusks were stuffed into an airmail cover and mailed from Kerala to Bombay—two tusks in an envelope meant to carry a few sheets of A4 paper. That would have been almost certainly an elephant below an year old. Babies in the trade. With the clouds of poaching darkening Asian skies, tuskers like Cross Tusks Junior were an absolute rarity. It was important that Yuki *san* saw the bull. But wildlife in India cannot be summoned at will. The spirit of the forest has to be savoured as it is served up.

On the day, the menu was a family herd fairly close to the dirt track. Five females, dust-brown and domed in outline. One of them still a sub-adult and another breaching the verges of adulthood. Three females had calved earlier, their sagging breasts a testimony of suckling. The two near adults may well have been daughters of the two younger adults. The third adult was a geriatric case, at least fifty-five to sixty years old, her ears folded twice over to the front, a deep fold indicating age. On both temples, the flesh had hollowed out into oil-pans of dark black and the skin hung around her like a leathery tent flapping in the wind. They stood at peace with the elements, testing the wind as it shifted every few moments. The Asian elephant uses this air swallowing technique as its sixth sense. The trunk swallows air which is then fed into the roof of the mouth, an action that is called a flehmen's response. Up on the roof of the mouth is a vomero nasal organ, the sixth sense of the elephant. The elephants had done their testing, got a few conservationists in the air, and with characteristic manners allowed us to be part of the scene. There is nothing more relaxing than to stand in an Indian forest and watch a herd of elephants. In their calm, unflappable manner they embrace mankind with a generosity that we have sadly not been able to reciprocate. Yuki *san* bowed thrice in reverance not merely with the thrill of seeing the beasts but in a way out of a sense of responsibility that he felt for the elephants.

'We Japanese have done so much to kill these animals,' he later confided touchingly, 'that I can only pay my respects to those still living. So-so.'

The big elephant populations in India are the southern and the eastern ones. Other than these two are the smaller populations in northern India along the foothills of the Himalayas and the central Indian population along the trijunction of Bihar, Orissa and West Bengal. Dalma is one of the small strongholds in Bihar. All conservationists must have done a little something that will ensure their name in gold once past the pearly gates. Dalma, according to Ashok, is his special little discovery. Just as every politician leaves office with a pet scheme mooted, unconcerned about its future deterioration, conservationists love to be involved in setting up protected areas. I suppose it gives them the happiness of doing something concrete and tangible; the minor delusions of grandeur. Ashok does not, in the normal course of things, believe in grandeur except after a long and steady flow of rum, and then he will tell you the story of Dalma.

The state was Bihar and the town near by Jamshedpur. Ashok was still in Tata Steel and not yet a full-time conservationist. Making steel must have been infinitely simpler and more straightforward. His weekend jaunt to the nearby forests of Dalma in southern Bihar was something that was looked forward to through the humdrum of the whole week. For one such visit in 1973 he had a special reason to be there. There were reports of elephants in Dalma. The Divisional Forest Officer, like all good bureaucrats faced with an issue without precedence, denied all existence of the elephants. As mammoths were not wont to roam in Dalma, the Asian elephant there lacked precedence. Not reality, however. For in the forests were herds of elephants. Ashok returned indignant. The DFO was furious.

'Bade babu! Bade babu!' summoned the imperious forester and his head clerk ran out in disarray. His was the most important post in a provincial office. To inform, conceal and act was his responsibility. The DFO only needed to sign.

'Hamar jungle mein haathi aur hamain ko nahin pata?' the DFO roared, disturbed that the discovery was made by an outsider. ('Elephants in my forests and I am not told about it?')

Bade babu was a seasoned veteran. *'Sahib, kabhi kabhi to haathi aata bhi hain, aur kabhi kabhi to chala bhi jaata hain, sahib.'* This was great wisdom: 'The elephant comes to the forest occasionally, but at other times it leaves the forest as well.' Man could not control Ganesha and wish to be told about its presence. The elephants had shown the intrepid *Bade Babu* a way out. The DFO, however, was now all pumped up and wanted to see the creatures with his own eyes. As he huffed and puffed his way up the incline, the herd shifted and came into view. Sinha sahib watched with some trepidation. Back in the safety of his bungalow and over half cups of tea he revived.

'To see these elephaants ees bhery threeling,' he confided in strong Bihari-speak, 'but the threel of seeing them bhery soon turns into pheear. That is the prhoblem!'

Ashok and I often recall Salim Ali's favourite repartee to those who did not believe in birds. It was common enough for people to ask him why he chose birds to tigers and elephants for a lifetime's work. His answer was unfailing.

'Elephants and tigers are very exciting, all right,' he would aver with a twinkle forming in the corner of an eye, 'but you will agree with me, won't you, that watching birds is perhaps . . . a little bit safer?'

Safety and the Indian elephant. It seemed all so strange when on repeated African savannah safaris I was taken to elephants as if they were inoffensive deer or antelope. Once in Zimbabwe a young male came sauntering up to the jeep in which I was, and shaking a few crusts of red earth from its body stretched its trunk tip to within a foot of my face. Suddenly the human smell hit him and he screamed in pure terror and backed away clumsily, pirouetting on rather unsteady legs. The elephant in India evokes images of domestication, the African one brings up memories of the wild bush. Yet it is the Indian one that to me is the wilder by a margin. Used to thick cover, less humans at close quarters and also perhaps resenting man for his captures and killings, Indian elephants are a capricious and idiosyncratic lot. The thought took me back almost to the beginning of my wild life. It was just after the Eravikulam and Sariska trips. Srishti was at it again and a small group of us were in Corbett National Park. The country's first national park spread a feast of spotted and hog deer out for us in its luxuriant *chaurs*. Million-coloured rollers twirled in the air on the lookout for insects, little green bee-eaters zipped ahead in front of them. The river spread hazily between the *chaurs* and the rest house at Dhikala, parts of it squelched circular by a regular troop of riding elephants that took the tourists to the grasslands beyond. The afternoon sun played upon the surface of the Ramganga. Corbett baked in the heat of a northern summer. The little water that was left in the river formed small pools and we splashed in their shallows, embracing the waters with the eagerness of addicts. My charges were three women and the lone deserter, Mohit Aggarwal. In the distance, the chital barked and acked. The rut fever was at its peak.

Mohit moved through the tall grass of the *chaurs* with the ease of an elephant. Not for him the indolent drenching of an afternoon dip. He was a photographer first. He crashed about trying to get to the watchtower where an afternoon spent watching the waterhole might well be lucky. The tripod weighed him down considerably and his cameras added to the weight. A silver streak played a rhapsody with the air in front of his nose. A male paradise flycatcher, black head and sterling silver body splaying across the *chaur*. The bird dipped its tail in a small waterhole ahead and then exploded into a sudden panic-stricken flight.

From the bushes to his left, a much larger shadow was detaching itself

'Lal Kaan,' whispered Mohit.

The rogue was well known in Dhikala, a heavily pigmented right ear giving it its identity. Lal Kaan. Red Ear.

Mohit broke out into a run. Lal Kaan did not like the look of the tripod. He paused for only a moment to snatch at the air in front of him with an angry trunk. Opening his mouth he let the air into it, sniffing out the unfamiliar scent that was bothering him. Knowing Mohit, he must have wheezed and hissed with worry. There was no more doubt. Lal Kaan let out a shrill trumpet and charged. Mohit ran with his life and equipment clutched to his bosom. Perhaps not quite in that order. In front of him a green watchtower loomed; sudden deliverance. Lal Kaan shrieked in anticipation of disappointment and ran into a bush.

'God!' Rivulets of terrorized salt water ran down Mohit's face.

The waters of the pool spread around us in circles of contentment.

'Where's Mohit?' Tara was the most concerned.

'Must have gone finding his shikras.' Pia was not.

'Must be jungie crows with you around,' Bharati would not allow Pia a moment of triumph. Pia had once referred to jungle crows as jungie crows and the name had stuck.

Around me, the trees suddenly seemed to be full of adult men. They hung, ripe and lascivious, watching the water sports with more than their due share of interest.

It was difficult to get out of the water without attracting more attention. The girls were furious with the male species—the whole jing bang lot of them.

Mohit was furious with frustrated males—especially the elephantine variety. Lal Kaan was a *makhna*, one of a large percentage of Indian male tuskers that do not bear tusks. The gleaming white ivory is a male preserve and a symbol of dominance and good health. The *makhnas* tend to get just a wee bit irritated by the lack of it. Much like men whose moustaches refuse to grow. They take it out on any weaker being around. Men without moustaches take it out on flies and mosquitoes. Lal Kaan was trying it out on Mohit. The elephant had disappeared quietly into the bushes when Mohit reached the watch tower. A full fifteen minutes later Mohit ventured down again, after testing the wind with his right nostril. Lal Kaan was waiting in the bushes below. With an agonizing shriek he flung himself at Mohit. The machaan was just at hand once again. Mohit returned four hours later, a shaking and nervous wreck. You could see that the elephant had won the battle of the nerves.

We were seated around a small dhaba in the middle of the Dhikala clearing and the girls were discussing male chauvinism while looking at a rather large and dirty pig. This was in actuality a wild boar, who had rather taken to humans and was used to hanging around the camp looking for a feedout. Buddhu or Idiot, as he was christened, listened to their chastisements with grave concern. Tara was the most relaxed of the lot, enjoying one of her occasional cigarrettes while Pia and Bharati sat with a bag of overripe plums between them, debating on whether Buddhu looked better than the local men or not.

Mohit arrived into the confusion like a tornado sneaking its way into the fold of a hurricane.

'What a day!' he heaved as he entered, threw his camera bag aside and with the same motion of his right hand picked up the bag of plums and fed the snorting wild boar on the side.

'You can say that again,' the girls chorused, 'and what bastards men are.'

Buddhu, the male chauvinistic pig, grunted his complete and harmonious acquiescence.

Tiger Tales

'The tiger sees you a hundred times for every time that you see the tiger.'
   —Old Indian jungle saying.

'Now, where the hell is that bloody tiger?'
   —New Indian tourist saying.

We were sitting in the shadow of the Satpuras. Around us the hills rose, ruddy and rugged. The earth was red with the fading heat and ten white *koroi* trees circled us, naked and leafless. A little further away were two dozen teaks; fine, large-boled trees with their leaves still quite intact. Still further away, the flaming flashes of a blushing *kusum* sprang out of the backdrop. The first rains had still not hit Melghat National Park, five hours off India's belly button, Nagpur. The days burned with central Indian summer heat, a dry, searing, leaf-crisping flame. Evenings were the only cool time to sit out and the five of us sat under a teak, thankful for the balm of falling dusk. Mohit and Alok flanked me. Alok has always reminded me of the rhino, in a philosophical sense. If said in Hindi it would be a positive insult, a reference to his considerable bulk. But for me he resembles the 500-million-year-old creature in his slow and unshakeable belief in the world he lives in. Every action is done with a stolidity of purpose and a solidity of form. You can trust him to carry on in the same fashion for the next 500 million years with no problem whatsoever. Alok was central to the formation of Srishti in 1987, in fact giving it its name. He was my partner in my early travails, including an infamous one at Sariska National Park when in order to see tigers we had spent two days inside the park with nothing to eat but two kilos of guavas. Spitting seeds and sprouting guava trees in our wake, we had come out friends. Gautam Malakar, a friend from the travel trade, sat a little further away. Madhav Gogate sat with his face towards us and his back to the irate grumblings of a group just returned from the forest. He wore a white bush-shirt over cream coloured pants, a parochial Maratha middle-class dress.

'Nothing in this forest. Nothing at all,' the tourists were clearly dissatisfied.

Gogate shifted uneasily in his seat. Above his head, a flying squirrel decided to complete a glide, tracing the outlines of the evening with its silken membranes. The squirrel does not actually fly like a bat, but glides sensuously, tree to tree, in search of food and a hollow home.

'I tell you! This Melghat business! Nothing to see at all. Absolute waste of time.' The fat tourist was lying on his back, belly to the sky, and expostulating with the stars. His friends and family gathered around him, soaking up the gloom of his words.

Gogate turned to face them.

'Excuse me, gentlemen,' he interrupted, 'what do you mean, nothing at all to see?' The flying squirrel was taking a return glide. The trees of Semadoh, the tribal hamlet inside the park, are a favourite with the creature.

'Nothing, *bhaisaheb*, nothing.' He was glad to have somebody to listen to him. 'It's a waste of time to come here picnicking, no?'

It was certain that Gogate thought this last statement to be correct. His face had turned strangely stern.

'What of the trees surrounding you, my friend? These magnificent teak, the *mahua*, the *koroi*?'

'Hah! you know what I mean! Not trees, not trees . . . wildlife!'

'The birds are calling all around you, you can see deer and gaur within five minutes of this camp, and you feel there is no wildlife!' A vein throbbed arthritically in Gogate's neck.

'Why are you joking, sir, please?' the man was still prone from his exertions of trying to view wildlife. 'No tigers, I mean. Four trips into this forest and we have not seen even one tiger. Not one only. What sort of forest is this, then?'

Gogate looked up to the squirrel for reassurance and then turned back a steely eye.

'My name is M.G. Gogate,' he was extending his hand to the fat one, 'Director of Melghat Tiger Reserve.'

The man sat up quietly and quickly.

'You see, I am a government servant. If you want to see me, just call me, I will come to where you are staying. But the tiger . . . ah, now, that is another matter altogether. We have still to include him in the government payroll.'

Gogate was enjoying this. The tourists were edging uncomfortably away.

'If you want to see the tiger, wait for the tiger to show

himself to you.'

The squirrel was poking its velvet nose out of the tree trunk.

'Don't look for him, for if you do so, you will never find him.'

We cheered silently, as a whiff of *mahua* crawled across the air.

~

The tiger is unquestionably Indian wildlife's star show. The elephant may be bigger, the pygmy hog more endangered, the red panda more cuddly, the snow leopard more mystic. But the tiger is simply the tiger. Lord of the Indian jungle. Sher Khan to Kipling. The eyes and soul of the forest. The animal the whole world wants to save. The target of the entire poaching mafia. One of the most endangered animals in the country, it symbolizes the unsaid aspirations and whispered hopes of tourists, diehard conservationists, first time wildlifers and R.K. Laxman's common man.

'It's just a pussy cat, *appa*,' Hamsini, Sukumar's two-year-old daughter, looking at her first animal picture book, was categorical. It sent her father and Lahiri-Choudhury, both good elephantwallahs, into paroxysms of mirth. The tiger men of India, Valmik Thapar and Ulhas Karanth, if present, might have rivalled male langurs in infanticide practices.

Valmik looms over the Delhi tiger scene like a bearded colossus. On select evenings as dusk descends on his Kautilya Marg residence, the waterhole within starts coming alive with wildlife. A typical evening would have at least four constant stars of tiger conservation in India. Ashok would be at the waterhole itself, a rum and water in hand (no ice, please), phone glued to his right ear as if it were an abnormal outgrowth of the tympanum. Brijendra Singh would be rather more discreetly placed from the waterhole, as befits aristocracy. An Honorary Warden of Corbett, Brij (in Delhi circles) or Kunwar Sahib (in jungle circles) is synonymous with India's first national park. His cravat would shine softly, catching the glint from his mini-handlebars that would twirl a few millimetres over his Scotch-pani. Sanjay Deb Roy, former head of Indian wildlife and Assam's answer to the Indian forester, who almost single-handedly brought the Manas National Park into international limelight, would be seated passively in the deepest chair. His glass would mirror the despair of a man who has just found out that his life's work is being undone by fellow men and an unforgiving circumstance. The fourth star would be a fickle star, changing with the seasons and times. This would be the man who is called the Director, Project Tiger; usually considered a choice abuse in a world where slinging slime at tiger officials is a daytime norm. Over the past two years, the urbane and unflappable Arin Ghosh has been replaced by the from-the-heart pragmatist P.K. Sen. Whoever the present incumbent, tiger evenings would inevitably find the person at the great Thapar residence, rubbing shoulders with a milieu that used him as a dart-board at all other times. Floating in between these stars would be the nebula of visiting scientists, conservationists and smaller beings. Bittu Sahgal, steel blue eyes and the stentorian voice of the country's most read wildlife magazine, *Sanctuary*. Ulhas

Karanth, quietly bristling over his drink with a pair of pugmarks swimming in his scotch. Joanna Van Gruisen, floating elegantly through the evening like one of her own rapturously wild photographs. Occasionally, a few foreign NGO representatives. Towering over the entire gathering would be the overpowering presence of Valmik 'Valu' Thapar, the scion of a remarkable media family, tigerwallah beyond compare and of late India's answer to David Attenborough.

'Have you been to Valmiki recently?' he asked me once, his beard glowering millimetres from my guilty face. I cringed and started inwardly. Guilty at having been to Valmiki and not seen the rampant destruction that Valu saw. Guilty at surreptitiously trying to avoid his rather large hands that waved me into submission by the strength of his convictions. And a secret guilt that should really be plaguing a large number of conservationists playing the save-a-wildlife game today: Are we really doing all we can to save this flagship of Indian wildlife?

It is rather surprising that despite the large number of tigerwallahs, the tiger continues to become more endangered. It was all very different in 1972, when the premier of the country took it upon herself to save the tiger in India. Being the daughter of Nehru, who was often seen cuddling a red panda or atop an elephant in Kaziranga, helped.

'Tiger,' she is reported to have said to her environment and forests minister, Dr Karan Singh, who went by that name among friends, 'Tiger, you have to save the tiger.' And so was born Project Tiger and a few thousand kilometres of paper fences went up around a few thousand square kilometres of paper forests. In a few years tiger numbers surged upwards. First slowly, an inch at a time, like the hesitant growth of a newborn, and then with the prodigious spurt of an adolescent. Some of this was because tigers being tigers responded to good protection by increasing in numbers. The rest was because bureaucrats being bureaucrats increased tiger numbers on paper. When the poaching wave started, the tiger was ready, two decades after protection, to slip back into the glamorized role of extinction mega-star. Even in Ranthambhor, the Mecca of tiger watchers, seeing a tiger was a tough job for nearly ten years.

I have in that respect been rather lucky with the tiger. While the world waits with bated breath for their first tiger, I saw my first one without specially looking for it. I was well into my teens but it was still my first trip into a protected area, even though my school in Chandigarh, Yadavindra Public School, stressed on the outdoor life. (That is perhaps the reason why half its scholars in that day and age turned cricketers and the other half terrorists.) Just out of school and Ranthambhor hit me with the full chill of the desert. It was zero degrees outside and shivering through the thin cotton T-shirt that I took, I learnt that desert nights can freeze. Ranthambhor itself is not desert; more an oasis of green in the parched brownscape of inner Rajasthan. Winter nights are still sub-zero and the morning dawns crisper than a starched cotton *chikan*-work kurta. Those were days when the stoutly moustached Fateh Singh Rathore, wild dog hater and tiger champion, ruled Ranthambhor like his personal fiefdom. The people on the peripheries must have hated the bristling twirl of his handlebars, the cocky feather in his leather hat, the darkly sullen monsoon clouds on his brow. The tiger loved it and responded by behaving like what it is ecologically—a cat.

The saddest thing about the threat facing the tiger throughout the world is the fact that it is a cat. The domestic cat is that supremely confident tabby, shunning domestication with the silken finesse that the English call feline. The wild cat, the world over, is a shy shadow, hunted and persecuted for a host of untenable reasons, skulking in the peripheries of human existence and once in a while vanishing into the shadows of extinction that inevitably build up around it. Allowed a freer reign, though, the cat should turn cat and reproduce. Any self-respecting feline—with the exception of Garfield—can have babies at a rate that could rescue the Parsi population overnight. The tiger in Fateh's Ranthambhor had demonstrated just that. In 1987, the park was full of tiger cubs gambolling on the heels of their famous parents. Every third bush held a tiger with a dozen jeeps surrounding it, every fourth waterhole had a full grown sambar splashing into the water and running for dear life from the leap of the big cat. In the first two visits I saw all of that and more.

Valmik and Fateh formed a famous combination. Valmik wrote and took photographs, perched rather precariously on the roof-bars of Fateh's gypsy. Fateh managed the park and took photographs as well. Between Jack Sprat and his rather unusual wife, they had turned Ranthambhor into an international success story. Tourists came in hordes, the first pull away from the usual African safari. The mysteries of the Indian jungle had begun to hold centrestage, albeit in the open, see-a-tiger-a-day forests of the Rajasthan diadem. After Kipling and Corbett, Indian wildlife was facing a new revival. And then the poaching crisis hit Ranthambhor. This was at a time when the world was not willing to accept the early doomsayers who talked of poaching or trade. TRAFFIC had just been set up in India, thanks to the vision of Thomas Mathew and Ashok, and alongwith the latter I found myself increasingly a central character in that sordid drama. We worked to expose the workings of an illegal trade. Valmik and Fateh showed the world the tragedy.

Those were the days when WWF-India was still small despite its recently constructed plush offices amidst the rich and famous of Lodi Estate. To me, it also seemed to have a heart, a *raison-d'être*. Exemplifying the philosophy was Thomas Mathew, a small dapper Malayalee, an engineer by training, a conservationist by choice and a conscientious underplayer by habit. If Tom, as he is popularly known, is given the credit for building up WWF-India from a card selling outfit and a Sunday morning caper for the aristocratic outdoorsmen of earlier times, it would not be a grave mistake. If some give him credit for trying to come back and set up a tiger protection programme when half the world was baying at WWF's heels, accusing it of going right back to its pedigree, this would not be very wrong either. It is to Tom's credit that India got its first wildlife trade monitoring programme. Those were heady days for Ashok and me. Ashok had much more of all the tiger stuff but you could not be in the thick of things and not get an occasional smell of the big cat. It was an intoxicating smell, much like that of the tigers of Beat 14 at the Delhi Zoo.

It is only by keeping animals that you realize how individualistic they can be, much like human beings. For most people, animals are soulless, idiosyncrasy-less generalities. They would do well to enter the grippingly powerful odour world of the big cats at the Delhi zoo, where, every Friday, the tigers become human. I was helping out the keepers during the zoo wardenship bit. It was early days for the Srishti team and apart from the normal duties of keeping away from the cages visitors who had particularly sadistic tendencies, we were to help out with a different beat every week. Helping involved feeding, cleaning, studying and evaluating. Kamal Naidu, the energetic zoo director during those days, was supportive despite an uncooperative union and financial crunches. So I ended up in Beat 14, the tiger beat on a Friday which was live animal feeding day. The treat was a live chicken brought to supplement the fourteen kilos of meat that the adult tigers used to consume at the zoo. The chicken, eaten unplucked and uncleaned, was to help the cats get their weekly roughage, biologically a sound proposition. I was slightly more sceptical about the live bit. The fact that this kept the tiger's hunting prowess intact for a possible re-introduction programme was patently hilarious. To think that an animal that entered the precincts of an Indian zoo would eventually be re-introduced seemed like Hans Anderson enough. To think that the Friday chicken was a lesson in hunting was complete lunacy.

The chickens were brought to Beat 14 trussed up and wings folded over backwards to make flight impossible. As the black metal doors creaked open, the mother of all smells hit the chicken broadside on. Inside, the three tigers got the smell of their bait as well and they prowled uneasily around, orange stripes turning anxiously upon each other. The smell spread rank and bitter and the chickens anaesthetized themselves, turning their eyelids over in mock horror. They were thrown in next to the bars and the tigers reached out for them in their own singularly characteristic manner.

The large male was the least fussy, eating the chicken in a few seconds of programmed swipes. The female was a follower of the Marquis of Sade. She swiped the chicken in and then with immaculate, imperious innocence plucked every feather off its body with twitches of her powerful teeth. As the chicken writhed in mortal agony, the tigress licked the blood off her jaws and flashed a Buddhist death mask grin at the victim. After the ritual, the prey was eaten. The young male went one step further. For him, the chicken was a toy to be swatted between two massive paws in a frenzy of pre-dinner histrionics. The bird was a bundle of anaesthetized nerves, twitching about in comatose agony. Friday was chicken day. Friday was the day of the individualistic tiger.

The smell of a tiger. And it had permeated the TRAFFIC-India office in those days. Ashok had with him an Iranian called Hormoz Asadi whose job it was to go into alleys where angels and gods feared to tread—normally at midnight, with no weapon and a bag full of money. He would then negotiate with tiger traders and their henchmen and set up a raid, all the while clutching the bag of money and then coming out with the bag intact at the end of a session. It was nerve-wracking stuff at best. The fact that the field investigator was not a biologist irked some. It was soon realized that the skills required were not exactly those of a field biologist. What was needed for the job was a first-rate tough crook. Perhaps we all qualified in some ways because the results were phenomenal. Wherever we looked, skins came out of the woodwork. Tiger and leopard, desert and leopard cat, fox and jackal, and sometimes even the elusive snow leopard. And on 30 October 1994, the conservation world stopped for a millisecond. From the narrow crowded lanes of Gali No. 11 in Sadar Bazaar and the Tibetan refugee camp at Majnu Ka Tila in Delhi, we recovered 400-odd kilos of tiger bone, fourteen tiger skins and 200 assorted mammalian furs. The trade was alive and festering in the capital of the city. It was ample proof of the size of the trade. It was also another reminder that nails were being driven into the tiger's coffin. Lead players sat up, drank their whiskies with a little greater panic and the best among them started to work seriously. For the first time the tiger circles of Delhi had lost their air of flippancy. The situation in India seemed very bad indeed.

In Nepal the situation was no different. I had ducked into a fur shop after setting a hotel on fire. The candle in the room had been toppled over by the wind and fire engines were beginning to circle in through the winding alleys. I had left the hotel a few minutes earlier and was blissfully unaware of what was going on. The job I was on was far more urgent and interesting than putting out hotel fires.

'You want tiger skin, sir . . . not leopard skin, sir . . . very good sir, but very, very bad, sir.'

Mir Ahsan was as eloquent as a Kashmiri in Nepal

could get. He had not yet put his finger on the fact that I was a fellow Indian. If Kashmiris think that way, that is. When he got to know, his cheeks reddened with the flush of a valley apple and he bowed. We were in Thamel, the raggedy-baggedy tourist back-packer district of Kathmandu. Mir and I were in the back portion of his shop viewing thirty to forty assorted fur coats and mammalian skins.

'*Mian*, why didn't you tell me you are from Hindostan, no. You wear the jeans like a westerner. And your hat. Oh, so confusing nowadays!' He wiped his brow with an embroidered piece of carpet cloth. Around him a riot of colour formed into papier mâché globes, hand-knit rugs and patchwork suede jackets.

'Have some *kehwa*, sir.' He poured a rich red tea out into a goblet. The spices floated out in a steamy vapour and warmed the air between us. Tea in Kashmir and Ladakh has always fascinated me. The people of the valley drink the *kehwa*, burning red with the scent of cinnamon and clove. The Ladakhis drink a snow-yellow tea with salt and yak butter taking the place of traditional sugar and milk. As different as the people. As close by as the two of us in a small Kashmiri shop. His hand reached out from behind the counter and pulled out a rich fishing cat coat.

'Now this, sir, is good stuff. Very, very cheap too.' I turned the skin over and pulled away part of the lining to feel inside for stitch marks. Twenty-five skins at least. These were large cats. Smaller cats such as the desert cat might end up thirty-five or forty to a coat. Forty wild souls on the back of a wild woman. The early seventies had seen acid-throwing protesters keep fur off the streets in Europe. Now the fashion seemed to be re-emerging.

'But tiger, Mir bhai.' Tigers were not made into coats, but furriers did deal in full tiger skins and I had information that one such piece lurked in a secret cabinet. The mythical snow leopard beat it to the draw, however. It was a soft white coat, smelling of damp snow and wet blood. Three animals. A creature that Raghu Chundawat had seen only seven times in five years. And he had done his doctorate on it from the Wildlife Institute of India. A being that wove Peter Matheissen's days and nights in Nepal into a mystical tapestry. Snow leopards. Floating ghosts among the snow clouds. And here they were, three of them in a single heap.

The Kashmiri was unwrapping a tiger skin slowly now from a rolled newspaper bundle. He was more interested in showing me the news items about Kashmir. It was a propaganda sheet about aerial acid attacks on citizens and the rape of schoolchildren. I had last seen such vicious stuff on Pakistan Television in Karachi.

'*Katra katra khoon ka badla lenge, mian*,' he stuttered emotionally ('We will take revenge for every last drop of blood').

Non-existent Kashmiri blood or the very visible stain that had dried chocolate on the inside of the tiger pelt, I wondered.

'If atrocities have been committed, it must be made right,' I assured him. 'I am not from your state but in my mind we are of the same country, the same race and are brothers.'

'Yes, yes, I know. It's not you, *mian*, it is those *saala kutta* government and army we are against.' His angst poured dark onto his face.

'This tiger skin, how much is it for?'

'Ten thousand, *mian*, but for you eight. *Theek*? Eight because we are brothers. Brothers against the *zulm* of India.'

I asked him more questions about the way he brought it into the country.

'Rolled up in cattle skin or in carpets. Leather or carpets. Easy across the border.'

'No checks?' I had to hear it from him.

'Checks?' He was vastly amused. 'Schoolchildren cross this border with polyester yarn wrapped around their legs. Trousers down, money got, back to Nepal. Easy, no? What checks?'

'What about shahtoosh, *mian*?' This was the king of Indian shawls, a light fluffy heirloom that can boil an egg wrapped in it, pass through an index finger ring and tell the whole world that you have arrived. It is perhaps the costliest wool in the world. It is also the underbelly wool of the highly endangered *chiru* or Tibetan antelope. Weaving shahtoosh shawls and indeed trading in them is a Kashmiri tradition. The wool is also bartered for tiger bones at the India-China border. A dead animal for another. Blood for blood.

The man's eyes burned bright and blue, clear like a spring sky in the valley. Shahtoosh must have brought to him the smell of home far away. The *kangris* burning coal in small clay-enclosed pots close to the skin, giving warmth and skin cancer alike. The small toy boats with a dream house inside on a mirror-blue lake. Kashmir of a day past and long gone.

'Not here, *mian*. In Srinagar we have plenty. Not here.'

Mir *mian* passed into a trance for his homeland.

Around him his friends and colleagues showed me five more tiger skins amidst heaps of skim of smaller beasts. By the time I got back to the hotel, my room had burnt down completely. A small world gone . . . while a bigger one lay bleeding at the furriers.

This was a time when the world community also started to point fingers. Why, they asked belligerently, is the tiger still endangered despite all the past donations and largesse? Where, they thundered, had all the money gone? The questions came from the media world, the genteel Western conservation world and the rough and tumble let's-do-it-overnight activist world. They came in droves to the doorstep of the largest tiger population of the world. Just as poachers did when tigers started drying up in the countries surrounding India. When tiger bone, so essential for the Oriental tiger bone wine, became a commodity hard to get. When chefs of tiger penis soup that was gulped surreptitiously in money-lined Japanese chambers found ingredients scarce. When a skin for the rich and famous to hang up behind them or use as a rug near the fireplace started vanishing from the markets. Welcome to India. Poachers and conservationists alike!

The Indian government, for the large part, did not extend a golden welcome to the conservationists. They were foreigners, mostly white men and women who were unfamiliar with Indian cultures. If only the money could be got into India without their infernal interference. Then, slowly, they realized that a balance would have to be struck and cold hauteur turned to mild warmth. One of the people to take the tiger by its bones was Michael Day, an advertising man in his early days and champion of the tigers soon after. His fortuitous conservation-coming in

Thailand was told and retold at many a dinner table soon
after his book started doing the rounds. Mike, when I met
him at Ashok's, was as impatient with the tiger's fate as
many of us in India were. He also had a grouse against
WWF, who he insisted were doing nothing to save the
tiger. In many ways we knew he was right. He was
voicing the inner feeling of a number of Indian
conservationists but putting it in the no-nonsense,
slightly arrogant, icicle-cold tone of a man with nothing
to lose. His Tiger Trust was a one-man, one-woman
business run out of a shed in Suffolk but his plans were
grandiose. He needed to save the tiger and he wanted to
do it in a hurry; WWF could go suck eggs if they did not
play along. There was only one regret that Mike had. He
had never seen a tiger in the wild.

'Show him one,' Ashok ordered paternally.

I took him to Corbett during the monsoons.

The crispness of the morning air was growing heavy
with heat. Only the gurkha seemed to be enjoying the
ramble through the brambles. The lantana bushes on
either side grew thick and spiny, woody stems pushing
sinuously along the air and clustering into
micro-bouquets of pink, yellow and white. Berries hung
by the bushel, dropping off as our bulks cleaved through
the bushes, parting the spines with the coarseness of our
own hides. Wild boars are better suited to this sort of
bush, digging low tunnels in the brush and rooting
half-foot furrows in the ground to expose tubers and
other culinary delights of the porcine variety. Boars love
bushes. I know that from painful experience at the Point
Calimere Sanctuary. Four hours of sweltering search for
the nest of the brahminy kite in the Palmyrah trees had

reduced me to a sweat-soaked sponge. The beach spread vast and soulless, the Indian ocean met it in an irritated manner. I crept into the confines of a welcoming bush to escape the scorching beach sun and the mocking vegetation. Thirty seconds later, I rocketed out again, this time backwards, propelled by the snout of a wild boar in utter panic. The poor sod had chosen the same bush for his own respite. All it wanted to do was escape from me. In doing so, it opened up a six-inch gash on my outer thighs. The Saligornia waved their fat, salty fingers at me out of the sand in sheer spite.

In the forest adjoining Corbett, the lantana brush was unbroken and altogether more mirthful. As it tugged into our flesh, I felt it grow more peaceful and relaxed.

Mike wrung out his bandana. He was sweating profusely, but kept up with the gurkha with the large loping strides of a person who desperately wishes to see a tiger. I knew from the groans of my soul that the tiger would not appear. What would Gogate say, otherwise?

'Look, *saab*, pug marks.' The tracker was good. The pug marks tottered fairly straight, a line of palm-shaped depressions on the cracked yellow soil. There were no claw marks. Retractable claws. A cat. Small for a tiger, and unaccompanied by larger prints. A leopard.

'*Guldaar!*' The tracker was all respect. We were out looking for a tiger but a leopard was always next best. A slight shiver of excitement ran through my body. The red on Mike's kerchief was soaked flush to his forehead.

We followed the line carefully, looking down with care and then around us with slightly greater apprehension. The sun beat down just as it should on a big-cat track. The line went forwards for three or four kilometres. All of a sudden it vanished: the magical air that surrounds the leopard. It was as if he had sprung into the air and ridden on a cloud to get away. We went forward for another kilometre and could not pick up the track.

'Let's get back.' Mike was keen to get into the park proper and get an elephant-ride chance on the tiger. Besides, the leopard had vanished completely.

'*Ooper chala gaya, sahib*,' the gurkha remarked originally. ('He's gone up into the mountains.')

We turned and walked back to Dhikuli. Soon the marks appeared again and beside them our own footprints, tracking the animal on the way up.

'What in the name of high heavens!' hissed Mike, the sweat breaking into running beads on his forehead. There below him were his own large bootmarks depressed half an inch into the soil. My smaller ked marks, shallow and spreading lightly, were beside his. The gurkha's hunter boots were the lightest, the micro-pressure of a tracker's feet mostly hidden by our overwriting. On top of all our prints, with a gut-wrenching, soul-chilling certainty, we saw the clear marks of the leopard's foot.

'He was just behind us, *saab* . . .' the gurkha stuttered.

'Hell!' Mike yelped, 'the bugger's walked on top of our footprints!'

'It's the smell. He would be wanting to smell his followers,' I explained, trying ineffectively to be a biologist.

Mike looked at me goggle-eyed.

'You mean he was tracking us while we were tracking him?'

It looked most certainly like that. The cat had sprung

away on hearing us return. With the litheness of a forest spirit, he had returned to the shadows, leaving his indelible marks on all of us. Pug marks.

'Can't let him get away with it, can we?' I had a usual mad idea forming malignantly in me.

We walked back past the original leopard trail, with human trails alongside obliterated by the returning leopard, all the way back to Dhikuli. I made sure that I stepped over the leopard's fresh marks carefully, erasing his manifest superiority over the human race.

~

Mike did not see a tiger in India.

This was unfortunate, for the *chaurs* between Dhikala and Khinnanauli are among the best places to see a tiger in India. Sitting in the old Dhikala rest house, I have heard a tiger roar through the tall elephant grass. Venturing unsteadily into the grasslands atop a park elephant, I have seen tigers on innumerable occasions. With the winter congregations of deer in the grasslands, the tiger is pulled into the arena like a gladiator of yore. He crouches unseen and unheard even if whiffs of feline smell may alert the herds for a fraction of a second. The momentary uneasiness will pass if the animal is silent. Through this magical world of hush and scream, tourists are taken sailing on elephants. With an expert mahout guiding his charge, the elephant seems to be silent as well. On a few occasions, the succulent temptation of a *rohini* bush will take the elephant away from its path. A strong word and a thwack later it is back on its course. A few feet down and the beast may stop to slushily let out a stream of urine. This time the mahout will normally let it be. In between these diversions, one mahout will sight the tiger. A good mahout has years of experience in looking through the grass and recognizing the hidden stripes, in reading elephant signs that indicate the presence of the tiger. Occasionally, the reactions of other animals in the vicinity alert the mahout. An alarm call of a sambar or chital in particular are good pointers. And then from the world of stalks and grass a ghostly shadow will slowly emerge. The most experienced tourists on the elephant will excitedly prod the others and whisper loudly, others will scream faintly and collapse into the arms of loved ones. If the elephant gets too close, the tiger may give a mock charge and be treated to a few more screams. And then the figure will slip away. Back into the forests where it can rest unhindered. By poachers or conservationists. Tourists or census takers. To be what it is best at being: an unseen spirit of the Indian jungles.

Ulhas Karanth, India's foremost tiger scientist, was certain that like Michael Day foresters were also not seeing tigers in India, not even pug marks. Ulhas is a belligerent field academic, not leaving to science alone what his words could well demonstrate. He conducted a very interesting test on a number of field forest staff. Giving them more than thirty pug marks of four tigers that had walked inside a zoo cage, he asked them to identify the number of individual tigers. One man got six, another got twenty-four. The remaining were all in between, and funnily enough nobody could identify all pug marks correctly. Very interesting indeed, considering that the method of counting tigers in India is by a pug mark census. So how many tigers are there in the wild? Nobody, in reality, has any answers. Four thousand, says the government, 3500 say conservationists. Radicals say less than 2500. And yet each is a guess based on how wrong the pug mark count is. Ulhas has suggested the use of camera traps to estimate tiger numbers, a method he has used successfully in Nagerhole. Granted that it is an expensive method, but it seems to be the only alternative. An alternative to men walking in the field and finding pug marks that are traced out with an accuracy depending entirely on their eyesight and application and are then analysed by another team, once again based on human senses so prone to error. But is there really a need to know absolute numbers? Most scientists feel that this is not needed to monitor a population and is needed only to answer parliamentary questions. Long term trends based on sampling techniques are many and well tested the world over. None of them need correct numbers to predict whether a population is going up or down. The politicians want numbers, though, and so do international donors. And so, each year, in all seriousness, the Tiger Census farce is played out across the country.

It was a census of birds that took Alok, Atul, Taresh and me into Chilla at the southern end of Rajaji National Park. I was the Regional Co-ordinator for the Asian Midwinter Waterfowl Census for northern India and the birds that congregated at the deep end of the Chilla Barrage had to be counted. Each year, apart from the normal counts, we had seen mergansers there, sleek deep-diving ducks that liked a combination of deep and fast-flowing water. The census was done in the early morning and the afternoon was spent in a well-deserved siesta. Come evening, it was time to see the mammals of the area. One night the team decided to try and see a tiger. In retrospect we should have never taken that night walk. Bound together by the gloriously brave thread of ignorance, we decided to start the walk just after dinner at the dhaba outside the rest house.

'Will there be tigers at night at the machaan, chowkidar?' I was resting my feet imperiously on an old reclining cane chair and sitting on another antique. The cane furniture of the rest houses is without doubt the most comfortable made anywhere in the world; wooden arms stained dark with years of sweat and heat, cane middles woven intricately by equally dark arms, and fine step-notches on the base that allow the chair to be reclined at angles that international airways would do well to copy. This one was in the Chilla rest house. Chilla is the southern end of Rajaji National Park that binds the towns of Haridwar and Rishikesh with the Himalayas.

'*Haan, saab*, of course, of course. There are always tigers at the machaan in the dark.'

I respected his grey hair that had turned colour watching tigers in the forest. I was completely and utterly wrong. Ten years of further forest wanderings awakened my suspicion. It was a little disconcerting to hear chowkidar after chowkidar separated by vast distances telling the same yarns, the same alcohol-sodden dreams and just about anything which would please you and ensure the tip. That in turn would ensure his tipple and happiness would descend on the forest post once more.

'Of course, *saab*. There is big male, *saab*. This is striped tiger, *saab*, not the other one, of course.'

'Which other one, chowkidar?'

'The spotted one, of course, *saab*.'

I was foolish enough not to let even that alert me.

Two kilometres in an unknown forest at night can be a terrifying experience. I had the two strongmen behind me. Alok, calm and unflappable, shone his pocket torch to the right. Atul, excited and vocal, shone his to the left. Tarun, a novice wildlife enthusiast, brought up the rear and shone his behind him, turning over his shoulder to keep up with the light. I had the onerous responsibility of leading the pack. This was part of an elaborate wildlife defence plan hatched during the rice and rajma dinner at the dhaba.

'You can't miss the path, *saab*.' The chowkidar was elated with his twenty rupees.

'But animals? Snakes?' I asked, fearful of running into some during the walk.

'Oh plenty, *saab*, crawling with them, *saab*, jungle full of them, *saab*.'

I was comforted. The torch parade was hatched.

As we set out, the weak moon sunk over the clouds and a few nondescript stars were left to guide the way. Our torches have never shone so fearfully and ferociously as they did then. Two hundred yards were covered by this strange eight-legged luminescent creature with four beams of light shining in all directions.

'What's that?!' shrieked Atul as a shadow fled past.

All four torches swung in unison to face east.

'Who's looking at the back?' I asked leaderlike and responsible for any rear attacks.

All four torches shone immediately to the rear.

There was nothing in either direction but the silence of a damp, dark, unforgiving tropical forest. I had to swing my torch away to the front to lead the way. Seeing a departing light, all the others followed me automatically and the path ahead was lit up brilliantly. The path was winding left, a hastily cut, slightly overgrown jungle path made with the sole purpose of catching waterfowl counters totally unawares.

'I think I see an animal here, Vivek,' exclaimed Alok pausing between every two words; measured, bottom-heavy words that could not be shaken by the situation around him. It was comforting to have him around.

'There is something to my left, I think.'

All torches turned west. The luminescent creature was turning upon itself. Still no wild beings had appeared. We were only halfway to the machaan but the tension had drawn us closer to each other.

'What about snakes?' screamed Atul a little hysterically.

All four torches shone at our hunter boots, cheap Indian army discards.

The creature had bunched upon itself, turned into a giant crawling millipede. It progressed at a very slow pace, revolving and turning its fearful lights on a leaf fall, a drop of dew, the crunching underfoot of a fallen twig. The whole world was suddenly dark, mysterious and forbidding. The forest immediately around was choc-a-bloc with its most nefarious creations.

As we inched forward, the machaan rose out of the night to greet us. The green paint was peeling off and it looked a positive ruin. We had just begun to climb its precarious six-inch footholds when Atul yelled from the bottom.

'What about leopards? What about them, eh? What if they come? All you city types . . .'

He left the sentence unfinished as we hurried down to help him barricade the tower. For an hour in the night, bone-weary and chilled with fear and the descending dew, we collected brambles and thorns, stout logs and thin branches and built what in the morning looked like a small garden bonfire heap. A small tabby cat could have leapt over it with consummate ease. It did not matter then; Atul Singh Nischal was satisfied. It would guard us against the marauding leopards of Chilla. As we went into the small watch room at the top, the forest welcomed us with the ear-piercing scream of a maniacal hyena. The striped hyena, denizen of the night, cruncher of bones and leftover meat, and the possessor of a call eerily reminiscent of a castle banshee.

Atul clutched painfully at my arm, his nails digging furrows of fear into it.

'*Chudail*,' he whispered hoarsely, '*chudaaaiiilll*.'

The *chudail*, we all knew, was a she-ghost. She stalked the forest uttering demented cries, luring unwary passers-by—who think them to be striped hyenas—up into trees and crunching them in a midnight snack. It was easy enough to distinguish the two of course. The hyena is a slouched, uncouth beast with its hair a mess and an evil leer stuck permanently on its powerful, short-set jaws. The *chudail*, on the other hand, is a beautiful woman with well combed hair and a lasciviousness that attracts even Himalayan sages. Her only physical deformity is that her feet are twisted at the ankles to face opposing poles. An easier distinction I could not come up with myself. Atul Nischal was not convinced, however, and the night was spent in cold misery, clutching at each other and waiting for the many creatures that could appear out of the forest. The missing tiger, the can't-jump-a-fence leopard, the canid *chudail*.

The light of the terai morning dispelled any nocturnal doubts that may have existed in Atul's minds. With a delighted whoop at the undamaged leopard barricade, he vaulted into the forest.

'I can smell chital,' he said, 'a whole herd of chital.'

We had still not had breakfast. I was worried.

'I will herd them to you. Now, all of you just crouch behind this bush and watch me. I will herd all the animals to you.'

'Now Atul, stop this,' I began, but he had gone already, huge loping leaps that catapulted him over the straggling lantana bushes and *adhatoda* blooms.

I could hear him crashing through the undergrowth like a tusker in musth.

'Now just you wait.' There was a loud crash. Then a welcome silence.

In the distance chital barked delicately, upset by the disturbance.

Alok and I looked at each other, eyebrows arching in total puzzlement.

From the forest fringes, a wail arose to clarify the situation. It was high pitched, the first call of the brain-fever bird, the dying rattle of a wild boar, the mating call of the jackal.

'Vii-ii-vv-eee-kk-kk,' it screamed, 'Vii-iive-ee-ee-kk.'

We rushed forward to help our mate. A herd of chital scattered at our approach. Till then they had been staring curiously at the form of Atul Singh Nischal. He had run very fast and hard between two thin sal trees and was now inextricably caught in a position of great acrobacy. His arms were splayed to heaven and his feet pointed rather alarmingly in totally opposite directions. His head was bent backwards and was trailing the forest floor. From his mouth, the jackal-boar cry emerged even more urgently.

'Vii-vee-ee-kk. Help. Please.'

~

Many years have passed and people have moved on in their lives to new responsibilities. Atul is a filmmaker and Alok a banker. Bharati fights waste of all sorts and plastics in particular; an environmental crusader, if that can be termed a profession. Mohit has formed a nature travel group, Asian Adventures, which runs some of the best and eco-friendly tours through Indian wildernesses. His photography is largely a forgotten passion but his love for the wild extends through his tours and camps. An integral part of his programme is running low-cost trips for children, the only hope left in a callous world. Rajesh is a specialist on the oak ecosystem of the Himalayas. And I wander about stopping illegal killing and trade of animals.

A variety of professions and a variety of species have played a part in shaping our lives. Yet, the first phone call after a wilderness outing by any of the group is greeted by a very familiar chorus.

'Saw anything?'

The person has only one of two choices.

'Nothing much. Just a few elephants, and a few

hundred deer and many birds and . . . well that's about all.'

Or—

'Tiger! Tiger! And at around ten feet. A full half an hour. Have you ever seen a tiger in Nagzira?'

May the Gogates and Sukumars of this world rest in peace. Let Lahiri-Choudhury and Ashok discuss this unfair cattiness in the salubrious surroundings of Saturday club. May I feel the odd twinge of regret at doing most of my work on charismatic mega fauna while the Andaman teal vanishes unsung and unhelped. The tiger has undoubtedly stolen Indian wildlife's star show.